A FLEDGLING DEMOCRACY

T0373729

MOHAMED ZAYANI
(Editor)

A Fledgling Democracy

Tunisia in the Aftermath of the
Arab Uprisings

جامعة جورجتاون قطر
GEORGETOWN UNIVERSITY QATAR

Center *for* International *and* Regional Studies

HURST & COMPANY, LONDON

Published in collaboration with the Center for International and
Regional Studies, Georgetown University–Qatar.
First published in the United Kingdom in 2022 by
C. Hurst & Co. (Publishers) Ltd.,
New Wing, Somerset House, Strand, London, WC2R 1LA

A Cataloguing-in-Publication data record for this book
is available from the British Library.

ISBN: 9781787387140

www.hurstpublishers.com

Printed in Great Britain by Bell and Bain Ltd, Glasgow

CONTENTS

About the Contributors   vii

List of Figures and Tables   xiii

Acknowledgments   xv

1. Post-Authoritarian Governance and Elusive Stability: 1
    Tunisia's Uneasy Transition
    Mohamed Zayani

2. The Tunisian Transition and Authoritarianism in the   31
    Middle East: Democracy is up to the Citizens, not
    the Neighbors
    Marina Ottaway

3. Transitional Bodies, Party Politics, and Anti-Democratic   59
    Potential in Tunisia: The Case of HAICA
    Enrique Klaus

4. Post-Islamism Politics in Tunisia: Ennahda's Evolution   87
    since the Revolution
    Fabio Merone

5. Tunisia's Re-Invigorated Civil Society: Changes   103
    and Challenges
    Zuzana Hudáková

CONTENTS

6. Mobilization in Tunisia Post-2011: From Political   127
    Protests to National Campaign Movements
    Irene Weipert-Fenner

7. The Violence of Endurance: Youth Precarity and Social   151
    Justice in Inner Tunisia
    Alyssa Miller

8. Changing Security Dynamics in Tunisia: Reconsidering   173
    the Battle for Ben Gardane
    Ruth Hanau Santini

9. What Can Tunisia's Past Tell Us About its Future?   187
    Critical Junctures and Political Trends
    Alexandra Domike Blackman

Notes   219

Index   267

ABOUT THE CONTRIBUTORS

Alexandra Domike Blackman is an assistant professor in Cornell University's Department of Government. She received her PhD from the Department of Political Science at Stanford University in 2019. Her research interests include the politics of religion and religious institutions and Middle East politics more broadly, including gender, the development of political parties, the evolution of authoritarian institutions, and the role of foreign and transnational forces in the region. Her dissertation research examines the impact of French colonial administration on local political and religious identities in Tunisia. She is author of the articles 'Religion and Foreign Aid' in *Politics & Religion* and 'Gender Stereotypes, Political Leadership, and Voting Behavior in Tunisia' in *Political Behavior*. She has several current projects on Tunisia including research on political elites' strategic response to gender quotas, political accountability in municipal governance, and the politics of drug depenalization.

Zuzana Hudáková is a post-doctoral researcher at the Center for International Studies (CERI) at Sciences Po, Paris, and a visiting lecturer at the Catholic University of Lille. Her research focuses on the dynamics of protest in authoritarian regimes and the use and effectiveness of United Nations sanctions. She holds a PhD from the Graduate Institute of International and Development Studies (IHEID) in Geneva, where she is also a research associate. Her recent publications include 'UN Targeted Sanctions Datasets, 1991–2013'

(*Journal of Peace Research*, 2018) and 'Civil Society in Tunisia: From Islands of Resistance to Tides of Political Change' (*Journal of North African Studies*, 2021). She is also a co-author of several policy briefs, including *The Effectiveness of United Nations Targeted Sanctions* (IHEID & Watson Institute, 2013) and *Amman Issue Brief: Arab Civil Societies after the Uprisings: Challenges during Political Transitions* (IHEID, 2012).

Enrique Klaus teaches social sciences and journalism at the Faculty of Communication, Galatasaray University (Istanbul). He holds a PhD in political sciences from the Grenoble Institute of Political Studies. He was previously professor at Science Po Rabat, International University of Rabat, and postdoctoral researcher (French Ministry of Foreign Affairs and ERC-TARICA) at the Research Institute for Modern Maghreb (IRMC) in Tunis. His research interests include political sociology of the media, praxeology of public space in the MENA region, elections and media in Tunisia, audio-visual regulation in North Africa, the Tunisian Press agency's reform, graffiti and comic books in the MENA region, and population control through state administration at the Syrian consulate in Istanbul. He authored several peer-reviewed articles and book chapters on these subjects, including (in French) 'The Polemic over "the Journalists' Black Book": Tunisia's Transitional Justice in the Face of Democratic Polysemy,' in *Justice and Reconciliation in the Maghreb Post-Arab Revolts*, ed. Éric Gobe (2020); 'Propaganda and Official Information in the Age of Media Pluralism: The Case of the Tunis-Afrique Presse News Agency,' in *Tunisia: A Democratization Above All Suspicion?* (CNRS Éditions, 2018); and 'The HAICA's Authority over the Tunisian Media Sector: A Transitional Anachronism?' (*L'Année du Maghreb*, 2015).

Fabio Merone is a political scientist specialized in the Middle East and North Africa region, and currently associate fellow at the Centre Interdisciplinaire de Recherche sur l'Afrique et le Moyen Orient at Université Laval, Canada. He has a PhD in political science from the University of Ghent, where he also held a post-doctoral research fellowship in the Department of Conflict and Development, Middle East and North Africa Research Group. His research interests include political Islam, Salafism, jihadism, and contentious politics in Tunisia and the Arab world. He was previously a political analyst and foreign correspondent based in Tunisia. He is the co-author of *Salafism after the Arab Awakening: Contending with People's Power* (Hurst, 2017). He is also the author of 'Between Social Contention and Takfirism: The Evolution of the Salafi-Jihadi Movement in Tunisia' (*Mediterranean Politics*, 2017), and co-author of 'Local (R)evolutions in Times of Democratic Transition: Reconstructing Political Authority in Tunisian Municipalities (2011–2014)' (*Middle East Journal*, 2016) and 'Islamist Parties and Transformation in Tunisia and Morocco' in *Social Currents in North Africa: Culture and Governance after the Arab Spring* (Oxford University Press, 2018), among numerous other journal articles, policy papers, and news articles.

Alyssa Miller is a Postdoctoral Research Fellow at the Institute for Middle East Studies at the German Institute for Global and Area Studies (GIGA). Her research centers on questions of kinship, transnational mobility, and social justice in Tunisia and the wider Middle East and North Africa region following the 2011 Arab Uprisings. She holds a PhD in Cultural Anthropology from Duke University and was an Andrew W. Mellon Postdoctoral Fellow at the Wolf Humanities Center at the University of Pennsylvania from 2019–20. Her publications include '"I Do Not Forgive!" Refusal and Hope in Tunisia's Democratic Transition' (*Comparative Studies of South Asia, Africa, and the Middle East*, 2021) and 'Kin-Work in a Time of Jihad: Sustaining Bonds of Filiation and Care for Tunisian Foreign Combatants' (*Cultural Anthropology*, 2018).

Marina Ottaway is a Middle East scholar at the Woodrow Wilson Center and a long-time analyst of political transformations in Africa, the Balkans, and the Middle East. She joined the Wilson Center after fourteen years at the Carnegie Endowment for International Peace (CEIP), during which she played a central role in launching the Middle East program. Prior to that, she carried out research in Africa and in the Middle East for many years. She taught at Georgetown University, the Johns Hopkins School for Advanced International Studies, the American University in Cairo, the University of the Witwatersrand in South Africa, the University of Zambia, and Addis

Ababa University. Her extensive research experience is reflected in her publications, which include ten authored books and six edited ones. Her most recent book, *A Tale of Four Worlds: The Arab Regions after the Uprisings* (Hurst, 2019) deals with the Tunisian transition. Other publications include coauthoring *Getting to Pluralism: Political Actors in the Arab World* (CEIP, 2012) and *Yemen on the Brink* (CEIP, 2010).

Ruth Hanau Santini is an associate professor of political science and international relations at the Università Orientale in Naples, Italy, and an associate fellow at the Middle East, Central Asia, and Caucasus Studies Institute at the University of St. Andrews. She was previously an associate fellow at the Johns Hopkins School of Advanced International Studies (SAIS), Bologna Center. She has worked at several European think tanks on European foreign policy, international security, and Middle Eastern politics. She was a visiting fellow at the Brookings Institute in the United States and Europe. She is the author of *Limited Statehood in Post-Revolutionary Tunisia: Citizenship, Economy and Security* (Palgrave, 2018) and co-editor of *Rethinking Statehood in the Middle East and North Africa: Security, Sovereignty and New Political Orders* (Routledge, 2019) and *Limited Statehood and Informal Governance in the Middle East and Africa* (Routledge, 2020). She was the principal investigator for the 'Participatory Challenges from Tunisia to Oman (STREETPOL)' research project and is currently a consultant for the World Food Program's Analysis and Early Warning Unit.

Irene Weipert-Fenner is project director and senior researcher on intrastate conflict at the Peace Research Institute Frankfurt (PRIF), which analyzes the causes of international and intrastate conflicts and looks for ways to solve them. Her current project is 'Struggles over Socioeconomic Reforms: Political Conflict and Social Contention in Egypt and Tunisia post-2011 in Interregional Comparison,' and her prior project was 'The Socioeconomic Dimension of Islamist Radicalization in Egypt and Tunisia.' She was a Visiting Professor for Middle Eastern Politics at the University of Marburg in 2019. She is the author of *The Autocratic Parliament: Power and Legitimacy in Egypt, 1866–2011* (Syracuse University Press, 2020). She coedited

Socioeconomic Protests in MENA and Latin America: Egypt and Tunisia in Interregional Comparison (Palgrave Macmillan, 2019), and she is the author of numerous journal articles and book chapters, including 'Unemployed Mobilisation in Times of Democratisation: The Union of Unemployed Graduates in Post-Ben Ali Tunisia' (*Journal of North African Studies*, 2020).

Mohamed Zayani is an award-winning author and professor of critical theory at the Georgetown University School of Foreign Service in Qatar. His works include *Digital Middle East: State and Society in the Information Age* (Oxford University Press, 2018); *Bullets and Bulletins: Media and Politics in the Wake of the Arab Uprisings* (Oxford University Press, 2016); *The Culture of Al Jazeera: Inside an Arab Media Giant* (McFarland, 2007); and *The Al Jazeera Phenomenon: Critical Perspectives on New Arab Media* (Pluto Press, 2005). His book *Networked Publics and Digital Contention: The Politics of Everyday Life in Tunisia* (Oxford University Press, 2015) was the winner of 'The International Communication Best Book Award' from the International Studies Association, 'The Global Communication and Social Change Best Book Award' from the International Communication Association, 'The Communication, Information Technologies and Media Sociology Book Award' from the American Sociological Association, 'The Sue DeWine Distinguished Book Award' from the National Communication Association, and 'The Toyin Falola Best Book Award' from the Association of Global South Studies.

LIST OF FIGURES AND TABLES

Figures

5.1. The evolution of the number of CSOs in Tunisia (1980–2020)   112

6.1. Number of annual protests in Tunisia, January 1, 1998–December 31, 2019   131

9.1. French, Italian, and Tunisian populations in Tunisia, 1871–1966   205

9.2. Pre- and post-World War I French population in coastal regions versus in interior regions   207

9.3. Pre- and post-World War I North African population in coastal regions versus in interior regions   209

9.4. Political mobilization for the secular and Islamist factions of the nationalist movement, March 1956   214

9.5. Ennahda share of the two-party vote (versus Nidaa Tounes), 2014   215

Tables

3.1. List of relevant transitional institutions   62

3.2. Private TV's performance in the 2019 elections   75

5.1. The changing composition of Tunisian CSOs by area of activity   114

xiii

ACKNOWLEDGMENTS

In addition to the authors whose work appears in this volume, the editor wishes to thank a number of scholars and colleagues who contributed insights and provided input: Amel Boubekeur, Edwige Fortier, Mongi Boughzala, Zouhir Gabsi, Reza Pirbhai, Rory Miller, and Clyde Wilcox. This project was developed in the context of a research initiative supported by the Center for International and Regional Studies. Grateful acknowledgement goes to the center's team who provided support for the project: Mehran Kamrava, Ahmad Dallal, Zahra Babar, Elizabeth Wanucha, Misba Bhatti, and Maram Al-Qershi. Invaluable assistance came from Suzi Mirgani, the center's managing editor, who deserves a special thanks for her generous time and editorial support at various stages of the project. Thanks are also owed to Alice Clarke, the managing editor of this book, and Daisy Leitch, the production director at Hurst, for all their work during the publication process, and to Ailie Conor for her editorial input.

1

POST-AUTHORITARIAN GOVERNANCE AND ELUSIVE STABILITY
TUNISIA'S UNEASY TRANSITION

Mohamed Zayani

A decade after the outbreak of the Arab uprisings, the Middle East and North Africa region continues to experience turbulent developments. The hopes for social and political change that fueled the uprisings have not materialized, nor has democratization taken hold, and turmoil continues across much of the region, resulting in the return of repression in some cases, the collapse of the state in others, or simply the perpetuation of the status quo. Shortly after its revolution, Egypt suffered democratic regression with the reinstatement of authoritarianism; Syria was mired in a relentless civil war; oil-rich Libya descended into chaos with warring factions playing into the hands of international and regional powers; and Yemen has endured a spiraling conflict and has been embroiled in a proxy war that is threatening its very unity and exacerbating regional tensions. In Lebanon, Iraq, and Sudan, popular protests deepened political disorder. Even wealthy Gulf monarchies felt the reverberations of the Arab uprisings. In countries where there have been attempts to undertake reform, as in the cases of Jordan and Morocco, such efforts have been modest at best.[1]

1

In the midst of the turmoil that ensued after the Arab uprisings, Tunisia charted for itself a unique path. Embracing a new political culture based on freedoms, pluralism, peaceful rotation of power, and civic engagement, it emerged as a lone 'success story' of democratization, peaceful transition, and civil rule.[2] Since 2011, the country experienced significant changes and rapid political transformation. It has set up transitional bodies and took constitutional measures that are conducive to building a nascent democracy, enshrining political freedoms, and instituting an orderly transition of power. With the political sphere liberalized, tens of political parties were formed and free elections were held at the local and national levels. Equally noteworthy are the country's various institutional reforms and its progressive new constitution, which upholds individual freedoms, champions women's rights, and protects the freedom of speech and of association. Tunisia also reformed state laws to enable greater civil participation and put measures in place to enhance access to information, help achieve public accountability, and expose corruption—steps that are indicative of a strong commitment to political reform.

Going hand in hand with the building of democratic institutions is the emergence of a vibrant civil society. The sphere of civil society action has expanded with newfound freedoms, relaxed legislation on associational life, and growing desire for civic engagement, seeking both recognition and an active role. Not only did civil society groups mushroom after the revolution, but the very role of civil society evolved. While not all associational life has been politically driven, there was a flurry of organizations that sought to enhance governance, promote accountability, fight corruption, and defend freedoms.[3] Through bottom-up input, active engagement, and vocal criticism, such organizations have played an active part in the country's democratic transition, putting pressure on the government and instituting a new culture of government accountability,[4] while at the same time serving as 'spaces of democratic learning.'[5]

The progress Tunisia has made toward a democratic transition is often relegated to its social cohesion (a homogeneous population and the absence of tribalism and sectarianism); its institutional strength (a tradition of state bureaucracy inherited from the colonial and pre-colonial periods); and its long commitment to modernization and the pursuit of progressive reforms since independence (investing in modern education, developing women's rights, and pursing religious moderation).[6] While the legacy of institutionalism, moderation, and openness helped the country effect a peaceful transition and spared it the unrest and violence that have racked other states in the region, adapting to the exigencies of a post-revolution era has proved arduous.

In spite of the country's achievements, daunting challenges remain which are impeding its transition and hindering its ability to consolidate the gains it has made since the revolution. Although Tunisia has fared better than other Arab states that were shaken by revolutions and although it managed to diffuse several crises, its transition has been uneasy, its democracy fledgling, and its outlook uncertain. As the country emerges out of decades of authoritarian rule, it is finding itself faced with formidable political, economic, social, and security challenges. Particularly noteworthy is the instability of the political scene, the slow pace of reform, deepening economic difficulties, enduring social unrest, the unrealized aspirations of the youth, the elusiveness of social justice, and the unfulfilled promises for development in the inner regions. As well as engendering a growing disconnect between the state and its citizens, these challenges are locking the country in a liminal state that is characterized by perpetual fragility. It is this state of fragility that this collaborative volume seeks to capture. Focusing on unfolding sociopolitical dynamics that took shape since the revolution, the contributions in this work shed light on how Tunisia navigated its first decade of democratic transition, and what the ongoing changes and challenges mean for a country that aspires to build a better future.

A Transition to Post-Authoritarian Governance

Throughout the transition period, the army remained outside the political scene. This allowed for the transitional process to unfold in line with the provisions of the Constitution, which eventually was made obsolete by ad hoc revolutionary measures and non-elected provisional structures designed to move the country to post-authoritarian governance. The day after Zine El Abidine Ben Ali fled the country, Fouad Mebazaa, the speaker of the parliament, was sworn in as acting president and the sitting Prime Minister Mohamed Ghannouchi moved to constitute a transitional government. Although the peaceful nature of the transition was welcomed, the improvisations that characterized this initial stage yielded a post-revolution government that is replete with remnants of the old regime. The half-measures Ghannouchi took in his first political test poorly meshed with the country's revolutionary momentum. In reaction, the protesters demanded more radical changes and an overhaul of the political system, including the departure of Ghannouchi himself, the dissolution of the legislative assembly, the banning of the ruling party, and, most importantly, the election of a new and more legitimate legislature to write a new constitution. Only a few weeks after the fall of Ben Ali, Ghannouchi bowed to the pressure and resigned. He was succeeded by a new interim government headed by Béji Caïd Essebsi, a minister under Habib Bourguiba, who was entrusted with leading the country during a short transitional period that was to culminate in elections by the end of 2011.

The emerging consensus regarding the need for a full-scale reform yielded an ad hoc transitional body that would institutionalize change and accelerate its pace.[7] The High Commission for Political Reform, which was initially established to reform undemocratic and repressive laws, merged with representatives from the Revolutionary Committee for the Safeguarding of the Revolution to form a transitional legislative body—the High Commission for the Protection of the Objectives of the Revolution, Political Reform, and Democratic Transition. Its mandate was to oversee democratic transition. Under this legislative body, a new Electoral Law was drafted and passed, an independent electoral commission was established, and a regulatory framework for campaigns and campaign funding was put in place. These gains helped channel revolutionary change and forge a 'constitutional political pathway' that would institutionalize democratization efforts and give public confidence in the process.[8]

During the eventful interim period that followed the short rule of Ghannouchi, a number of measures were taken to put an end to institutions and establishments that were considered pillars of authoritarian rule and to work toward creating new political frameworks. Thus, the secret police agency was dissolved and the ruling party, which dominated the country's political scene for decades, was dismantled. Most significantly, the government gave in to the pressure to elect a National Constituent Assembly that would be tasked with drafting a new constitution and to hold elections within a year. This new elected body was an important first step toward establishing a fledgling democracy in which politics would no longer be the prerogative of a particular party, class, or group, and where inclusiveness and pluralism are fostered.

This same period was marked by an unprecedented political momentum. Thousands of non-government organizations and civil society associations were established and more than a hundred political parties were legalized, including the previously-banned moderate Islamist party Ennahda. The country's first democratic elections of a National Constituent Assembly on October 23, 2011 ended the interim period. Expectedly, the ballot box brought Ennahda to power. Short of an outright majority to lead, though, Ennahda formed a three-party ruling coalition (that came to be known as the Troika), forging an alliance with the two secular parties, the Congress for the Republic (CPR) and the Democratic Front for Labor and Liberty (FDTL). Hamadi Jebali, then Ennahda's secretary general, was sworn in as prime minister; the dissident human rights activist Moncef Marzouki was elected as president; and longtime opposition figure Mustafa Ben Jafaar became the speaker of the National Constituent Assembly.

The Perils of Power

With the Ennahda-led government in power, Tunisia entered a new post-revolution phase that differed markedly from the harmony and solidarity that characterized the first months following the ousting of Ben Ali. Notably, political partisanship increased, cleavages between parties deepened, and ideological splits among the country's political adversaries intensified. The ascension of Ennahda to power and the way it dominated the political scene created resentment and, even within the ruling coalition, there was much unease. The situation took an unexpected turn in 2013, when a wave of political violence increased tensions and threatened the country's peaceful transition toward democracy. The assassination of Chokri Belaïd, a member of the National Constituent Assembly from the secular opposition, marked the beginning of a period of political instability that put the Troika government in a difficult position. The opposition blamed Ennahda for the deterioration of the situation in the country and called for broad-based participation in the political process. Unable to form a new cabinet of independent technocrats, Prime Minister Jebali resigned to be succeeded by Ali Larayedh, another prominent figure of Ennahda.

The assassination of a second opposition figure, Mohamed Brahmi, in July of that same year plunged Tunisia in a deep crisis. Political violence threatened to destabilize the country, disrupt its institutional reforms, and thwart its peaceful transition to democracy. These developments had unmistakable reverberations, widening the rift between the country's political camps, undermining the Troika's ruling coalition, and weakening Ennahda's position further. With the suspected involvement of Salafis in the political assassinations, Ennahda was blamed for the rise of Islamic radicalism in the country and taken to task for adopting a lax attitude toward hardline Islamist movements and the ultra-religious conservatives who advocated Islamic rule. A series of deadly attacks by jihadi Salafis and extremist groups in Mount Chaanbi in 2013 and the repeated targeting of security forces added to the tension, drew more criticism of the Ennahda-led government, and further united the opposition.

Deep resentment against, and vocal criticism of, Ennahda gave momentum to the beleaguered opposition parties. The mounting tensions that characterized this juncture were evident in the mass anti-Ennahda demonstrations that took place in the summer of 2013. These coalesced around the Irhal movement, which demanded that the Ennahda government resign, the National Constituent Assembly be dissolved, and a government of national salvation be formed. Several opposition figures, political players, and activists joined forces to oppose the Ennahda-led government, staging demonstrations in the Bardo public square in Tunis, across from the seat of the National Constituent Assembly. With intense anti-Ennahda popular protests and the suspension of the assembly's work, the country sank into an acute political crisis that risked derailing the transitional process. A tug of war ensued. While the demonstrators and the opposition invoked popular legitimacy, Ennahda held on to its electoral legitimacy. As the crisis deepened, the path to building a lasting democracy became more uncertain than ever.

The pushback against Ennahda came at time of increased rejection of political Islam in the region. In post-Mubarak Egypt, the Tamarod protest movement and the intervention of the army led to the ousting of an elected president, Mohamed Morsi, the ostracizing of the Muslim Brotherhood, and the reversal of the country's democratic transition. In Tunisia, the apprehension toward Islamic politics and deep distrust of Ennahda (whose advent, its critics feared, would entail rolling back the gains of a civil state) were matched only by Ennahda's own fear of the return of repression as the dramatic events in Egypt made patently clear. The depth of the crisis, which crippled interim institutions and jeopardized the country's peaceful transition, evinced the perils of power and attenuated Ennahda's position. Opting for political pragmatism, Ennahda signaled a willingness to enter into talks and negotiate an agreement with the emboldened opposition, to make political concessions, and to work on forging a path forward toward the completion of democratic transition. Civil society played an important mediation role, diffusing the tense political situation, smoothing differences, and building consensus among the country's major political players. A national dialogue platform was brokered by the National Dialogue Quartet, which was led by the Tunisian General Labor Union (UGTT) and comprised of the Tunisian Human Rights League (LTDH), the National Bar Association (ONAT), and the Confederation of Industry, Trade and Handicrafts (UTICA). Broad-based consultation and several rounds of tough back-and-forth negotiations ended the stalemate and led, in December 2013, to a historic agreement on a consensual political roadmap for a more stable transitional phase. Ennahda's constitutional compromises entailed stepping down voluntarily.

7

Effectively, one critic noted, Ennahda's succumbing to popular and political pressure 'was inherently undemocratic, but it was seen as a way to provide stability and ward off violence.'[9] The voluntary resignation of the Ennahda-led government and the dissolution of the ruling coalition made way for the appointment of a caretaker non-partisan government of technocrats headed by Mehdi Jomaa.

The adoption of a political roadmap and the ratification of a modern and progressive constitution during this transitional period paved the way for the much-awaited legislative and presidential elections in October 2014 and the establishment of a new government. More than a hundred parties competed to gain seats in the Assembly of the Representatives of the People, the legislative body that supplanted the National Constituent Assembly. Among these was Nidaa Tounes, a hastily formed party that was led by Essebsi. Widely perceived as the successor to the former ruling party, Nidaa Tounes succeeded in bringing under its umbrella heterogeneous 'liberal' voices, including secular opposition figures and old regime elites, positioning itself as the main secular party and a political counterweight to Ennahda. The ballot box favored the rise of Nidaa Tounes, which reaped a double victory. With 86 out of the 217 seats constituting the legislature, Nidaa Tounes took control of the parliament, while its founder Essebsi was sworn in as president. This ended the four-year initial transition period and ushered in a new phase, but also brought in different challenges.

Mounting Political Uncertainties

The country's efforts to institute a procedural democracy that guaranteed a peaceful rotation of power had its limits. Politically, Tunisia's democratic transition did not translate into a strong political culture as the reconstituted political scene remained fragile and political stability elusive. This is reflected in the kind of political tensions and the sense of mistrust that reigned in spite of the pragmatism of several key political players and the power-sharing agreements between the country's leading parties.

It is from this perspective that we can understand the rapprochement between Ennahda and Nidaa Tounes. Although the dynamics of the elections and the mutual distrust between the two leading parties suggest that the victory of the one would force the other to be in the opposition, in effect, the unfolding of the political situation yielded a different arrangement. The political antagonism that fueled the election campaigns gave way to a ruling coalition of the two parties and a search for political consensus. The narrow victory of Nidaa Tounes impelled it to enter into a 'bargained competition' with its archrival.[10] The arrangement was guided by the desire of both parties to reintegrate the post-revolutionary political scene, manipulate the political system to their advantage, and consolidate their political positions—though such compromise was a source of frustration among these parties' supporters and their electoral bases.[11]

While the political culture of national consensus served the country well during this period, both parties steered clear of controversial issues, which impacted how the transition unfolded. In the absence of an effective opposition, both parties were more keen on consolidating their political positions than they were willing to build democratic institutions, such as establishing the constitutional court or undertaking bold reforms, including structural economic reform.[12] Further slowing the pace of reform was the inherent weakness (and opportunism) of many of the political parties, including Nidaa Tounes. Resting on political alliances, the party that coalesced around Essebsi was held together less by a common political vision than a staunch opposition to what Ennahda stood for, the kind of society it favored, and the politics it adopted. Nidaa Tounes garnered support among the voters not only because its victory would reign in Ennahda's dominance, but also because it promised to end the status quo and bring about change. Once in power, though, the party shattered almost as quickly as it had been formed as it fell prey to internal power struggles and was paralyzed by infighting. Inevitably, the emergence of splinter parties fractured Nidaa Tounes, which eventually imploded and, by the 2019 elections, was eclipsed from the political scene.

These divisions were symptomatic of the reconfigured political scene. Even credible parties, and subsequent iterations of these parties, which were established by the opposition during Ben Ali's rule—such as Moncef Marzouki's Congress for the Republic, Mustapha Ben Jafaar's Ettakatol, and Ahmed Nejib Chebbi's Al Jomhouri—were fractured and either failed to win seats in the parliament or had an insignificant political presence. Many of the new parties that emerged after 2011 proved to be rather elitist formations that lacked a clearly articulated vision and a popular base, resulting in weak parties and a fragmented opposition. Further undermining the new political culture was the fact that such fragmentation made the exercise of power more dependent on individuals than on political party institutions. Many parties, including established ones, were unable to function as institutions or to build lasting democratic processes within the parties themselves. Even leftist parties with a long political history and whose anti-liberal discourse continued to have an appeal—like the Workers Party (PCOT), which became part of the Popular Front (a coalition of left-wing and Arab nationalist parties)—eventually fell prey to infighting and political ambitions. In the 2019 legislative elections, the representation of the leftist parties was reduced to a single seat, which inevitably meant the disintegration of the Popular Front. Largely shaped by its radical politics, much of the political left failed to move away from its ideological positioning and its historical grudge against the Islamists.

By and large, the reconstitution of the political scene and the inherent weakness of political parties consolidated the position of Ennahda, the country's predominant party, which managed to position itself at the center of the reformulated political scene, drawing on its long political experience, its organizational strength, and its disciplined rank and file. Ennahda has adopted a strategy of moderation, pragmatism, and gradualism that enabled it to remain a key political player—though its rule has also been marred with various missteps, shortcomings, and failures. Significantly, although the fragmentation of the political scene has put the party ahead of the other political players, it deprived it of a strong political partner it could rule with or compete against, forcing it to enter into tenuous coalitions, thus making it all the more politically accountable during a difficult transition that was breeding growing discontent. Additionally, while Ennahda remains a central player in the political scene and, compared to other parties, has maintained its electoral appeal, its power base, and its unity, it 'has also been losing voter support, the trust of potential allies and the loyalty of party officials.'[13] Internally, Ennahda has suffered mounting tensions. All along, there have been discordances and disagreements between various streams within the party: between the conservative elements of the party and the moderate wing; the leading members of the once exiled branch of the party and the party leadership that remained in the country and faced regime oppression; founding figures who claim historical legitimacy and a reformist fringe that bemoans the democratic deficit within the party and calls for change. Co-founder Rachid Ghannouchi's 'patriarchal' dominance over the party (and his influence over the national political scene, being the speaker of the parliament) and mounting discontent over the lack of commitment to democratic practices within the party have exacerbated these internal frictions, resulting in a number of high-profile resignations from the party.[14] Ennahda's internal politics have not only increased distrust within the party and at times affected its cohesion and discipline, but have also made decisions at the shura council, its highest institutional body, often unpredictable and hard to manage.

A Crisis of Governance

The problems that plagued the political scene were not without effect. Although the country's key political players were able to navigate various challenges during the transition, there has been much uncertainty. For many people, the country's reconfigured political scene is far from assuring. Increasingly, there is disillusionment with mainstream party politics and distrust of politicians. This was evident in the number of independent lists that emerged with the 2018 municipal elections and, more so, in the 2019 presidential elections that brought to power Kais Saied, an independent candidate from outside the ranks of institutional party politics who advocates political decentralization, more representative governance, and bottom-up social and political change. The legislative elections yielded a heterogeneous mosaic with no decisive victory for any party, giving Ennahda a narrow lead over a new party, Qalb Tounes (whose founder, Nabil Karoui, is a former member of Nidaa Tounes), followed by four smaller parties: the Al Karama Coalition (*karama* meaning dignity), a socially conservative alliance; the Free Destourian Party, an anti-revolution party, which includes a number of figures of the Ben Ali regime; the Democratic Current, a progressive party; and the People's Movement, a Pan-Arab party. This resulted in a fractured parliament. Political disagreements, internal tensions, and fragile coalitions made the negotiations for forming a government all the more difficult. Within the space of only a few months after the 2019 elections, three proposed governments stood in front of the legislature for a vote of confidence. Political tensions, deepening partisan divides, and the absence of a constructive opposition have not only heightened political uncertainty but also deepened the country's crisis of governance. The dissolving of several municipal councils, which failed the test of shared governance and were paralyzed by partisan politics, speaks of challenges that are lurking at all levels of government.

Nowhere was the ineffectiveness of political life more patent than in the workings of a polarized parliament. Whereas in earlier phases of the transition, favoring inclusiveness over partisan politics helped foster a culture of political compromise—as epitomized by successive unity governments and recurring coalitions between key political parties and prominent political players—the new parliament was marked by confrontational politics, schisms, and fragmentation. Repeated scenes of chaos and political bickering became the hallmark for the nation's legislature, which deepened people's disillusionment with political parties. Further complicating the country's political scene is the discord that developed between Carthage, the Kasbah, and Bardo. The political crisis goes back to the forced resignation of prime minister-designate, Elyes Fakhfakh, who stepped down after barely five months in office, amid allegations of conflict of interest, to avert a no-confidence vote. The backing of Ennahda and its allies for his successor Hichem Mechichi fed political rivalries and deepened disagreements. A power struggle ensued when, following a government reshuffle in January 2021, the president refused to summon newly appointed ministers to swear the oath of office, citing violations. A prolonged deadlock ended with Saied invoking Article 80 of the Constitution, which empowers the president to take measures deemed necessary if the country were to face an imminent danger. Accordingly, the president dismissed the prime minister and top government officials, and suspended the parliament. He further consolidated his executive powers, announcing that he would rule by decree and undertake public prosecution during an undefined transition period, pending political overhauls and constitutional amendments.

These developments were met with mixed reactions. Those who supported the new measures welcomed a fresh start. A paralyzed political scene, an unresponsive political class, and a struggling economy left broad sections of Tunisian society exasperated with a decade-long transition (and nine successive governments) that failed to deliver on the promises of the revolution. In the absence of a constitutional court to adjudicate constitutional disputes, these measures were a *fait accompli*, though several parties, political forces, and civil society groups considered Saied's actions a presidential overreach and denounced the July 25 measures as an assault on democracy. What effect these developments are likely to have on the country's transition is hard to tell; what is certain, though, is that ten years later, Tunisia remains in a liminal state.

The Prospects for Transitional Justice

Significantly, the country's political problems run deeper. Tactical arrangements and tenuous coalitions between the ruling parties in Tunisia's post-authoritarian context did not amount to a national consensus to address the nation's problems. Nor did national dialogue efforts lay the groundwork for a real national reconciliation between pre- and post-2011 political actors and players. Further affecting the transitional process is the slow pace of reform and the difficulty of achieving transitional justice and reconciling the country with its troubling past in ways that could pave the way for a new start. One of the steps the country took toward democratic consolidation was to establish a Truth and Dignity Commission in 2014 to investigate human rights violations during the period 1955–2013. The ostensible aim of transitional justice was to reestablish justice for both the victims and the perpetrators, and, in the process, restore dignity and recreate trust. Such reconciliation was deemed necessary for the country to move toward democratic transition.

But the process was far from smooth. From its outset, there has never been a political or popular consensus about the committee, which often lacked internal support and complained about the non-cooperation of government agencies and the impunity of certain figures. This affected both the work and the legitimacy of the committee. There was fear among those who were associated with the old regime(s) of what the committee's probing eye could yield, but there was also apprehension among the defenders of the revolution that justice was not being served and that achieving national reconciliation (even if it means whitewashing corruption) was taking precedence over accountability, which runs counter to the spirit of the revolution. Failure to adopt measures that would immunize the revolution as the country moved out of the immediate post-revolutionary period proved to be fertile ground for anti-democratic forces to resurge and for the lurking deep state to regain momentum. The new dynamics that have developed since 2014 facilitated the return of old guard political elites, anti-change forces that have a vested interest in the perpetuation of the existing system, and business networks that capitalize on state resources and channels to consolidate their position and further their economic interests.[15] There was fear that the complacency of the political elite was robbing the revolution of its momentum. Those fears were intensified with the contested 2015 amnesty law (known as the Administrative Reconciliation Law), which indemnifies civil servants who committed financial crimes under the former regime under the pretext of improving the investment climate and maintaining political stability. The law triggered a wave of protests and was criticized for creating a 'culture of impunity' that undermines both the pursuit of justice and anti-corruption efforts.[16]

Expectedly, the transitional justice process was not free of political agendas as various political factions attempted to manipulate the process for political ends, which pointedly entailed reckoning with the country's past (and acknowledging past wrongs), reexamining hegemonic state narratives, and coming to terms with competing versions of Tunisia's modern history and national identity. Particularly contentious is the issue of how the state relates to religion, which took a salient political dimension with the deep schism between the Islamists and the secularists.[17] These dynamics made transitional justice as much a legal process as a political project.[18]

Added Challenges and Stalled Reform

Significantly, the success of the democratic transition is contingent not only on efforts to implement the process of transitional justice to redress past abuses (truth seeking, the recognition of past wrongs, determining the responsibility of the state and of individuals in past abuses, issuing apologies, and ensuring retribution), but also to reform the very state institutions that facilitated or permitted these abuses or were complicit in the abuses. This is the case with the security apparatus and the judicial system, which were instrumental for the old regime's durability. Thus far, attempts to reform these establishments to ward off future transgressions has proved a slow and arduous endeavor.[19] These shortcomings, which prevented a full implementation of transitional justice, leave the door open for the recurring of abuses. Notwithstanding the pushback from human rights activists and the vigilance of civil society, these risks are real. For instance, the controversial draft law that legalizes impunity for the security forces and undermines the rule of law drew much opposition for fear of democratic backsliding.[20] The fact that, a decade after its revolution, the country still operates under emergency laws that give authorities extensive and exceptional powers is raising concerns about potential abuses and the recurrence of the excesses of the past, which could adversely impact democratic consolidation efforts.

Ironically, as much as the mounting security challenges mobilized the country's security apparatus, they also made the need to reform the security sector itself less pressing. This is not to underplay the security threats Tunisia has been facing. After the revolution, a number of factors undermined the country's security. The deficient capabilities of the nation's small army, the legacy of a security system that was subservient to an authoritarian regime, and the fragmentation of the country's intelligence services,[21] coupled with the weakness of the state during the transition period, engendered an added security weakness. While Tunisia has been spared the kind of violence and destruction that plagued other Arab nations in the aftermath of the 2011 uprisings, it endured a number of deadly terrorist attacks by jihadis. The assassination of two opposition figures in 2013 mired the country in a deep political crisis, which risked derailing its transition. Tragically, Tunisia was the scene of two of the region's deadliest attacks in 2015, one in the Bardo Museum in the capital Tunis and the other in a tourist resort in the coastal city of Sousse. That same year, there was a suicide bombing inside a presidential guard bus a few blocks away from the Ministry of the Interior in the heart of the capital.

The most challenging security threats, however, came from the borderlands. Since 2012, sporadic deadly attacks in and around Mount Chaanbi on the country's western border made concrete the risk of terrorism and highlighted the threat of jihadi violence.[22] While the nature of these security threats is new to the nation, the problem of porous borders predates the revolution. For years, Tunisia's western borders with Algeria and southern borders with Libya have been appropriated by smuggling networks, which thrived in border towns in the absence of a genuine commitment on the part of the state to develop the unprivileged and neglected inner regions. With neighboring Libya descending into chaos, these challenges were compounded by the inflow of militants, networks of illegal immigrants, arms trafficking, and militant incursions. Recurring violence and continuing instability in post-Gaddafi Libya had a spillover effect. This was made patent during the assault on Ben Gardane in 2016, when a group of Islamic State militants infiltrated the country through the southern border with Libya with the aim of gaining a stronghold and establishing an Islamic emirate. Although improvements in the security environment have contributed to the country's political stability during the critical transitional period, security remains a challenge in the absence of a comprehensive strategy. This is all the more so considering the sluggish reform of the security sector,[23] not to mention the continuous resistance on the part of various actors and stakeholders who benefit from the perpetuation of the current system to tackle issues of security governance and carry out changes as part of the broader democratization process.[24]

Economic Malaise

Despite the change the country has undergone, the transitional period did not bring about the kind of stability, progress, and prosperity that people hoped for. Since 2011, Tunisia's economic problems have deepened and the country remains gripped by economic hardship. Particularly disconcerting is the persistence of problems associated with the underlying causes of the revolution, including the unrealized aspirations of the youth, the unfulfilled promise for inclusive development in the inner regions, the persistence of social inequalities, and growing socioeconomic disparities. Overall, the country's economic outlook has deteriorated and both the micro and macroeconomic indicators are far from assuring: high unemployment rates, exploding external debt, large fiscal deficits, high levels of public spending, significant fiscal instability, and low economic growth rates—all of which hinder the prospects for sustainable long-term economic growth.[25] When it comes to the everyday lives of people, the acceleration of inflation, declining purchasing power, and the erosion of living standards are producing considerable frustration.

Young people in particular are facing an uncertain outlook, as many have been excluded from political life and deprived of economic opportunity. The post-2011 Tunisia did not live up to the expectations of youth, leading to disillusionment with what the revolution had achieved for them. Further marginalization of youth, who were primary actors during the revolution, and their limited participation in decision-making processes during a critical period of change led to increased disenchantment with the transition. By and large, there is distrust of the political class, which continues to be dominated by an older generation, and a disconnect from the state and state officials and institutional actors, as they failed to take heed of the real causes that led to the revolution.[26] Demands for employment and dignity were largely unmet after the revolution, leading to youth disillusionment and growing social discontent.

Economic hardship and the lack of real prospects for betterment at home have lured more young people into migration.[27] They have also fueled waves of social protests to pressure the government to pay attention to people's hardships and to remedy their situations and, more broadly, to demand economic and social rights.[28] While many of these protests are local or related to a specific group and a particular field, others have been organized around economic sectors and activities that continue to disprivilege the inner regions and divert resources away from local communities, including the Kamour protests and those in the mining region.[29] Although, increasingly, there have been nation-wide protest movements and coordinated campaigns aimed against government policies, such as the one that erupted in 2018 to protest against the deteriorating economic conditions and the government's austerity measures, these were not sustainable. While such expanding forms of contention do put pressure on the government to act, by and large, social activism and popular demands for socioeconomic justice have been met with attempts to discredit and marginalize them.[30] The social effects of the country's deepening economic problems often brought the government in confrontation with the UGTT, the nation's main labor organization, which leveraged its ability to call for strikes to regain its political weight and enhance its bargaining power. Although the labor organization has a long history of activism and a broad legitimacy, its positions on socioeconomic issues have been a source of contention, with some criticizing the union for being 'a spoiler for difficult reform efforts,'[31] while others consider it a stabilizer. The pushback by the union, as well as growing discontent and activism by those who had economic grievances, made it difficult to implement economic reforms. For the government's many critics, such reforms are meant to implement policies mandated by foreign financial institutions and international donors advocating a neoliberal economic model to the detriment of a declining middle class and the impoverished working class.

One of the manifestations of the country's socioeconomic difficulties is the amplification of the informal economy. Over the years, sprawling networks of informal trade and the persistence of a parallel economy developed at the expense of formal economic activity with detrimental fiscal effects on the state. In impoverished regions on the borders with Libya and Algeria, entire towns and communities rely on smuggling and on illicit goods for their livelihood.[32] The proliferation of these networks of informal trade is impelled by the lack of economic opportunity and the scarcity of job opportunities. Efforts to fight these cross border activities have been undermined by the absence of long-term solutions for a region where promises for socioeconomic development have not been fulfilled. Seen from the perspective of these disadvantaged inner regions, the persistence of economic difficulties and uneven development is indicative of a lack of political will on the part of the state to remedy the consequences of policy choices and political decisions the inhabitants of these regions have endured for decades.

In Search for Social Justice

High unemployment rates and low job creation in disadvantaged areas point to an absence of social justice when it comes to the disenfranchised inner regions. Regional disparities persist between the urbanized richer coastal regions and the less developed and rural regions in the interior, accentuating the problem of unfair distribution of wealth. This is the case with the mining region, where a short-lived social movement developed in 2008. The state's extraction of phosphate in this resource-rich region did not go hand in hand with efforts to develop the region nor did it translate into economic opportunity for the local population. Demands for inclusive regional development and equitable distribution of wealth have not amounted to much. In spite of various newly announced government projects designed to benefit the inner regions, such initiatives were not substantive and remain inadequate for the growth of these areas, which suffer from poor infrastructure and substandard services when it comes to health, education, and welfare. Faster and more inclusive growth is still needed to help narrow the disparities between regions.[33] Significantly, dealing with the country's inequalities requires more than quick fixes. The revolution has made apparent the need for a new social contract that redefines the role of the state and its relationship to its citizens. While politically this move has been facilitated by the transition from autocracy rule to institutional democracy (even if proven fragile so far) and the upholding of civil rights and freedoms that are provided for by the Constitution, there are impediments at the level of the state and limits when it comes to the economy. State capacity is lacking and the ability to deliver essential government services in vital sectors, such as education and healthcare, is limited. The stagnation of the economy and the limits of the country's very economic model have impeded growth, hindered the ability to create high value jobs, and undermined developments efforts. Deep changes are not easy to implement, as regional development requires, among other things, major structural economic reforms.[34] The success of these efforts also requires rethinking governance, modernizing public administration, and reducing the bureaucracy within a bloated and inefficient public sector, which largely serves the interests of the old ruling cliques and business elites and is plagued by corruption.[35]

Corruption was one of the factors that fueled the 2010–2011 protests. After the revolution, corruption increased and became more widespread, plaguing nearly every sector of the economy, ranging from illicit enrichment and the misappropriation of public funds to the petty corruption that has become an inevitable part of carrying out day-to-day transactions and facilitating the rendering of services. The 2019 corruption index ranks Tunisia as 74 out of 180 countries.[36] So rampant and endemic has corruption become that the state has made fighting it a national priority, enacting legislation that deters corruption and establishing anti-corruption agencies such as the Commission of Inquiry into Misappropriation and Corruption, the National Anti-Corruption Commission, and the Judicial Financial Pole. Widespread corruption has not only prompted the successive governments that assumed power in the post-revolution period to take measures to fight it,[37] but also mobilized civil society actors and watchdog groups like I-Watch and Raqabah.

In spite of state initiatives, government measures, and civil society pressure to increase accountability, corruption has increased. Hindering the efforts of anti-corruption agencies is their lack of the necessary training, resources, and capacity to effectively deal with corruption and to enforce laws. Government anti-corruption efforts have also been undermined by political considerations; in some instances, anti-corruption campaigns have been carried out selectively, leaving untouched influential members of the business elite and steering clear of certain economic and administrative sectors where corruption is rife. The persistence of corruption is weakening trust in the state's ability to safeguard social justice and pursue good governance, undermining faith in the state's institutions, eroding values of transparency and accountability that are central to democracy, and undermining open government plans. It is also deterring foreign investment, affecting economic recovery, and hindering economic growth, all of which have direct implications on the country's democratic transition.[38]

Despite proactive economic policies to stimulate growth and revive the economy, there is no political will to tackle challenging economic issues or undertake serious economic reform. Many of the economic measures that have been taken seem designed more to contain people's anger than as real or structural reforms. For example, pressure from the unions, resistance to change, and the political cost of reform led to increased state subsidies to several mismanaged and underperforming national corporations and the recapitalization of a number of public banks—spending that has further ensnared the country in a vicious borrowing cycle.[39] The inability of the economy to generate growth and add value is perpetuating a cycle whereby social pressure and popular demands for tangible progress are impelling the government to continue to provide quick fixes. These social tensions have taken their toll on the economy, engendering the disruption of vital economic activity, eroding an already declining productivity, and affecting economic growth. In the critical mining sector, phosphate extraction and exports have decreased due to economic grievances, local protests, and political divisions. Other sectors have also faced tremendous difficulties. Tourism, a key sector and the lifeline of the economy, has been adversely affected by the transitional uncertainty the country is experiencing, but has also been hard hit by a surge in terrorism as well as travel restrictions following the outbreak of the global COVID-19 pandemic in 2020. These problems have been compounded by decreasing investment. The business climate is not assuring due to internal and external factors. Frequent labor protests and widespread worker discontent in the face of rising living expenses and persistent hikes in prices have negatively affected the business investment environment and the flow of foreign investment (FDI) into the country and led to the closure of numerous foreign companies, while the economic fallout of the upheaval in neighboring Libya has negatively affected the expandability of Tunisia's economy.

Mounting socioeconomic difficulties have weighed heavily on the country's democratic transition, leading to political uncertainty, while the kind of instability that marked the political scene during the transition prevented effecting deep reforms. In much the same way political progress has been undermined by the deterioration of the economy, the recovery of the economy has been hard to achieve considering the hesitant steps the successive post-2011 governments have taken to tackle growing social demands and chronic economic problems. Even when there is political will to move forward, there has been little tangible progress on the economic reform front. As the revolution and its aftermath are not yielding concrete changes and improvements in the daily lives of ordinary people, the country is running the risk of 'reform fatigue.'

Overview of the Individual Chapters

A decade after its revolution, Tunisia continues to be a fragile democracy. While the country made substantial gains, many challenges remain, pointing to an arduous path forward. These changes and challenges are the focus of the eight contributions to this volume.

In Chapter 2, Marina Ottaway focuses on the imperfections of Tunisia's democratic experience and what they mean for a country in the throes of change. Placing the new Tunisia in the context of the region's persistent authoritarianism, she outlines the underlying reasons that helped it transition from an authoritarian system to what she describes as a 'struggling democracy.' These reasons, she argues, are specific to Tunisia and range from a deeply embedded (formal and informal) political pluralism that survived decades of authoritarianism to central political players who value pragmatism over idealism and from a small professional army that was insulated from politics to fortuitous events that played out favorably for the country's democratic transition. While the path Tunisia followed has helped consolidate its democratic gains, imperfect as these may be, such gains, Ottaway notes, came at a cost: save for the constitutional guarantees for individual freedom, including the freedom of speech, the revolution did not alter people's reality, unemployment continues to be high, and dignity remains elusive. These challenges make the process of change all the more uncertain; they also underscore the complex nature of the democratization process and the unstable nature of transitions. Ultimately, Ottaway concludes, while the case of Tunisia may be unique in the Middle East and North Africa, by and large, the country's uneasy transition is not fundamentally different from others in its imperfections as many of the difficulties the country has been facing are typical of newly established democracies.

While Ottaway dissects the intricacies of fast-paced developments in Tunisia's political life and the trials and tribulations of its democratic transition, in Chapter 3, Enrique Klaus offers a critical examination of the transitional bodies that were established after the revolution in order to overcome the legacy of decades of authoritarianism and consolidate the country's democratic transition. Focusing on the High Independent Authority for Audiovisual Communication (HAICA), which was set up in 2013 to regulate the Tunisian audiovisual sector and guarantee the freedom and pluralism of the media, Klaus highlights the limits and contradictory nature of this important transitional body. While in principle the HAICA's legitimacy rests on its independence and neutrality, in practice, its workings obey complex dynamics that lie at the intersection of media positioning, political power play, and business interests. This is evident in the political maneuvers that led to the creation of the HAICA, the long and arduous negotiations associated with instituting this transitional body and determining its constitution, and the discordances between its members, whose appointment was along partisan lines. These dynamics, Klaus argues, have undermined the legitimacy and independence of the regulatory body and tainted its work. If anything, the kind of polarized pluralism that shaped the HAICA and came to define the audiovisual sector resulted in a problematic overlapping between the political sphere and the media sphere. The chapter highlights how the uncertainties these logics engendered have implications not only on the country's evolving media sector, which is being appropriated and instrumentalized by key political players and stakeholders, but also on the country's democratic transition as a whole.

The fast-paced historical changes Tunisia has undergone since the revolution yielded various transitional institutions that could potentially alter the nature of governance in Tunisia, but also compelled the country's political players, both old and new, to adapt to the demands of a constantly reconstituted political scene or else face the risk of effacement. Nowhere is this more conspicuous than in the case of Ennahda, which moved from being a banned Islamist party, with its members either imprisoned or in exile under Ben Ali, to being a key political player after the revolution. The transition thrust Ennahda to the fore and brought it to power through various power-sharing agreements and government coalitions. Ennahda's post-revolution political trajectory and its integration in and adaptation to the political process—the focus of Fabio Merone in Chapter 4—is noteworthy because of its potential implications for the country's political transition, but also for what it tells us about evolving models of mainstream political Islam. Merone explores how the changing political dynamics in Tunisia impelled Rachid Ghannouchi's party to pursue a strategy of 'professionalization' that is premised on separating its charitable work and da'wa activities as a movement (haraka) from its political activities as a party (hizb), and, further, what it means for Ennahda to embrace post-Islamism. More than merely a secularization of Islamic politics, Merone argues, Ennahda's official decision to move to the center of the political spectrum— and to position itself as a relatively conservative national party with a political agenda rather than an Islamic movement fighting for its survival—amounts to a process of de-ideologization, which affirms the party's acceptance of Tunisia as a civic state. Compared to the rest of the Arab world, Merone concludes, political Islam in Tunisia is taking hold in unique ways. The political evolution of Tunisia's main Islamist party and its ability integrate state institutions and take part in democratic governance, which sets it apart from other versions of political Islam in the region, is a manifestation of its 'Tunisianité' and a reflection of a strong national identity that is associated with a long tradition of moderation and reform.

Going hand in hand with the momentous changes in the political scene and the notable transformations in institutional politics are sociopolitical dynamics that developed outside formal party politics, including the injection of new life into the associational sphere. In Chapter 5, Zuzana Hudáková examines the profound changes civil society has undergone since the revolution and the role civil society organizations played in the country's democratic transition. Whereas under Ben Ali, the state pursued a 'heavily-regulated' approach to associational life and civil society was predominantly constituted of state-controlled or state-funded associations that were used by the regime to perpetuate authoritarianism and enhance its control over society, after the revolution, the associational sphere became more diverse, autonomous, and vibrant. Facilitating the increase in associational life and the surge in bottom-up activism are new laws that organize associational life, an increase in citizen participation, the injection of foreign aid, and the influx of foreign funding. In spite of these gains, Hudáková notes, the burgeoning post-2011 civil society in Tunisia is not without limitations. While many new organizations have been professionalized and have proven adept at influencing policy and mobilizing networks, the least institutionalized ones remain marginal, lacking in resources and experience, and not rooted in the community. Notwithstanding the democratizing potential of civil society and their role in strengthening institutions and improving governance, Hudáková concludes, their impact has been limited when it comes to 'deep structural issues that require government intervention and political, social, and economic reforms.'

In spite of the diversity and heterogeneity of civil society, much of its thrust lies within the sphere of civil and political rights. The parochial view of public interest that many civil society organizations traditionally adopted and the inadequate attention these organizations paid to social and economic rights left many individuals and groups to fight their own battles for socioeconomic rights and to intensify their collective action and escalate their activism.[40] Complementing Hudáková's exploration of how organized forms of activism in a reconfigured civil sphere have integrated into the very workings of shared governance is Irene Weipert-Fenner's contribution on extra-institutional modalities of assertion and disruptive forms of contestation in Chapter 6. Specifically, Weipert-Fenner examines the evolution of collective popular action and social protests since the revolution. Thus, initial political protests were motivated by the demands of a new political system that breaks with authoritarian practices and promotes democratic governance. In subsequent years, disenchantment with the country's socioeconomic condition and unfulfilled promises for change further increased social discontent and intensified local activism by independent actors and local groups. With the government's adoption of austerity measures, though, outbursts of local discontent and regional waves of contention—which typically emerged independently of formal organizations and were articulated around pressing issues like unemployment and development for the marginalized inner regions—acquired a national dimension with networked forms of mobilization supported by various organizations and civil society actors. While fragmented forms of contention continue unabated, deeper networks have emerged and consolidated their efforts around coordinated nationwide protests that are more strategic and more sustained. Significantly, Weipert-Fenner notes, these overlapping dynamics make changing forms and logics of mobilization during the country's transition as important to note as transformations in the political scene.

Many of these forms of protest are youth-centered and youth-driven. Although young people were key players in the 2011 revolution and youth issues were one of the drivers of the popular uprising, for most of them the promises of the revolution remain unfulfilled with rising unemployment, endemic corruption, and deepening regional unbalance. These dynamics are explored in depth in Chapter 7 by Alyssa Miller, who takes a closer look at the plight of disposed youth in underdeveloped and socioeconomically marginalized regions, focusing specifically on youth precarity. Miller provides a vivid account of the struggles of precarious rural youth in Tunisia's inner regions and their efforts to draw attention to their issues and to claim their right to dignity, social protection, and a better life. She focuses on Kasserine, an inner governorate in the arid western-central region that suffered generations of underdevelopment that contributed to the perpetuation of an informal economy with bordering Algeria, but also a region where vulnerability has kept the revolutionary spirit alive. Drawing on ethnographic work she conducted in Tunisia and participant observation of protest movements and sit-ins that are often marginalized, delegitimized, and even criminalized, she illustrates how Kasserinois youth relentlessly struggle to lift themselves up and face up to a government they view as having failed its citizens. By shifting the focus from 'resistance' to 'endurance,' Miller's contribution deepens our understanding of how youth overcome adversity and seek social justice even as they continue to suffer from systemic exclusion and the state's indifference to their conditions.

Enduring regional inequalities and systematic marginalization, which were accentuated by unequal redistributive policies that favor the coastal regions over the inner and southern regions, have had implications on the very notion of citizenship and belonging. The revolution brought in hope for a reconfigured relationship between the center and the periphery as well as between the state and its citizens. These dynamics are at the center of Chapter 8, in which Ruth Hanau Santini draws attention to evolving notions of citizenship. These are intertwined with changes in the very practices of state institutions that are impelled by the changing security dynamics in post-revolution Tunisia. Focusing on a jihadi attack on the southern town of Ben Gardane, on the border with Libya, which was carried out with the aim of establishing an Islamic State emirate in North Africa, Santini illustrates how both the state and citizens reacted in the face of a tenuous security situation. The state's coordinated response to the attack and the ability of the state's security agencies to adapt to these challenges is indicative of a change in the very conception and practice of security from 'regime security' in an authoritarian context to 'state (or republican) security' in a post-authoritarian context. Significantly, Santini notes, the case of the Ben Gardane attack also hinges on the broader issue of 'societal security,' which is evident in the reaction of the inhabitants of the town, which has historically been viewed as 'disloyal to the post-independence statist project' and, over the years, came to represent the kind of inequality, underdevelopment, and marginalization that plagues the inner regions. The support the security apparatuses received from the residents, who fiercely defended their town, signals the emergence of 'a new pact' between the authorities and the town's inhabitants, and, more broadly, between the post-revolution state and citizens whose lived experience has been shaped by decades of state disavowal. For Santini, the reaction of the townspeople—taking pride in defending their homeland and constructing narratives of bravery around the battle of Ben Gardane—points to how state security is henceforth inextricably linked with societal security, identity politics, and the very conception of citizenship.

In the concluding chapter, Alexandra Domike Blackman delves into history to reflect on Tunisia's transition, highlighting enduring legacies that can help better explain post-revolution political developments and outcomes, whether it is state legitimacy, inclusionary politics, or political stability—relative as these may be. She points out social and political trends that evince a certain historical persistence, drawing attention to 'critical junctures' that continue to have an enduring effect on Tunisia's political path and to shape societal inclinations and policy choices. These historical legacies, Blackman notes, are noteworthy 'not only because of their continued importance in Tunisian politics but also because the post-revolutionary period represents an opportunity for a break with past patterns.' Significantly, such 'institutional and behavioral path dependence' is not inevitable, which makes it hard to predict with any certainty how the country's political transition will unfold. Eschewing determinism, Blackman argues that the enduring effect of these historical developments on the political outcomes can change (and, in fact, the revolution brought in notable discontinuities), but reversing the course of development of some of the country's taken-for-granted sociopolitical realities comes at a cost. For example, while the reversal of women's gains may be difficult in a country that has a long history of commitment to women's rights, the weakening of kinship networks in Tunisia (following decades of Ottoman *beylic* rule centered around prominent families, colonial bureaucratization and state centralization, and post-independence government policies) undermines decentralization efforts and democratic consolidation at the local level, as such legacy is not conducive to the emergence of effective subnational political structures for democratic governance. Both individually and collectively, the chapters that constitute this volume offer an in-depth look into how Tunisia navigated its transition. Together, these grounded reflections paint a complex picture of a country in the throes of change.

2

THE TUNISIAN TRANSITION AND AUTHORITARIANISM IN THE MIDDLE EAST
DEMOCRACY IS UP TO THE CITIZENS, NOT THE NEIGHBORS

Marina Ottaway

For a decade, Tunisia appeared to be transitioning from the authoritarianism that marked the first half century of its independence into a struggling democracy. Then, on July 25, 2021, President Kais Saied dismissed Prime Minister Hichem Mechichi and suspended the elected parliament for a period of thirty days, arguing that the exceptional measures he took were called for by the unconstitutional actions of the parliament and the paralysis of the government in the face of a mounting economic crisis. A month later, he extended those provisions, with no roadmap or indication that he intended to revert to the political process envisaged by the Constitution. Rather, Saied made it clear that Tunisia needed to return to the strong presidency it had prior to the 2011 uprising. Whether the president's action constituted an executive overreach, as his detractors claim, or a correction of the course of the revolution, as his supporters maintain, Tunisia's experiment with democracy appeared to be over.

The reversal of the democratic process in Tunisia and the seeming willingness of much of the population, including civil society organizations, to accept it should not obscure the fact that, for nearly a decade, the country had been remarkably successful in installing a democratic system. It is therefore important to understand the causes of that success, but also its costs, because both help explain the predicament the country is facing.

Tunisia did not become a perfect democracy, where the voices of all citizens count equally in determining the actions of the government—but no such democracy exists in the world, and I suspect it never will. Nor was Tunisia a participatory democracy, in which citizens take part directly in policy discussions and decisions— but, then again, participatory democracy is also an ideal concept that does not have many real-life examples, particularly on a nationwide scale. More modestly, the Tunisia that emerged in the decade following the revolution is a country where the various political players abided by democratic procedures and where the government broadly respected the law. Some segments of the population had a strong voice and the ability to influence government decisions, while others had much less clout. Furthermore, policies were not always determined by the noble pursuit of 'national interest,' but by a process of bargaining among politicians who themselves were influenced by different interest groups. In other words, Tunisia had joined the world of democracy as it is in practice, not democracy as an ideal. Even such qualified democratic transformation was a long shot.

There had been no slow buildup of democratic demands or enduring struggles to build opposition organizations and structures of shared governance. The leadership at the top did not appear particularly divided, a factor found to facilitate transitions from authoritarianism elsewhere.[1] There was no pressure for change from neighboring countries or regional organizations. On the contrary, Tunisia is part of a region where authoritarianism, whether benign or malign, thrives. The country is sandwiched in between Libya, which has been mired in a decade-long civil war, and Algeria, which is caught between a military-dominated regime and protesters that cannot win but do not want to give up. The political climate in neighboring countries and, in fact, in the broader Middle East and North Africa (MENA) region did not help Tunisia solidify its political achievements, either by example or by pressure—as was the case at one point in Latin America, where latecomers to democratic transitions benefited from the new regional context.[2]

Tunisia was truly the outlier, the exception among countries where the hopes raised by the 2011 uprisings were dashed by the success of authoritarian regimes in reestablishing their control, as in Egypt, or by descent into conflict and chaos, as in Libya, Yemen, and Syria. A number of factors and conditions accounted for this initial success, including a deeply embedded political pluralism that had survived repressive regimes; agency, in the form of capable leadership; an element of luck; and a degree of pragmatism as major players accepted the politics of the possible rather than of absolute principles and ideals. These internal factors were crucial, particularly considering that international context had at best a minor impact. Significantly, however, Tunisia paid a price to become democratic, trading formal democracy for failure to carry out the substantive reforms many of its citizens expected. In the end, this price was too high, leading to an anti-democratic reaction and the near-collapse of the country's democratic experiment.

Authoritarianism and Its Resilience

The Tunisian transformation took place in a context marked not only by the prevalence of authoritarian regimes but also by their remarkable capacity to persist in the face of challenges. Before the 2011 uprisings, change appeared unthinkable. The authoritarian regimes of North Africa had been exceedingly stable for decades. Tunisia had only two presidents, Habib Bourguiba and Zine El Abidine Ben Ali, since independence in 1956. Algeria was still ruled by military and civilian figures who had earned their credentials during the war against France, which ended in 1962; and after ten years of extremely bloody conflict against Islamists during the 1990s, that generation reaffirmed its control and still maintains it to this day. In Libya, Muammar Gaddafi had ruled for over four decades—from 1969 until he was overthrown and killed in 2011, leaving behind a country nobody has been able to govern. Further afield, the Moroccan monarchy had managed to maintain power, enacting only minor reforms through a succession in 1999. Egypt had experienced the Nasserist coup d'état that changed the character of the regime in 1952, but since that time had seen power transferred in an orderly manner to a succession of military officers—each the vice-president of his predecessor. In the Levant, the same pattern of stable authoritarianism prevailed, and, in the Persian Gulf region, monarchies adhered to closed political systems based on hereditary rule.[3] Tunisia and the countries of the MENA region, in other words, were perfect case studies of what scholars defined variously as authoritarian persistence, robustness, resilience, and other terms suggesting that incumbent rulers were not about to leave the scene. A vast scholarly literature on that topic had developed before 2011, inevitably leading to a wave of rethinking in the subsequent year, followed, when democratic transitions did not materialize, by the conclusion that the earlier analyses of authoritarian resilience had indeed been correct.[4]

The inevitable corollary of stable authoritarianism was the weakness of popular mobilization and political organizing. By and large, there was not much underground organizing, except on the part of some Islamist groups that appeared to be as focused on preaching as they were on politics. In most countries, including Tunisia, legal non-governmental political parties existed and participated in elections, competing with each other in the limited political space the regimes were willing to leave open, but conscious of the fact that their position was bound to remain marginal and their influence nonexistent. Beholden to the regime for their existence, some of these parties even positioned themselves as loyal opposition parties. Political parties that had been operating before 2011 often tried to explain their poor electoral results after the uprising by arguing that they had not been able to organize freely earlier. In so doing, they confirmed that they had limited themselves to operating in the narrow space the government allowed them, rather than trying to push the limits. The exception, as we shall see, were Islamist parties and, in the case of Tunisia, the labor unions.

34

The problem of demobilized societies, which authoritarian regimes had deliberately promoted, was compounded by the suddenness of the uprisings. Most democratic transitions are slow processes, not sudden events and even less so the outcome of revolutions. Studies of democratic transitions are unanimous in concluding that violent eruptions are unlikely to usher in democracy. Some even believe that any kind of mass mobilization is dangerous, while Isobel Coleman concludes—after considering the examples of India and South Africa and musing on the impact of Martin Luther King Jr. on the civil rights movement in the United States—that peaceful mass mobilization can help lead to a democratic transition.[5]

The Arab uprisings, at least initially, were not revolutionary upheavals by people determined to do anything, including using force, in order to overthrow existing regimes and set their countries on a new course. Nor were they the culmination of a long process of popular mobilization for change. Even Islamists, the most organized of all the groups and the ones with the largest popular following, were taken aback by the uprisings and in some countries, including Egypt, had trouble deciding how to react and whether to join in the protest. In sum, the Arab countries that experienced uprisings were unprepared for either revolution or peaceful democratic transitions.

To be sure, socioeconomic conditions were bad; but bad conditions do not inevitably lead to uprisings and revolutions, and even less often to democratic transitions. Furthermore, as many analysts have pointed out, socioeconomic problems were chronic ones that had existed and been denounced for decades—they were not the results of a sudden crisis. Above all, what was missing in most countries were people and organizations prepared to act in a systematic, organized fashion. On this point, Tunisia was the exception, although the organization was provided not by devoted revolutionaries, but by the labor union federation, the Union Générale Tunisienne du Travail (UGTT), whose top leadership had a history of accommodation with the government that was at odds with the more uncompromising position of its activist rank and file.

The protesters in various countries were quite successful in mobilizing people in the short run. Social media proved to be a powerful tool for rapidly reaching the younger part of the population, although several studies have pointed out that traditional media, such as satellite television, and old-fashioned methods, such as word of mouth, helped bring crowds to the streets.

Because of the lack of previous experience, strong leadership, and organizational structures, protesters in most countries were not able to build on the initial success. One of the least sufficiently told stories of the 2011 wave of uprisings is how quickly protesters were excluded from all decision-making processes. They undoubtedly triggered a process of change, but they could not control it. The dedication of many of the young people is unquestionable. They courageously occupied the squares, defying repression at high personal costs. Although the protests have been described as peaceful and for the most part remained so, governments did not hesitate to use force. But despite their determination, they could not control the process of change. This was also true in Tunisia.

One obvious reason is that protesters were not armed, nor did they want to be, and governments had all the means of repression at their disposal. But even more importantly, people participating in the uprising were organized for protest, not for exercising power. Social media summoned crowds effectively but did not tell them what to do; without plans for the next steps, crowds became ineffective. Ideology also hampered some of the youthful protesters, who rejected hierarchy and strong leadership in favor of the notion that power should be widely distributed. This idealism was one of the reasons why protesters elicited much sympathy around the world. The hard reality, however, is that even peaceful political change involves a transfer of at least some power from the old regimes, a transfer that cannot take place unless protesters succeed in generating power themselves. Modern history is rife with examples of how movements that meant to give power to the people ended up as top-down authoritarian regimes when new elites succeeded in generating and mobilizing power.

The movements that triggered the uprisings did not have, and were reluctant to acquire, the characteristics needed to become effective players in the process of change. Instead, it was those few preexisting organizations with a strong structure that continued the process the protesters had started—notably, the Muslim Brotherhood and movements it inspired and, in the case of Tunisia, the labor unions.

Paradoxically, the political parties that called themselves democratic—and thus felt entitled to become the major beneficiaries of a reform of the political system—were ineffectual in seizing the opportunities created by the challenge to existing regimes. This is particularly striking in countries with functioning political parties that had been contesting elections regularly. Such parties had adapted to functioning in a subordinate position to the regimes, without challenging them, and were thus poorly positioned to try to build up mass support. Egyptian secular parties of the right, left, and center contested elections not by trying to build their constituencies, but by negotiating with the government on how many seats they would be allowed to win and where. When the uprising created more political space for these secular parties, they were slow to adapt to the fact that winning votes required building popular support rather than negotiating with the government and they became fearful of being outcompeted by the well-organized Islamist parties.

Given the weaknesses of the protest movements and of the mainstream political parties, incumbent regimes had all the advantages. They controlled the security forces, the judiciary, and the bureaucracy—which, in authoritarian countries, is not a neutral, rule-based institution but a political tool of the regime. In other words, the stable authoritarian regimes of the Arab region had considerable resources to maintain their position, while the protesters had few to challenge them.

Last but not least, authoritarian regimes had not maintained themselves in power for so long without acquiring a great deal of political sophistication. In Egypt, the military—the power on or behind the throne since the 1952 coup d'état—sacrificed President Hosni Mubarak by coaxing him into resigning because he was the lightning rod for the protesters. By pushing him out and elevating to center stage the Supreme Council of the Armed Forces (SCAF), which had operated quietly until then, the military gained popularity without sacrificing any power—'the army and the people are one' became a popular slogan in the streets of Cairo. In Morocco, King Mohammed VI ordered the writing of a new supposedly more liberal constitution, held elections, and allowed the Muslim Brotherhood-inspired Party for Justice and Development to form the government when it won the plurality of the vote, confident that ultimate power was still in his hands, not in that of the elected government.

The Tunisian Exception

Tunisia followed a different course after the uprising. It experienced a change of regime—or, at least, as much of a change of regime as is likely to occur without a violent revolution that wipes out the old elite. Tunisia was unlike any other country in the region. The differences between Tunisia and the countries of the Gulf and the Levant are obvious; those between Tunisia and its neighbors in North Africa less so, but extremely significant and deserve close attention.

Structural Differences: Embedded Political Pluralism

The power structure in Tunisia before the uprising was simple. Power resided where it was supposed to be: in the presidency. It was an authoritarian system, to be sure, but without hidden actors, a deep state, or a military establishment lurking in the background. What you saw was what you got. In Algeria and even Morocco, on the other hand, there was a clear difference between what citizens called '*le pouvoir*,' the place where power ultimately rests, and '*le gouvernement*,' the official authorities who are, in reality, subordinated to '*le pouvoir*.' In Morocco, even after the 2011 rewriting of the constitution, power ultimately remains in the hands of the king and his entourage—what Moroccans call the *Makhzen* and what I will refer to as the palace. In Algeria, the situation is more convoluted because ultimate power resides not in a visible entity like the Moroccan palace, but in a network of elderly military and security officials and their civilian associates, whose claim to power often goes back to the role they played in the war for independence over half a century ago. In Egypt, ultimate power was in the hands of the military and security forces, even when the country was run by civilians. There was much speculation toward the end of the Mubarak presidency about whether the military had lost its clout, speculation that came to an abrupt end when the military forced him to resign. In all these countries, elections were held regularly and prime ministers and cabinets came and went, but '*le pouvoir*' was immutable. In Tunisia, power and government coincided and the president was the supreme authority. This difference proved crucial after the transition. Whereas Mubarak's resignation only peeled away a surface layer and the Moroccan king's constitutional revisions did not touch the real power of the palace, Ben Ali's unexpected flight to Saudi Arabia left a real power vacuum. It is not clear whether Ben Ali really meant to go into exile or, as he claimed, he meant to escort his family to safety in Saudi Arabia and return, but was blocked from doing so; the fact is that he left and never came back.

The absence of a hidden power or deep state was, to a large extent, the result of President Bourguiba's strict policy of keeping the military weak and, above all, out of politics and under civilian oversight. The military, as a result, developed an ethos of political neutrality. At no time after 2011 did it give any sign of wanting to violate this tradition, making it possible for politics to unfold.

Another of Tunisia's crucial characteristics, which set it aside from other countries, is that it was politically pluralistic, although it was fairly homogeneous in terms of ethnicity and religion. Sunni Islam, in a non-doctrinaire, popular form, was the religion of the vast majority of Tunisians, and the Berber population was too small to be a significant factor as it is in Morocco and Algeria.[6]

But politically, the country was pluralistic, with three major trends—that can be schematically represented as the left, the Islamists, and the center—competing for the allegiance of the population. All three trends had a strong presence and a long history in the country; they all had a degree of organization (either legal or clandestine) and counted among their leaders figures with a long experience in politics. Tunisia had a genuine left, represented more by the labor unions than by the handful of leftist parties that seemed unable to overcome their divisions. The UGTT was founded in 1946, but the origins of left-wing unionism in the then French protectorate go back as early as 1924—although initial organizing attempts by French labor unions broke down repeatedly over differences about the colonial situation, which the French unions accepted while the Tunisian organizations naturally opposed. Nevertheless, despite the many tensions, the French unions carved a leftist imprint on the UGTT that is still evident above all in the regional branches.

After Tunisia became independent, the UGTT developed a complicated relationship with the government, with the group's central leadership more willing to be coopted while the rank and file members and local branches remained activist. Without entering into details, suffice to say here that through the ups and downs of its relationship with the government, the UGTT remained a strong organization with an interest in broad socioeconomic issues, not just strictly labor issues, and was willing to join other groups in fostering reform.[7]

The Islamist trend also had deep roots. Tunisia had a long tradition of Islamic learning, represented by the Zeitouna Mosque, a prominent religious institution.[8] Rachid Ghannouchi, co-founder and leader of the Ennahda party, had a Zeitouna education and had become a respected theologian with reformist ideas before becoming a politician. The party survived Ben Ali's repression and, although many of its leaders were in exile or jail, it sprung back immediately when restrictions were lifted.

Both the left and the right have a genuine following and are well rooted in the society. In addition, the country had a lively but fragmented secular center represented by people who had been close to the Bourguiba regime or managed to keep moderate parties alive under Ben Ali. This center was represented by many small political parties, usually dominated by a single personality, all competing with each other rather than cooperating. In 2014, much of the center coalesced around Béji Caïd Essebsi and his new Nidaa Tounes party, which succeeded in winning the largest number of votes in both the parliamentary and the presidential elections. United only by a desire to counter Ennahda, Nidaa Tounes splintered even while Essebsi was president and disappeared after his death in 2019, but the secular center still exists. Tunisia has had a pluralistic political scene and an active civil society. This was reflected in the intervention of the quartet—a coalition including the UGTT and other civil society organizations—in an attempt to resolve the impasse among the political parties mired in discussions in the National Constituent Assembly in 2013. I will return to this point.

Both the political pluralism and the absence of social pluralism were important to the outcome of the transition. Once elections were freed up after 2011, people cast their votes on the basis of political preferences, rather than affirming their identity, as happened in many ethnically or religiously divided countries. Political identities are divisive enough, but not as much as ethnic and sectarian ones can be. Political identities were quite distinct and well rooted. The government was authoritarian and rejected pluralism in its functioning, but this did not prevent members of society from being pluralistic in their political ideas.

Pluralism was a major factor in the Tunisian transition, involving a number of civil society organizations as well as political parties. The literature on democratic transitions is rich in reminders of how important civil society organizations are to democracy; but in most countries, civil society organizations are new and often ephemeral, formed during the transition with the encouragement and financing of foreign donors.[9] Not so in Tunisia.

Agency and Leadership

Tunisia's post-independence history left it with the legacy of a weak military under civilian oversight, of social homogeneity but with embedded political pluralism, and of organized strength in parts of civil society. Some of these characteristics were the result of clearly identifiable earlier policy decisions—for example, the political neutrality of the Tunisian military. Others were the result of circumstances—for example, as a relatively flat country, Tunisia did not offer shelter in the mountains to the original Berber population, which was assimilated as a result, while it remained distinct, and at times rebellious, in Algeria and Morocco. Whatever its historical differences and structural characteristics, however, Tunisia was not destined to automatically experience a successful transition to democracy. Those characteristics did not protect it from authoritarian leadership between independence and 2011.

The structural characteristics made it possible for leaders to make choices that, in the end, led Tunisia to become what it is now. The outcome was not predetermined; conditions lead to change only with the help of agency and leadership. People make choices, and a crucial one in the case of Tunisia was the choice by most of the actors to settle for the politics of the possible and reject doctrinaire positions. And as a reminder that we cannot always explain everything 'scientifically,' it is important to admit that an element of luck also played a part at times.

The issue of leadership arose as soon as President Ben Ali left the country on January 14, 2011. The reaction of members of his government—Tunisia did not have a higher power or deep state operating behind the scenes—was to try to minimize change by turning to the mechanisms prescribed by the Constitution to ensure an orderly succession if a president died or became incapacitated. The speaker of parliament, Fouad Mebazaa, became the interim president, while Prime Minister Mohamed Ghannouchi remained in his position. Within days, though, this arrangement started disintegrating. The protesters, who wanted regime change, would not accept this approach, which was designed to maintain the continuity of the system. Particularly unacceptable to them was the fact that the interim government was made up entirely of members of Ben Ali's ruling party, the Democratic Constitutional Rally. Many of the new government officials started leaving the party, which was then dissolved by its central committee on January 20. Protesters considered the move to be cosmetic, since members of the former party were still running the government. Amid continuing unrest, Prime Minister Ghannouchi was forced to resign and the president—who continued to act in an interim capacity until the election in October—appointed Essebsi in his place. A secular, centrist politician of the Bourguiba generation, Essebsi was no revolutionary. He had held numerous high positions in the Bourguiba regime. Under Ben Ali, however, he had only served as an ambassador and later for a while as speaker of the chamber of deputies. This gave him sufficient distance from Ben Ali to make him moderately acceptable to those demanding change.

Essebsi was an astute politician who understood that he was not governing under normal circumstances. Citizens were highly mobilized, and the major challenge to the cabinet was less the young people in the streets than the multitude of special committees and organizations that had sprung up, demanding a voice in the transition. At this point, Essebsi made a critical decision. Rather than trying to suppress and disband these groups, he decided to give them a role. For this, he turned to Yadh Ben Achour, a jurist and member of an old and respected Tunisian family. Ben Achour had been appointed by Ghannouchi during his brief time in power to head the Higher Political Reform Council, which was expected to steer the country to a new constitution. Essebsi specifically asked Ben Achour to find ways to integrate the growing number of rival committees into the work of the Higher Political Reform Council. In Ben Achour's own retelling of the story in an interview, this appeared an impossible task, because the groups had widely different ideological positions and demands, ranging from those advocating a turn to liberal democracy to those advocating revolution. Nevertheless, he managed to bring them together in a 'High Council for the Realization of the Goals of the Revolution, Political Reforms, and Democratic Transition.' The awkward name reflects the variety of demands of the council's members, who, in the end, included: representatives from twelve political parties; eighteen civil society organizations, including trade unions, professional associations, and nongovernmental organizations (NGOs) in the human rights and women's rights realm; and 'national figures' chosen on the basis of unclear criteria, all for a total of 155 people. The only thing they had in common was the understanding that they needed to find a way to move forward toward a new political system and that they thus had to agree on a process even if they did not agree on the end point. After much discussion, the motley high council agreed to hold elections for a National Constituent Assembly under the supervision of an independent electoral commission; the constitutional assembly would write the new charter but also act as an interim parliament, supervising the formation of the new government and legislating as needed. The duration of the National Constituent Assembly was not clearly specified, but it was generally assumed that it would last for about a year. Getting to the elections was not a smooth process. The date had to be postponed from July until October 2011 to complete preparations, leading to accusations that this was done for political motives, but, in the end, Tunisia arrived safely at the elections, with much grumbling but great flexibility on all sides.

The Imponderable Factor

Good luck, as I argue, intervened at various points. It affected the difficult negotiations among members of the high council. It affected the result of the elections, which were held under a system of proportional representation and gave no party the majority of the seats. Ennahda won 37 percent of the vote and could not possibly rule alone or impose its constitution. To be sure, the inherent political pluralism of Tunisia ensured that many parties would be represented in the National Constituent Assembly, but a difference of a few percentage points in the way votes were distributed could have influenced the dynamic of government formation—this is what I call luck, for lack of a better word.

The Politics of the Possible

The National Constituent Assembly elections were followed, after much bargaining, by the formation of the Troika government, a compromise solution that gave Ennahda the prime minister position, while the Congress for the Republic Party, which received 8.71 percent of the vote, assumed the presidency and the Ettakatol Party, with 7.03 percent of the vote, nominated the speaker of the National Constituent Assembly. Remarkably, the left had no representation in the Troika: its strength resided in the labor unions, while its parties were small and fragmented and failed to receive enough votes to earn them a role in the new government. Eventually, almost two years later, this led to the formation of the National Dialogue Quartet, which gave the left a vehicle for exercising its real political weight that was not represented in the National Constituent Assembly.

Despite the power-sharing agreement represented by the formation of the Troika, the work of the Constituent Assembly was slow and marked by much dissension. The pluralism embedded in Tunisian society guaranteed that nobody was excluded, but there was mutual suspicion among representatives of various trends. Secularists and Islamists were suspicious of each other, Ennahda and the left saw themselves competing for the support of the populace, and the UGTT suspected Ennahda of trying to infiltrate the labor unions. Secularists feared that Ennahda would try to enact a constitution that imposed shari'a on the country. This fear might not have been genuine, however, but rather a ruse to stir up anti-Islamist sentiments—for example, rumors started circulating that Rached Ghannouchi wanted to bring back polygamy, long outlawed in Tunisia.

The work of the National Constituent Assembly went on without an end in sight. By early 2013, grumbling was mounting that the assembly has outlived its mandate, particularly in the ranks of the left. The malaise mounted further following the assassination of a prominent leftist leader and critic of the government, Chokri Belaïd, in February. Suspicion fell on Ennahda, despite its denials—in fact, it was later proven that the assassination had been carried out by the radical Ansar al-Shari'a.[10] The assassination of a second leftist critic of the government, Mohamed Brahmi, on July 25 brought the country to the brink of a major crisis, with large anti-government demonstrations in the streets of Tunis, the withdrawal of some sixty members of the National Constituent Assembly, and the UGTT's threat to call a general strike. The fact that a coup d'état in Egypt a few weeks earlier had brought the military to power, eliminating the Muslim Brotherhood from politics, contributed to the feeling that the entire region was about to explode again.

Once again, good leadership prevailed against considerable odds. The UGTT chose politics over the raw power of the street and gave up the general strike and, instead, brought together three other civil society organizations: the employers' federation, called the Union Tunisienne de l'industrie, du commerce et de l'artisanat (UTICA), the order of lawyers called Ordre national des avocats de Tunisie (ONAT), and human rights group Ligue tunisienne des droits de l'homme (LTDH). These formed a National Dialogue Quartet, announced on July 30. The national dialogue was not a new idea for the UGTT, which had called for one as early as June 2012. The formation of the quartet, of which the UGTT was the most important member, can be considered an opportunistic move by the organization to enhance its political role since it was not represented in the National Constituent Assembly, but it was also a realistic maneuver because, as one of the country's most important organized forces, it had to be part of the political process. It was also a powerful reminder of the importance of civil society organizations, particularly a genuine and well-embedded civil society, to a democratic transition. The UGTT had legitimacy and credibility.

The national dialogue worked. From August till January 2014, when a new caretaker government was formed, the original four members of the quartet were joined by twenty-one political parties, including the members of the Troika and, most notably, Ennahda, in an attempt to find a new way forward.

The quartet managed to impose a timetable on the National Constituent Assembly to finish its work, and to convince Rachid Ghannouchi that Ennahda should give up its control of the cabinet and accept the formation of a government of national reconciliation. Ghannouchi managed to bring along the Ennahda leadership despite the reluctance of its more radical members. In the clearest, and probably only, example of the impact of the regional context on the Tunisian transition, he was acutely aware of the fate that had befallen the Egyptian Muslim Brotherhood when it had refused to negotiate a compromise with the military, as Ghannouchi had advised President Mohammed Morsi to do. Ghannouchi knew that Ennahda had the right to form the government under the rules of the Constituent Assembly but that it no longer had the political support needed to overcome the crisis. As a result, he chose the politics of the possible despite internal dissension within the party. Ennahda thus agreed to relinquish its control to an interim government. Mehdi Jomaa, a so-called technocrat with no ties to Ennahda, became prime minister on January 10, 2014. Work on the Constitution had also proceeded at a rapid pace and, on January 26, the National Constituent Assembly approved the new charter.

The Constitution, like the new cabinet, represented a significant compromise for Ennahda, eliminating all references to shari'a as a source of legislation—shari'a is mentioned as a source of legislation in most Arab constitutions, including the one written for Iraq under US supervision—and limiting references to Islam to a statement that Islam was the religion of Tunisia, which was also present in the 1956 Constitution. It also declared Tunisia to be a civil state based on citizenship, the will of the people, and the supremacy of law. Ghannouchi, in an interview with the author and in other statements, justified the omission of any references to shari'a on the grounds that the concept is too broad and complex to be a useful guide to legislation, since it represents thirteen centuries of interpretations by different schools of Islamic thought, and not a single, agreed upon code of Islamic law. While his statement that shari'a encompasses many different interpretations, controversies, and contradictions is widely accepted, the agreement not to mention shari'a in the Constitution represented a major concession that complicated relations between Ghannouchi and the hardliners in Ennahda. It did, however, make it possible to reach an agreement with secular parties and move the Tunisian transition another step forward.

The Constitution called for a degree of power-sharing between the president and the prime minister, although favoring the latter. Essebsi, who was elected as Tunisia's first president under the new constitution, made a deliberate attempt to center more power in his own hands, even calling for a constitutional amendment to shift the balance of power between president and prime minister, but nothing came of it.

Parliamentary elections were held in October 2014, closely followed by the vote for the president. Ennahda, which in 2011 had confronted a large number of mostly quite small parties and easily won the plurality of the vote, faced a major adversary in 2014: a broad umbrella party called Nidaa Tounes, organized by Essebsi after he stepped down as prime minister following the 2011 elections. Nidaa Tounes was a loose coalition of disparate forces, held together by opposition to Ennahda and Essebsi's personality and his political acumen. Compared to the highly organized Ennahda, Nidaa Tounes was at a disadvantage, but Essebsi was an experienced politician and offered a rallying point for Tunisians who remained suspicious of Ennahda's true intentions despite the enormous concessions it had made by giving up control of the government and accepting a

47

secular constitution. Running without a real program on an agenda of opposition to Ennahda, Nidaa Tounes gained eighty-six seats in parliament while Ennahda gained sixty-nine, with the rest divided among a number of much smaller parties. Presidential elections were held in November and, with more than a dozen candidates competing, nobody won the majority of the vote in the first round. In the run-off elections between the two top candidates, Essebsi received 55.68 percent of the vote and Moncef Marzouki, the president under the Troika agreement, 44.32. Officially, Ennahda had not presented a candidate for the presidential election: in Ghannouchi's opinion, the country was not ready for an Islamist president and he saw Egypt as a warning of what might happen if an Ennahda candidate ran and won.

The arithmetic of the parliamentary election results presented Tunisia with another major challenge. Although Nidaa Tounes, as the party with the largest number of votes, was entitled to form the cabinet, it discovered that it could not form a coalition that could win a vote of confidence in parliament without the participation of Ennahda. In February, after several attempts at forming a minority cabinet, Essebsi accepted the politics of the possible and agreed to the presence in the government of the party he had previously demonized.

The Undoing of Success

The first, crucial phase of the Tunisian transition came to an end in January 2015. Not that Tunisia could be considered a consolidated democracy at that point, or even in 2020, despite having gone through a new election and a new process of government formation in keeping with the Constitution. In fact, there is reason to question the usefulness of the concept of consolidated democracy in general, in view of the challenges even countries long deemed to be democratic are facing around the world. In any case, even so-called consolidated democracies are in constant transition; for example, US democracy was different under President Donald Trump than under President Barack Obama.

To understand the reversal of the Tunisian transition, it is necessary to explore two key questions: what factors contributed to its initial success and what was the cost of that success?

Lessons from the Tunisian Success

The outcome of the Tunisian transition was the result of four broad factors, already discussed: favorable structural conditions; timely interventions (agency) and good leadership; an element of luck; and major actors embracing the politics of the possible rather than absolute principles and ideologies. A small number of individuals— interestingly all older men in a country of young people—set aside their own beliefs and ideologies to make possible solutions that, at times, departed from prior agreements but were crucial to the outcome; without Ghannouchi agreeing to give up control of the government in 2014 and Essebsi eating his words a year later in order to form a government with Ennahda, the initial outcome in Tunisia would have been quite different and a lot bleaker.

On the other hand, factors that some analysts have deemed crucial to the transition had only secondary importance. Most notably, street protest was relatively unimportant. True, without large crowds on the Avenue Bourguiba Ben Ali would not have felt threatened and would not have decamped to Saudi Arabia, but behind those crowds were the organized forces of the UGTT with a long history of activism that began in Sidi Bouzid and brought the protest to nearby towns, provincial centers, and, finally, Tunis.[11] The leadership needed to transform street action into effective political pressure, which was provided by better structured organizations. The fact that organized political forces, including the UGTT, quickly superseded the spontaneous street action of the protesters made the transition possible. Mass action was a facilitator at the beginning, but not the major factor in the transition. However, these dynamics contributed to the perception of betrayal among protesters, particularly youth groups that felt they had carried out a revolution but had then been shunted aside, without reaping the benefits. The bitterness is evident in conversations with young Tunisians.

Another factor that played only a minor role, if any at all, in the transition was external influences. The transition was the result of a genuinely domestic political process. Tunisia never attracted much international attention, particularly in comparison to its larger or more troublesome neighbors. The United States considered it a country that France, and more broadly Europe, should handle, while France itself was not overly concerned. The Gulf countries, when they began trying to spread their version of Islam in the Maghreb, looked at Morocco more than Tunisia. Tunisians felt neglected—many a delegation visited Washington, pleading for more assistance—but they wanted economic aid, not political interference. Tunisia did allow foreign democracy promotion NGOs to operate, including the International Republican Institute (IRI) and the National Democratic Institute (NDI), but their role was marginal in the big picture, although they might have helped some political parties to organize better. Indeed, it is difficult to imagine how foreign organizations could have helped devise a transition so deeply dependent on the country's structural conditions and an entrenched civil society that included labor unions steeped in the language of Marxism-Leninism.

The existence of strong domestic organizations, on the other hand, was important. There has been a lot of emphasis on the role of social media in organizing the 2011 uprising in all countries in the region, but there has not been a serious discussion as to whether social media could do much beyond convening people. The follow up to protests were political steps in which experience counted more and organizations that could remain active over the long run were more important than enthusiasm and instant communications. The UGTT and, to a lesser extent, other members of the quartet provided leadership and organization. Young activists who insisted that loose networks relying on social media were superior to tightly structured hierarchal organizations, which authorities could penetrate and destroy, were proven wrong in Tunisia.[12]

Finally, the flexibility demonstrated by many individuals and organizations proved crucial to the initial success of the Tunisian transition. The road to democracy is not linear and does not necessarily include only steps that are in line with democratic principles. A transitional body like the High Council for the Realization of the Goals of the Revolution, Political Reforms, and Democratic Transition was constituted of organizations and individuals chosen on an ad hoc basis because they were vocal, not because they were representative or had a special reason to be included. Then, in 2013, when Tunisians had already formally elected a National Constituent Assembly, they turned to a self-designated quartet of non-representative organizations—why was the Order of Lawyers, a professional organization with a small elite membership, included, for example?—and allowed it to essentially dictate for a few months what the democratically elected authorities should do. The conundrum is that while non-democratic steps can lead to democracy, they can also easily lead to the reinforcement of authoritarianism.

The Cost of the Tunisian Transition

Many protesters who took to the streets in Tunisia were greatly disappointed by the outcome, and the young were particularly disillusioned. Protesters wanted concrete results. They wanted jobs, better living conditions, and the elusive 'dignity.' They also wanted democracy, but not as an end in itself. They got the democratic system, but not the rest. This is the paradox of a democratic outcome: democracy is not a set of concrete results, but a process based on the principles of popular participation, majority rule and protection of minority rights, and rule of law. Respect of those principles can lead to different outcomes based on the balance of political forces and the degree of engagement of different groups at a particular time. Studies of democracy as is, rather than democracy as an ideal, show that even in countries that have free elections, power is not distributed equally among citizens, but rather that those with greater resources in terms of money, education, and experience have disproportionate influence. This does not mean that, as citizens, we should dismiss the shortcomings of democracy as inevitable and not try to do anything to mitigate them. But it means that, as analysts, we should not measure the situation in any country against the parameters of an ideal democracy. This entails accepting the fact that for many people demanding urgent change, a democratic system is at best a partial solution and for many no solution at all.

Foreign advocates of democratic transformations are as torn as domestic ones between the principles of democracy and the concrete outcomes. For successive US governments, democracy has been not only a principle but also a means to achieve concrete outcomes, and when strict adherence to democratic norms threatens to lead to unwanted results, Washington often conveniently bends the rules. US policy toward democracy in Egypt and Palestine offers good examples. The United States began vigorously promoting democratic transformation in the Middle East, the so-called freedom agenda, after the invasion of Iraq in 2003. In late 2005, parliamentary elections in Egypt, which were freer than usual at the urging of Washington, saw about 20 percent of the seats going to Muslim Brotherhood members or sympathizers running as independent candidates. Shortly afterwards, in January 2006, legislative elections in the Palestinian territories saw Hamas, which refuses to recognize the legitimacy of the state of Israel and is considered a terrorist organization by Washington, win seventy-six seats. Fatah, which controlled the Palestinian Authority and had US support, only won forty-three seats. Not much was heard about the freedom agenda after those two elections. Advocates of democracy are rarely, if ever, willing to support a democratic system to the detriment of the concrete outcomes they want.

With these general considerations in mind, I will explore the costs of the democratic transition in Tunisia, not by attempting to measure the situation there against the standards of an ideal democracy, but by seeking to evaluate how the democratic process Tunisia followed has been an obstacle to attaining other goals Tunisians appeared to value, judging from demands made during the protests. This discrepancy eventually led many Tunisians and, above all, parties and organizations of civil society to remain relatively passive when the country turned back toward authoritarianism after July 25, 2021.

The first cost was the slow and uncertain pace of the process of change because of the need to negotiate and compromise among the many political forces. It took over two years, a major crisis, and the intervention of the UGTT-led quartet before the National

Constituent Assembly agreed on a new charter. In autocratic Morocco, the commission appointed by the king in March 2011 had a new document ready by June 17. It is possible, though difficult, to prove, that the protracted process of negotiation initially solidified a commitment to the Tunisian Constitution. But it is painfully evident that the slow pace of the transition and the accompanying instability created doubts about the future of the country and had significant negative economic consequences. For example, before 2011, both Tunisia and Morocco had started manufacturing parts for the French auto industry. After 2011, new investment in the production of auto parts, and even in the assembling of cars, was directed almost exclusively to Morocco as investors did not trust the stability of Tunisia. Economic stagnation contributed heavily to disillusionment among Tunisians.

The second cost was the extent of the compromises that Tunisian leaders and organizations made to resolve successive impasses. True, compromise and bargaining are intrinsic to all democratic systems, in which by definition no group gets everything it wants. A democratic transformation is not a revolution that sweeps away the old regime. Thus, the complaint of many Tunisians, and even foreign analysts, that members of the Ben Ali regime are still in positions of influence or that they have not paid restitution for their corrupt acts under the old regime are correct and understandable, but they also depict a situation that is probably inevitable, short of a revolution— which in any case is not necessarily a good road to democracy. The transitional justice measures that are now prescribed to countries in transition have worked imperfectly in all countries, including South Africa, despite its trend-setting, high-level Truth and Reconciliation Commission. But there are degrees of compromise and degrees of imperfection and Tunisia had a fairly high number of problems in a process that is typically flawed. Flexibility was key to the initial success, but the cost led to the reversal. The third cost for Tunisia making the transition possible was the weakening of the distinction between the ruling coalition and the opposition. The post-2014 elections government included the two major rival parties because, as noted earlier, Nidaa Tounes could not form a cabinet capable of winning a confidence vote in parliament without the participation of Ennahda. The parties that remained in the opposition, like the Popular Front and the many small centrist ones, could not provide an effective counterbalance to this alliance. Democracy does not function well without a strong opposition, which opens up the possibility that the incumbent government could be voted out of power. Also, parties or coalitions of parties that remain in power for too long usually become complacent or corrupt, which is bound to weaken the democratic process. By the time Saied suspended the parliament, the democratic institutions no longer provided the balance among countervailing forces that could have allowed them to address mounting problems.

Finally, some of the leaders who had been crucial to the success of the transition started to undermine it by trying to remain at the center of all decisions. Essebsi started undermining confidence in political institutions by calling for a stronger presidency, presumably so that he could continue to be the savior of the nation. As the co-founder and former head of Nidaa Tounes, Essebsi looked the other way when his son's ambition to turn the party that brought him to power into a 'family-dynasty,'[13] which ultimately weakened it institutionally and contributed to its downfall. Similarly, Rachid Ghannouchi, whose leadership of Ennahda had been a major factor in the initial success of the transition, came to see himself as indispensable both to the future of his party and to that of Tunisia. Even when members of Ennahda started losing confidence in Ghannouchi, he was not predisposed to allowing enough space for others in the party to come to the fore.[14]

Should the July 25 measures prove to be the point of no return, the ultimate responsibility with the authoritarian turn in Tunisia rests with the president. As I argued earlier, conditions are important, but the final determinant of what happens is agency—that is, how people choose to act. None of the costs of the transition made it inevitable that the president would try to impose an authoritarian solution on the country; it was his choice to do so.

Democratic Transition in Context

The Tunisian transition and its reversal were the result of domestic processes, but they did not take place in a vacuum. A transition can be influenced by foreign factors in several ways; it can be influenced indirectly by cultural elements that come from the outside but become embedded in the country over a long period or it can be helped and encouraged by changes in neighboring countries. Influences can also be direct in the form of intervention by other countries that impose certain changes or alter the balance of power among domestic actors. Although none of these factors had a major influence in Tunisia, it is worth exploring them briefly here.

Cultural Influences

Some historical cultural influences facilitated the transition in Tunisia, although it is difficult to judge their importance. The idea of a secular government, for example, is not as alien to Tunisia as it is to Saudi Arabia, and nor is the idea that people have a right to choose their leaders. Neither Bourguiba nor Ben Ali governed remotely democratically—nor did the French, as a matter of fact— but the concepts of secularism and democracy have become part of the cultural heritage of Tunisians together with many other traits. Tunisia is not unique in this respect: everywhere, encounters with other countries and cultures and historical experiences leave a residue. For example, the 2011 Moroccan constitution lists in its preamble 'the convergence of its Arab–Islamist, Berber (amazighe) and Saharan-Hassanic (saharo-hassanie) components, nourished and enriched by its African, Andalusian, Hebraic and Mediterranean influences'[15] as constituent parts of the Moroccan national identity. Not all influences are manifested in dramatic ways. The French influence in Tunisia, for example, is reflected in the details of the political system that the National Constituent Assembly chose: the sharing of executive power between the president and the prime minister and proportional representation rather than a first-past-the-post electoral system for the parliament bear the imprint of the French system. It was unsurprising for a former French protectorate to make those choices.

The Demonstration Effect

The indirect influence of the context was particularly weak in Tunisia. The country was not dragged toward democracy by events in other countries. On the contrary, it experienced the region's first uprising in late 2010 and influenced others. As Samuel Huntington has pointed out, democratization comes in waves, as an example of a successful transition (or even an attempted one) encourages people in other countries in that region to also demand change.[16] As military dictatorships started collapsing in Latin America in the 1980s, more countries felt the pressure to follow suit. However, not all countries caught in the wave make it safely to shore; instead, many are sucked back into the authoritarian sea. The initial wave of democratization that followed the collapse of socialism in Eastern Europe is now giving way to the restoration of authoritarianism, for example. Tunisia started the wave and rode it a long way toward the shore, even while other countries failed immediately. The difference, as argued, was the domestic situation.

Direct Interventions

Direct interventions to influence the initial Tunisian transition and its subsequent undoing have been relatively unimportant, particularly compared to those in other North African countries. No country intervened militarily in Tunisia, as they did in Libya, and even attempts to influence the situation politically were subdued. This helped Tunisia, because benign neglect by the international community allowed a domestic process to unfold.

Tunisia always received relatively little international attention. The United States never had much interest in the country, considering it a European concern. Europeans, including France, had limited interest themselves. The country was small and uneventful. When Gulf countries started meddling in North Africa they also focused on the larger countries. Saudi efforts to impose a Wahhabi influence on the Maghreb, for example, targeted Morocco above all.

The lack of international attention and thus assistance was an economic problem for Tunisia. It had enjoyed moderate growth before the uprising, but it suffered grievously afterward because of instability and lack of investment. Economic recovery remained slow and this contributed to a loss of confidence in the government. As a result, the reaction to the turn to authoritarianism was subdued, with organizations that had been key to the initial shift toward democracy sitting on the sidelines.

Would the political outcome in Tunisia have been different if the US had mounted a vigorous democracy promotion program? While one can never prove a counterfactual assertion, there are reasons to doubt it. The impact of direct democracy promotion in any country is uncertain. It is telling that the examples of successful democracy promotion mentioned by US officials and analysts are always the same: Germany and Japan in aftermath of World War II. Both were countries where the old regime had been utterly destroyed by the war and which were under American occupation. Even in those two cases, there is still much controversy about how much of their success was owed to the United States and how much to domestic factors. The latter certainly contributed substantially to the outcome, as seen by the fact that the two countries developed different political systems and different political cultures.[17] In any case, there are no clear examples of successful democracy promotion in recent years, including in countries where the United States has been an occupying power. Iraq after 2003 developed a political system based on elections, but much of the power in the country has never been in the hands of elected officials: much continues to reside with armed militias, religious authorities, politicians who have given their allegiance to Iran, as well as the religious establishment in both Iraq and Iran. And the outcome of democracy promotion in Afghanistan hardly merits discussion. When it comes to the Tunisian transition, the country's experience supports the idea that democracy, as a system based on popular participation, arises from a domestic process, and that outside influences and even direct support are of secondary importance. The success or failure of a democratic transition is up to the citizens, not its neighbors.

3

TRANSITIONAL BODIES, PARTY POLITICS, AND ANTI-DEMOCRATIC POTENTIAL IN TUNISIA
THE CASE OF HAICA

Enrique Klaus

The Independent High Authority for Audiovisual Communication (commonly known as the HAICA) is a transitional body in charge of regulating the Tunisian audiovisual sector. Created in 2013, the HAICA is one of several post-Ben Ali era institutions, which many international observers consider a guarantor of the democratic character of the system that is to emerge from a no less democratic transition. Taking issue with such view, this chapter offers a critical analysis of audiovisual regulation in post-revolutionary Tunisia and pinpoints its less-than-democratic dimensions. The aim is not to join the HAICA's many politically motivated critics but to shed light on the dynamics that shaped the workings of this transitional body and defined its relationship with the country's key media players and its political elite.

The HAICA is a revealing case study of the transitional institutions set up post 2011, such as the Independent High Electoral Commission (ISIE), the National Commission of Investigation on Corruption and Malpractice (CICM), and the Truth and Dignity

Commission (IVD) in charge of transitional justice. In the interlude between Zine El Abidine Ben Ali's departure and the adoption of the 2014 Constitution, these institutions were designed to put Tunisia on the road to democracy.

Compared to other transitional bodies, the HAICA is of particular heuristic interest insofar as it induces us to question the nature of the so-called 'young Tunisian democracy.' As a guarantor of freedom of audiovisual communication, the HAICA's mission is to organize one of the essential principles of the new democratic system—the freedom of expression. Moreover, unlike other bodies which tend to intervene on an ad hoc basis, the HAICA plays a more systematic role in regulating audiovisual content. While each transitional body intervenes on a specific issue (such as instituting transitional justice in the case of IVD, organizing elections in the case of ISIE, and curbing corruption in the case of CICM), the HAICA's mission is manifold: guaranteeing pluralism, preventing media concentration, protecting young TV viewers from inappropriate content, defining audiovisual ethics and journalistic probity, defining audiovisual standards, and drafting operational guidelines for what can or cannot be said or shown in the media. Finally, the HAICA appears to be significant for transitional governance—which the country's 'elites' seemed to want to conceive of, at least institutionally, as a second independence—as is demonstrated by the massive recourse to 'independent administrative authorities' (henceforth IAA) to deal with the burning issues of the transition entrusted to these bodies.

However, as we shall see in the case of the HAICA, convenient as it may be, this type of institutional approach is not as democratically friendly as it may seem:

> While appearing to be indispensable tools for overcoming authoritarianism, the independent authorities are part of dynamics of political change that generate uncertainties, induce calculations and introduce a power play by various actors that go a long way toward weakening their legitimate claims and, in fact, calling into question their call for neutrality and impartiality.[1]

Recourse to IAAs is based less on the urge to comply with democratic norms than on the promotion of various other internationally promulgated norms (administrative reform, withdrawal of the state, the adoption of best management practices from the private sector, etc.).

It must be evident by now that, contrary to many analyses of post-2011 Tunisia, I do not subscribe to the thesis of a democratic Tunisia born from the rubble of the Ben Ali regime. Instead, I offer a critical reading that brings into question the democratic legitimacy of one of the transitional institutions on which many hopes were founded in 2011 as such, and the way it was implemented in Tunisia.

The case of the HAICA gives us insights into the democratic nature (or lack thereof) of the Second Republic of Tunisia. A threefold hypothesis informs this chapter: (a) The study of transitional institutions that were operative in the fall of the old regime and the establishment of constitutional bodies in the making reveals much about the nature of the regime that is currently in place; (b) Like the other transitional bodies, the HAICA has a hybrid nature in the sense that it carries out democratic missions while relying on mechanisms that deviate from this norm; and (c) The work of the HAICA is based on the promotion of both a 'limited pluralism' (according to Juan Linz's definition of authoritarianism),[2] and a 'polarized pluralism,'[3] which makes the consolidation of effective democracy particularly difficult.

To explore these hypotheses, I will start with an inquiry into the peculiar relationship that IAAs have with the democratic principle. I will then try to uncover the shady elements that characterize the work of an audiovisual regulatory authority. I will then look more specifically to the HAICA by considering the context in which Decree-Law 116 (henceforth DL116) that gave birth to the HAICA was drawn up. In this chapter, I make the case that the motivations for creating this body were dictated less by democratic necessities than by political rivalries within the enlarged elite group after Ben Ali's ousting. This lack of a democratic and legitimate legislative basis has had direct consequences on the composition of the HAICA, particularly its politicization, thus inevitably undermining the very principle of 'independence' on which this type of institution is based. I then show how the combination of all these undemocratic elements has had a direct impact on teamwork and collegiality within the council, thus limiting the institutional effectiveness of a structure that many (the author including) initially thought could make democratic miracles. Finally, I propose a critical review of the HAICA nine years after its creation, drawing attention to how its failure to disentangle the strategies of its political players and the broader audiovisual community has undermined the prospects for establishing a democracy based on the informed choice of citizens.

Table 3.1: List of Relevant Transitional Institutions

Acronym	Name	Creation date	End date
CICM	The National Commission of Inquiry on Corruption and Embezzlement	Jan. 28, 2011	Nov. 13, 2011
HAICA	The Independent High Authority for Audiovisual Communication	May 3, 2013	May 3, 2019 (extended)
INRIC	The National Authority for Information and Communication Reform	Mar. 2, 2011	July 4, 2012
IVD	The Truth and Dignity Commission	Nov. 10, 2011	Dec. 31, 2018
ISIE 1	The Independent High Authority for Elections	Apr. 18, 2011	July 19, 2013
ISROR	The High Commission for the Protection of the Objectives of the Revolution, Political Reform, and Democratic Transition	Feb. 18, 2011	Oct. 13, 2011

Audiovisual Regulation, Limited Pluralism, and 'Euphemized' Censorship

Originating in the Anglo-Saxon liberal tradition, audiovisual regulation has emerged internationally as the solution to liberalizing the airwaves and putting an end to state monopolies. Audiovisual regulation is characterized by a contractual approach[4] to policies that allows the replacement of a system of *a priori* censorship with a system of *a posteriori* control. It is with this rationale in mind that audiovisual regulation has been promoted in Tunisia since 2011. It is based on an institutional arrangement allowing the state to disengage from the administration of the audiovisual sector and to delegate it in large part to an IAA. The latter acts as a screen, so to speak, between the state, which holds the broadcasting frequencies, and private media, which have the usufruct of these frequencies.

In established democracies, IAAs constitute the institutional form of New Public Management (NPM),[5] which uses private sector management models to improve the efficiency of the public sector. As such, it 'manifests itself in the creation and strengthening of sites of expertise that are internal to the state and aims at reforming and, in fact, transforming the administrative system.'[6] Thus defined, the objective of the NPM is less the question of democracy per se than that of the performance of state action through its submission to the managerial principles of the enterprise.

These innovations in policymaking are often conceived of as a sort of 'democratic given,'[7] whereas they constitute 'very unfulfilled political forms' that are certainly not insensitive to the type of regime in which they are inserted.[8] This is all the more true since the IAAs constitute 'frameworks that have little visibility in the public space and are largely decoupled from the official institutions of participatory democracy.'[9] Some critics go as far as to consider them as 'authoritarian isolates' within democracies.[10] This is at least the view of Gilles Massardier, who questions the classic definition of authoritarianism as 'limited pluralism.' He notes that the IAAs, and more generally the public policy networks that are supposed to broaden participation in policy making, are based on limited pluralism mechanisms: disconnection from the electoral market, relative confinement of decision making, emergence of new rulers who are not elected, but appointed, and 'whose legitimacy rests solely on being "concerned" with particular fields that are undergoing reform.'[11]

Such is the case for established democracies. But how about young democracies or 'democratizing' states? Since the 1990s, many international organizations have made extensive use of IAAs in their endeavors supporting democratization.[12] However, as the example of the HAICA will illustrate, 'in general, the NPM is often poorly adapted to the institutional contexts it is supposed to reform and generates perverse effects in the implementation phase.'[13] In particular, the importation of the neo-managerial formula on which the NPM is based 'does not mesh well with socio-political realities in which the economic success of capitalist firms has relied on the support of powerful state administrations through forms of corporatism and patronage.'[14] The case of Nabil Karoui's Nessma TV channel, which will be discussed in the penultimate section, illustrates these dynamics.

With regards to the principle of audiovisual regulation, it is set in such a way as to link the media to the regulatory authority. The guidelines—commonly known as *cahier des charges*—for granting audiovisual licenses contain several provisions with regards to commercial activity (legal form, advertising framework), programing (respect of societal norms and national identities), or the relationship between the media and politics (especially when it comes to electoral campaigns).[15] While these guidelines are largely based on normative principles valued by international organizations, they do not constitute a democratic guarantee. On the contrary, a careful consideration of these guidelines reveals certain elements that are not compatible with democratic norms.

The guidelines entrust the regulatory body with the task of producing normative rules governing the audiovisual sector. Effectively, it puts limits on the freedom of communication. By enumerating standards of audiovisual decency, the regulatory authority is helping define the contours of a legitimate culture that tends to be purged of certain social realities and practices that are nevertheless current in society. In the case of a largely conservative society such as Tunisian society, the HAICA's actions may lead to the narrowing of pluralism as defined in its societal dimension. Pushed to their extreme, such constraints could lead to the promotion of an idealized and 'unanimist' image of society whereby those individuals who engage in peripheral practices or values that are not appreciated by the prevailing morality are ostracized. In the case of Tunisia, this includes practices related to alcohol consumption and drug use, which are widespread,[16] or, for that matter, certain trends that do not conform with the heterosexual matrimonial beliefs preached by

Islam.[17] This could result in TV programing and offerings that do not adequately mirror society or provide a window on the outside world.[18] If anything, it helps to promote an idealized image, the empirical basis of which lies within the conservatism of (admittedly) a large part of the public. This risks reviving the old regime's tendency to offer Tunisians media programing that is constantly out of step with reality, in a dystopian relationship with their individual existence.

The adoption of audiovisual regulation does not mean the elimination of censorship—'an organized form of control over the content of cultural productions'—but only its redeployment under other forms.[19] Such transformations—as J.M. Méon points out in the case of the French Conseil supérieur de l'audiovisuel (CSA),[20] which has some commonalities with the HAICA—do not necessarily do away with censorship since, practically, 'advising or describing is nonetheless prescribing, which effectively means preventing the diffusion of certain content.'[21]

While the regulatory authority requires TV channels to rate their programs, it does not go out of its way to ensure or enforce compliance.[22] Entrusting media organizations with such a task can help internalize the criteria defined by the regulatory authority. In the case of the HAICA, this is ensured by the guidelines, which require applicants for a license to submit a file including 'a concept of self-regulation within the company' (Article 5). It also requires TV channels to use the appropriate signage for certain programs, according to the classifications defined by the HAICA.[23] Far from being optional, this signage is coercive insofar as any contravention exposes the operator to sanctions. The HAICA thus has the power to impose sanctions to ensure compliance with this signage and all the normative provisions on which it is based, all the more so since 'defining the criteria according to those of the CSA means above all preventing legal risks.'[24]

The internalization of control makes the exercise of authority invisible and therefore 'impossible to identify a single "censorship bureau."'[25] Thus euphemized, censorship is all the more 'soft' since it was legitimized in the case of France by the injunction to protect youth against the backdrop of recurrent debates on the impact of violent images on minors. While such a debate has only occasionally surged in Tunisia, the reference to children's rights in the audiovisual guidelines speaks of such an endeavor to legitimize censorship.

On the whole, the audiovisual regulatory authorities exercise a moderate but real form of censorship: 'even if the system of TV signage leads to effective censorship of certain content, it is usually not denounced considering the conditions under which it was developed and legitimized.'[26] In the case of Tunisia, and in the absence of a true legitimacy, what prevailed were the least democratic aspects of the audiovisual regulation.

The HAICA's Legislative Basis and Democratic Deficit

Contrary to what one might think, audiovisual regulation was introduced in Tunisia in 2011 in a very undemocratic fashion, as the circumstances of its adoption were the result of a 'coercive policy transfer.'[27] The intense presence of nongovernmental organization (NGO) consultants and the lack of consultation of the existing media are only one facet of this coercion.[28] Indeed, this innovation needs to be understood in the context of the political 'fluidity' of the immediate post-Ben Ali period,[29] that of a 'coordinated transition' leading to an order that is reflective of a balance forged by 'the set of strategic moves coming schematically—but not exclusively—from two poles: the elites of the Ben Ali era and emerging elites.'[30]

The authorship of DL116 that gave birth to the HAICA was disputed between the National Information and Communication Reform Commission (INRIC) and the High Commission for the Achievement of the Objectives of Revolution, Political Reform and Democratic Transition (ISROR).[31] Functioning as a proto-parliament, ISROR quickly took up the issue of the media, which its chairman considered as one of 'six laws of liberation.'[32] But in March 2011, a draft document was leaked leading to a tension between the ISROR and the INRIC, whose chairman resented the encroachment of the ISROR on his territory. To diffuse the tension, the ISROR was then compelled to consult with the INRIC, which introduced some amendments to the proposed law.

In September 2011, on two occasions,[33] the bill was discussed without being put to a vote for lack of a quorum. As a consequence,

DL116 could not be adopted in a (proto)democratic way or voted on by an assembly that was constituted of unelected members of a transitional body whose legitimacy rested on the ability of the emerging elite and the old one to work in a consensual way.[34] Additionally, and unlike the Electoral Law that gave birth to the ISIE, DL116 did not benefit from the democratic veneer of the ISROR.

Significantly, on November 2, 2011, DL115 and DL116 were promulgated by then acting President Fouad Mebazaa. This was the case despite the fact that the agreement between the Chairman of ISROR Yadh Ben Achour and would-be Prime Minister Béji Caïd Essebsi before he assumed office was such that ISROR was to work on the drafting of legal documents designed to organize the National Constituent Assembly's elections that were held ten days earlier. Once this deadline had passed, there was no obligation on the part of President Mebazaa to act on or circulate the draft legislation. In fact, due to the tumultuous relations with the ISROR, the question of the balance of powers was never resolved. Even if one considers DL116 to be emanating from the INRIC, there is nothing that compels the latter from endorsing the recommendations of an advisory body. Legally, it had no obligation to promulgate DL116.

Although DL116 holds Mebazaa's signature, it is hard not to sense the maneuvers of Essebsi. As many observers noted, the latter had an ascendancy over the former: 'Upon his arrival at the Kasbah, [Essebsi] became the true head of the Executive even if, theoretically, Mebazaa had much more extensive powers. This was due both to the personalities of the two men and to the nature of their past relations. For interim President Mebazaa, Béji Caïd Essebsi, who was seven years older than him, will always remain the elder.'[35] As a former chairman of the House of Deputies (1997–2011), Mebazaa (who was then 78 years old) knew that he had no political future in post-Ben Ali Tunisia. As for Essebsi, despite his advanced age, he had regained a second youth when he was called back from retirement to manage the country's transition.

What could have been Essebsi's motivations to promulgate DL116? It is difficult to detect a genuine desire to participate in the democratization of the media sector, as this would likely have drawn even more acerbic criticisms against the constitutional authorities,[36] and as he will probably find himself intervening on behalf of his ally Nabil Karoui, the owner of Nessma TV, to resolve his issues with the HAICA. Far from any obligation, the motivations of Essebsi to impose the HAICA seem more strategic on the part of a former statesman with reignited political ambitions. The strategy consisted of playing the 'democratic' institution card, while knowing that it would be up to those in charge after the elections (that had just been organized) to proceed to its effective implementation. Instituting the HAICA could thus be a democratic test of the new political elites, in particular Ennahda.

Unavoidably, this maneuver led to politicizing the very existence of the HAICA. The outcome of the elections was such that Ennahda had no choice but to form a ruling coalition. Expectedly, when it comes to an institution guaranteeing the freedom of expression, ideological divergences between the members of the ruling coalition on such a sensitive matter were bound to erupt—not to mention the benefits Essebsi could reap from the promulgation of DL116 in terms of 'democratic' respectability at the international level.

More than a simple test, and far from any democratic desire, the promulgation of DL116 is a 'political coup' as it illustrates 'the ability of the various actors to play by the book and abide by the norms while disavowing them, to rely on their capital and resources, institutional and otherwise, to emerge victorious from various power struggles.'[37] Expectedly, such dynamics were bound to complicate the effective implementation of the HAICA.

Sacrificing Independence: The Politics of the HAICA Appointments

During the seventeen months between the arrival of the Ennahda led-Troika to power and the HAICA's appointments, Essebsi's stratagem seems to have partly worked. Admittedly, the coalition did not collapse, but the negotiations within the coalition were contentious to say the least. Very early on, Ennahda sought an alternative to DL116 in order to reform the media sector, but such a move led Rachid Ghannouchi's party to be perceived as an enemy of democracy, and was regularly denounced as such by civil society.[38]

Beyond the circumstances that led to its adoption, Ennahda's reticence can also be explained by the sense of political mistrust that lies in DL116, as evidenced by the processes for appointing members of the HAICA, which reduces the number of political appointees (two members) to the benefit of legal entities (two members) and professional bodies (four members).[39] This was all in theory; in practice, though, things worked differently. This is all the more important to note, considering that the process unfolded within the rule of a government coalition whose modus operandi involves arbitrations and concessions, which unavoidably engenders the politicizing of appointments in a body whose defining characteristic is 'independence.' In theory, Ennahda was to recuse itself from making such appointments and only the heads of its coalition partners, Moncef Marzouki and Mustafa Ben Jafaar, would exercise the power of appointment. In practice, though, as the author was told on several occasions, to become the chair of the HAICA, it was necessary to 'go through Montplaisir,' in reference to Ennahda's headquarters.

Negotiations on the appointments opened in July 2012, in the wake of the INRIC's self-dissolution, and were concluded on May 3, 2013. Effectively, it took nearly a year of negotiations—interspersed with aborted announcements, maneuvers, open letters from the INRIC, and two 'general strikes'[40] by the media—for the HAICA to finally be instituted.[41] There were several reasons for such protracted negotiations. First, there was no consensus among coalition members on the three candidates to be appointed. The Congress for the Republic and Ettakattol proposed candidacies mainly from the academic world or from the ranks of the Left. For its part, after two decades of repression, Ennahda did not have a presence in the media as the sector was largely dominated by the former regime, with whom journalists of left-wing sensibilities coexisted as best as they could, and who categorically rejected the Islamists. By co-opting media personalities linked to the former regime, Ennahda sought to smoothen the relationship with the Tunisian Union of Media Executives' (STDM). Second, during the summer and autumn of 2012, a number of events and developments made the issue of the HAICA members' appointments less pressing: the initial draft of the Constitution (published on August 14), the attack on the US Embassy (September 14), and the initiation of the National Dialogue Quartet (October 16).[42] At the national and regional level, the hopes carried by the euphoria of the 'Arab uprisings' had started to wear out: 'the new geopolitical situation [was] becoming unfavorable to Muslim Brotherhood-inspired groups and, in the case of Tunisia, the relentless pressure of Ennahda's ideological adversaries was a reminder for many Nahdaouis of the kind of repression they suffered under Ben Ali.'[43] Finally, these developments compelled Ennahda, which was itself evolving, to be more cautious so as not to lose control of an institution whose workings and dynamics it was only beginning to grasp.[44] It was obvious that Ennahda had a political vision of audiovisual regulation, as evinced by the stalled negotiations over the appointment of the HAICA chair, the only member with a tie-breaking vote.

There is no doubt that the politicization of appointments has led to a distortion of the (already ill-defined) principle of independence. After ten months of negotiations, the HAICA was less the emanation of a search for independence than a reflection of the precarious balance of political forces, to the detriment of a civil society that lacked adequate representation in the HAICA council. Inevitably, this was bound to have a direct impact on the level of collegiality among the HAICA's members and the effectiveness of its regulatory action on the audiovisual sector.

Chronicle of a Sclerosis: Collegiality within the HAICA

The introduction of audiovisual regulation in Tunisia was at the origin of many professional dynamics in the audiovisual sector. This section will focus on those relating to the members of the council. Due to its limited duration and its novelty, the exercise of a mandate within the HAICA is based on a specific professionalization pattern. As audiovisual regulation had not been the subject of any training in Tunisia, its exercise was based on knowhow acquired in the practice of related activities. In terms of its composition, the HAICA brought together different legal, academic, and journalistic occupations. Such eclecticism was not without consequences on collegiality within the council. Far from being anecdotal, this issue is central to the viability of the institution as well as to its conformity to democracy, so much so that 'the organic independence of IAA stems from the collegiality which allows collective deliberation on sensitive subjects' and 'allows for the guarantee of objectivity in debates and decisions.'[45]

Beyond this, specific personal traits and professional experiences also condition the professional socialization to audiovisual regulation, since members had to be 'recognized' for their 'integrity' and 'independence' (Article 7, DL116). Eligibility within the HAICA rested on having a career in or around the media and a trajectory reflecting a certain degree of commitment to activism. This was the case with Rachida Ennaïfer, who had sixteen years of experience in journalism and a history of activism within professional and feminist associations. The same goes for Riadh Ferjani, a media sociologist with an academic interest in dissecting the mechanisms of censorship under Ben Ali's rule.[46] Save for these two, though, the other members did not necessarily have an activist background.

If arbitration and compromise among the political players during the transition could account for why only a minority within the HAICA had an 'activist' profile, finding candidates who had both the professional qualifications and activist profile was not an easy matter in such a post-authoritarian context. Combined with the politicization of such appointments, these specificities undoubtedly reduced the chances of fostering the necessary collegiality required for the smooth functioning of the HAICA, even before it was confronted with an external adversity (as will become clear below). During its first year of existence, the internal situation was so deleterious that the HAICA resorted to the services of a consultant in interpersonal relations to be at least minimally functional. But this was to no avail, as evidenced by the recurring resignations. In only two years of existence, the HAICA had recorded four resignations.

The pressure point of these resignations crystallized around the licenses granted in July 2014. The dispute within the council essentially concerned the granting of a commercial license to El Hiwar Ettounsi, a media outlet initially benefiting from an associative license, thus enabling it to earn advertising revenue and to obtain a capital gain—not to mention the fact that its owner, Tahar

Ben Hassine, very early on joined the ranks of Nidaa Tounes, and remained a member of its executive board until December 2013, in flagrant violation of the provisions of the DL116.

Mohsen Riahi, who was appointed by the STDM, was the first to resign on July 8, 2013, citing a lack of transparency in the licensing process as the reason for his resignation.[47] One month later, on August 5, judge and deputy-chair, Raja Chaouachi, followed suit, officially to reassume her judiciary functions.[48] These two seats remained vacant beyond the time limit mandated for their replacement.[49] The stakes involved in the 2014 elections prevented Rachida Ennaïfer and Riadh Ferjani from resigning earlier, although they also contested the result of the July 2014 vote.[50] They jointly resigned on April 27, 2015, one week after El Janoubiya TV—owned by businessman Mohammed Ayachi Ajroubi, founder of the Tunisian Movement for Freedom and Dignity and an influential figure in the world of football—was granted a commercial TV license. In a joint communiqué published in 2017, the two resigning members denounced the failure of the council, citing specifically its heterogeneous composition and the agendas of its members—all of which undermined collegiality and hampered the work of the HAICA: 'All the conditions were […] present for the failure of efforts to regulate broadcasting [in particular] a heterogeneous Council composed of people of very disparate levels and with personal ambitions inversely proportional to their competence. What better ground for all kinds of political infiltration and submission to different lobbies!'[51] To save face, Hichem Senoussi, a HAICA member who later became a self-declared spokesperson for the HAICA, would tell anyone who wanted to hear it that the resigning members represented the minority during the licensing votes and that they did not accept what the majority vote yielded.

This double resignation had the greatest impact because of the perceived independence of these two members and their commitment to democratic principles—elements that are not evident in the HAICA.[52] Beyond this symbolic dimension, their departure has weakened the HAICA, which being reduced to a five-member council, saw its decisions invalidated by the lack of quorum. The status of the HAICA drew much criticism from STDM, which announced that it no longer wished to collaborate (even though, in effect, there was no collaboration).[53] MFM and Nour radio stations as well as Al-Insan and Tunisna TV channels took advantage of the situation to resume broadcasting illegally. All these developments undermined the HAICA's authority in the Tunisian audiovisual sector.

Significantly, the HAICA was further weakened by an external adversity it faced all along. From its first steps, it found itself in a hostile environment populated by actors who were always prompt to politicize its action and to question its independence. The HAICA was immediately caught in a vice between, on the one hand, government officials who were bent on reducing its prerogatives, particularly regarding the issue of appointing the public media's CEOs, and, on the other hand, the owners of private media companies created during the Ben Ali era, who coalesced under the STDM. The latter rejected the HAICA's guidelines and, over the years, have increased pressure on politicians to defend their anti-regulation cause.[54] Noticeably, since 2015, the deputy-chair of the STDM (also the head of Nessma TV), Nabil Karoui, has distinguished himself by the populism that marked his actions against the HAICA, including threats to discontinue the broadcasting of the popular Turkish drama series *Harim al-Sultan*.[55]

The HAICA and the Specter of 'Political Parallelism'

These assaults would certainly not have borne fruit without a convergence of interests between media owners and political actors bent on weakening the HAICA, which obviously failed to keep the media (especially TV) free from political influence and vice versa. In their 2016 'Media Ownership Monitor' report, Reporters Without Borders and the Tunisian El Khatt Association listed no less than six TV channels with links to political personalities or political parties.[56] On the side of pro-Islamist forces, in addition to Al Janoubiya, Zitouna TV was created in 2012 by Sami Essid, a businessman close to Ennahda, and Osama Ben Salem, son of the Nahdaoui minister of education during the Troika. On the other side of the spectrum were a handful of media ventures that evolved at the intersection of business and politics. This was the case of the aforementioned

El Hiwar Ettounsi, which merged with Ettounsiya at the end of September 2014 after it managed to obtain its license. The merger, clearly aimed at circumventing the HAICA, took place during an opaque transaction between Tahar Ben Hassine, a media owner and former member of Nidaa Tounes, Sami Fehri, a former business partner of a prominent member of the Ben Ali clan, and Slim Riahi, a controversial businessman who is also the founder and president of the Free Patriotic Union (UPL) and president of one of the biggest Tunisian soccer teams, le Club Africain (2012–17). Hannibal TV was founded in 2005 by Larbi Nasra, a controversial figure and former member of the Ben Ali clan. Since Ben Ali's departure, he put his TV channel at the service of the counter-revolution. In 2014, only a few months after he sold 90 percent of his shares to members of his family, he founded his own political party, the Voice of the People of Tunisia. Also part of the heterogenous camp that constitutes the legacy of the Ben Ali era—the so called secular 'modernists'—was Nessma's boss, Nabil Karoui, who was also a founding member of Nidaa Tounes, and later the founding president of Qalb Tounes. Interestingly, some of these media players have also one more thing in common—having bid for the presidency: Slim Riahi in 2014 (5.55 percent of the vote) and 2019 (0.13 percent), Larbi Nasra in 2014 (0.20 percent), and Nabil Karoui in 2019 (27.29 percent). Equally worth noting is Hachemi El Hamdi, owner of the London-based Al Moustaqilla TV and presidential candidate in both 2014 (5.75 percent) and 2019 (0.75 percent).

These dynamics are indicative of the extent to which the HAICA failed to prevent (or to reduce) the degree of 'political parallelism' in the (re)structuring of the audiovisual sector, thus falling into the category of systems based on 'polarized pluralism,' in which the media functions as 'a battleground between contending social forces.'[57] According to Hallin and Mancini, countries with a high degree of political parallelism are characterized by the fact that 'media are still differentiated politically, [but] they more often are associated not with particular parties, but with general political tendencies.'[58] This can be illustrated by the findings of the HAICA report on the coverage of the 2014 elections by private TV channels.

Table 3.2: Private TV's Performance in the 2019 Elections[59]

Channel	Legislative Elections	Presidential first round	Presidential second round
Al Moustaqilla	No coverage	Extreme political polarization	Equidistant
Zitouna	Blatant political polarization	Blatant political polarization	Pro-Marzouki
Moutawassit	Blatant political polarization	Blatant political polarization	Pro-Marzouki
Nessma	Nuanced political polarization	Blatant political polarization	Pro-Essebsi
Tounisna	Blatant political polarization	Blatant political polarization	Equidistant/ low interest
Telvza	Blatant political polarization	Blatant political polarization	Equidistant/ low interest
Hannibal	Blatant political polarization	Nuanced political polarization	Equidistant
El Hiwar	Imbalances with no identifiable political orientation	Imbalances with no identifiable political orientation	Pro-Essebsi
TNN	Nuanced political polarization	Nuanced political polarization	Pro-Marzouki
Al Insan	Low interest in the campaign	Low interest in the campaign	Pro-Marzouki/ low interest

Table 3.2 reveals the various strategies of TV channels for aligning their coverage of the elections with their owners' partisan interests. Thus, the channels coming from the Islamist movement (Zitouna, Moutawassit, and to a lesser extent Al Insan) focused their coverage on a 'blatant or nuanced' polarization and campaigned for Ennahda's presumed candidate, Marzouki. Al Moustaqilla's balanced coverage of the second round of the presidential election can be attributed to the fact that its owner, El Hamdi, had abandoned his campaign after his party's poor performance in the legislative elections, whereas the channel openly supported him in the first round (extreme polarization). As for the 'anti-Islamist' clan, Nessma

TV, which showed relative restraint during the legislative elections, clearly put its popularity at the service of Essebsi's campaign. The latter had officially announced his candidacy on Nessma on April 28, 2013, and his campaign was run by Karoui & Karoui, the advertising agency of the conglomerate to which Nessma belongs.

Under these conditions, the HAICA failed its first 'test of public validity,'[60] which could have conferred on it some degree of legitimacy. Admittedly, one week before the start of the legislative elections, on September 22, 2014, it sought to reassert its authority by imposing a fine on the nine 'private' operators who refused to recognize the HAICA's guidelines or abide by them.[61] In view of table 3.2, such a move did little to remedy the situation. During the campaign, the HAICA multiplied the fines against the media, mainly for political advertising, the publication of polls (banned in Tunisia), and violating electoral silence. However, it is not clear whether these fines were actually paid. During both the 2014 and 2019 elections, the HAICA proved to be an ineffective electoral referee. Its only consolation, perhaps, was the poor performance of the politicians/media owners in question—with the exception of Karoui, whose case deserves attention.

To introduce a second illustration of the HAICA's failure to contain the political footprint on the Tunisian media sector, let us return to the concept of 'political parallelism,' which Mancini distinguishes from the phenomenon of instrumentalization of the media.[62] In their work on Libya, Anja Wollonberg and Carola Richter considered that 'the two phenomena are interrelated, but materialize on different levels: Whereas instrumentalization of media refers to the concrete and specific action of influencing media content, political parallelism is to be found on the structural level, as financial, organizational, or personal affiliations between media and interest groups.'[63] In their view, the instrumentalization of the media should be seen as 'one possible, particularly strong outcome of political parallelism instead of competing concepts.'[64]

No other actor on the Tunisian political–media scene illustrates this trend better than Karoui, whose Qalb Tounes party came second in the 2019 legislative elections. After putting it at the disposal of Essebsi, the Nessma boss kept using his television channel to facilitate his own political ascension. In 2015, in the midst of the crisis of the Nidaa Tounes party, Karoui was the 'exceptional guest' in a series of two interviews opportunely featured on prime time before the airing of the daily episode of the popular drama *Harim al-Sultan*.[65] During these interviews, he posed as a victim of the political maneuvers and personal ambitions of the president's son, Hafedh Caïd Essebsi, in a party of which he claims to be a founding member, though he never held any official position within the party (which would be in violation of DL116). In order to maintain a semblance of legality, he repeatedly announced his resignation from Nessma, even though his imprint was all the more obvious.

The summer of 2016 was a painful turning point, one which Karoui finally managed to turn to his advantage. On July 10, Transparency International's Tunisian branch, I Watch, revealed fraudulent financial arrangements (tax evasion and money laundering) associated with the Karoui group.[66] Going on the offensive, Karoui used his channel to carry out a smear campaign against the members of the association.[67] That same summer, the loss of his son Khalil in a car accident led Karoui to distance himself from the channel and turn his efforts toward the creation of a charitable foundation named Khalil Tounes, bearing the name of his son. Karoui crisscrossed the country's disadvantaged regions where he distributed food, household appliances, or money for carrying out personal projects to the most destitute. These actions were extensively covered by Nessma, conveniently right before the airing of *Harim al-Sultan*, under the worried eyes of the powerless HAICA and Karoui's political opponents, including then Prime Minister Youssef Chahed.

The popularity of these 'philanthropic' activities alarmed his opponents within Nidaa Tounes and the HAICA, leading to a number of punitive measures. On December 25, 2017, the HAICA ordered the suspension of a TV program, also named *Khalil Tounes*, for an entire month and on June 20, 2018, it imposed a TND 250,000 fine on Nessma because of the promotional dimension of Karoui's appearance on the show. As these measures had no effect, the HAICA announced on July 18, 2018 that it ceased its efforts to bring Nessma into compliance with the guidelines. However, on October 5, 2018, the HAICA again summoned Nessma's representatives over the same issue. The situation escalated and on April 25, 2019, police raided Nessma's studios to support the HAICA team, which came to seize its equipment and close the station for failure to comply. Karoui then publicly accused Chahed of being behind the maneuver and took advantage of being momentarily under the spotlight to warn that such a shut-down would disrupt the philanthropic activities of Khalil Tounes and prevent the distribution of thousands of meals to needy families during the holy month of Ramadan.[68]

The HAICA's chair denied the accusations of being manipulated by the politically ambitious prime minister and justified his decision by pointing to Nessma's repeated negligence that had become more and more prejudicial during an election year.[69] Four days later, Karoui was received by President Essebsi in a mediatized appearance. Shortly thereafter Nessma was back on the air and, in a climactic development, Karoui announced a month later that he was running for president.[70] The Chahed-led government then sought to counter Karoui's rise with an amendment to the Electoral Law prohibiting association leaders from standing as candidates. The law was passed, but remained unsigned by President Essebsi who died on July 25, 2019. Earlier that month, Karoui's personal assets (and those of his brother Ghazi) were frozen as part of the judicial investigation following the three-year-old I Watch revelations. Karoui reacted by announcing the creation of Qalb Tounes. On August 2, 2019, he officially submitted his candidacy. Three weeks later, on August 24, the HAICA and the ISIE decided to ban Nessma, along two other channels (Zitouna and Al Quran Al Karim Radio) from covering the elections on grounds that they were broadcasting illegally. That same day, Karoui was unexpectedly arrested and detained in connection with a judicial investigation into money laundering charges against him. Having qualified for the second round of the presidential race, he was released on the eve of a televised presidential debate that would bring him face to face with candidate Kais Saied. Despite his defeat in the presidential elections, his party managed to come second in the legislative elections (with 14.55 percent of the vote) behind Ennahda (with 19.63 percent). Undoubtedly, Nessma contributed to such political positioning and success.

Considering the fragility of the Tunisian transition, the polarization and politicization of the media sector is likely to continue unabated. In the months preceding the July 25, 2021 power grab, the HAICA and DL116 were points of contention at the center of intense political rivalries within a deeply fragmented parliament. After the 2019 elections, governmental instability, realpolitik, and converging interests helped overcome the kind of antagonism that characterized the electoral campaigns, giving way to an alliance between Ennahda, Qalb Tounes, and Al Karama Coalition. Despite the severity of the country's economic difficulties and the acuteness of the COVID-19 crisis the country was facing, the priorities of the ruling majority in the parliament seemed to be elsewhere. On May 4, 2020, Al Karama Coalition proposed a bill to amend DL116 that would deregulate the media sector by removing the requirement for television and radio stations to have licenses and would also give the parliament the power to elect members of the HAICA. If endorsed, such an amendment could potentially subordinate the HAICA to key players in parliament, thus undermining the very idea of audiovisual regulation. In effect, it would have engendered a de facto regularization of: Nessma TV, which is partially owned by the leader of Qalb Tounes; Zitouna TV, which is widely perceived as being close to Ennahda and Al Karama Coalition; and Al Quran Al Karim radio station, which is owned by Said Jaziri, a member of parliament from Al Rahma party.

When Al Karama's proposed bill was adopted at a parliamentary subcommittee on July 8, Elyes Fakhfakh's government reacted by introducing a comprehensive bill, which was initially drafted in 2016 as part of a collaborative endeavor designed to establish the Audiovisual Authority (ICA) provided for by the Constitution (Article 127). The government's countermove made Al Karama Coalition's bill irrelevant. Interestingly, before the new bill came to the floor, Ennahda and its allies pushed for a no confidence vote against Fakhfakh, who was then forced to resign. His successor put the last nails in the coffin. On October 19, one day before the government-introduced bill was scheduled to be debated in parliament, it was withdrawn at the request of Hichem Mechichi. A former adviser to President Kais Saied and the new head of government, Mechichi gradually withdrew from the tutelage of his political mentor to get closer to Ennahda and its allies. The deal was as follows: Mechichi would facilitate the adoption of this amendment and give the dominant political actors in the parliament a free hand over the media sector, in exchange for political support. Expectedly, perhaps, the controversy surrounding the bill was such that the discussion was postponed sine die. With the center of power shifting from Bardo to Carthage, it did not take place.

On July 25, 2021, after months of institutional and political deadlock and against the backdrop of a deteriorating health situation, Saied announced the freezing of the parliament. Three days later, he issued a decree dismissing the head of state TV channel Al Wataniya, reportedly for refusing to allow potential supporters of the president to enter the studio.[71] This maneuver was assuring for the HAICA, which was emboldened to resume its action against non-compliant media outlets owned by the president's political opponents. The HAICA's decision to seize the equipment of Zitouna TV on October 6, 2021 earned it a rebuke from its critics for attempting to take advantage of the July 25 political developments.[72] The day after Karoui was released on October 26, 2021, following his third incarceration since 2019,[73] the HAICA announced the closure of Nessma TV for illegal broadcasting, suspicions of financial irregularities, and management's assumption of a dual political and media role. Interestingly, with the exception of Hannibal TV, which reached a provisional agreement with the HAICA for its regularization, these media outlets found ways to circumvent the HAICA's decision by continuing the broadcast, communicating on social networks, or registering their audiovisual material likely to be seized under the name of independent production companies' channels.

Conclusion

Generally, audiovisual regulation is a challenging process. It requires the regulating authority to walk a thin line between two fields that are often in tension—what Pierre Bourdieu calls the political field and the media field. In the case of Tunisia, these difficulties range from the specificity of the audiovisual regulatory authority (discordance within the HAICA that reflects its constitution), to the media field (political appetites motivating the creation and governance of certain channels), to the political field (lack of a legal basis for the DL116 and the politicization of the process of appointing members of the HAICA). One of the main reasons for the HAICA's failure is common to all transitional or constitutional bodies and is succinctly articulated by the president of the IVD, Sihem Ben Sedrine: 'Despite the fact that [independent constitutional bodies] are clearly framed by the Constitution, neither the state's regulatory system nor the architecture of its organizational chart inherited from the former regime made provision for them, and the public administration continued to function while ignoring their existence altogether.'[74]

The slow pace of institutional reform aside, the lack of progress on IAAs seems to be part of an undeclared policy aimed at ostracizing the IAAs. In this respect, the variable of political culture in post-2011 Tunisia needs to be brought into the equation in order to better understand why the ruling political elites were ambivalent when it came to integrating the IAAs into their power politics, as the foregoing analysis suggests. By and large, the new political culture that has taken hold is characterized by its peculiar relationship to the rule of law: the latter is not perceived as limiting action, but rather as a constraint to be overcome. For example, during Essebsi's presidency, media tycoon Karoui consistently downplayed his relationship to Nidaa Tounes and, conveniently, when he formed his own party, Qalb Tounes, he downplayed his managerial and decision making role within Nessma TV. Similarly, Zitouna TV resorted to using independent production companies in order to outmaneuver the HAICA. The parliament's handling of DL116 is yet another example of this peculiar relationship to the law and the peculiarity of the political culture that is taking hold; within parliament, 'the democratic culture has often been reduced to voting, often at the expense of compliance with the spirit of the law, as if voting were the only criterion of democratic functioning.'[75]

Feeding this political culture since 2011 has been the convergence of interests among the members of the ruling political elite, who are bent on neutralizing constitutional counter-powers aimed at institutionalizing the country's transition. In the absence of a true democratic culture, it has been particularly difficult for the HAICA to accomplish its regulatory role. Ironically, its workings have been sabotaged by the very political players who instituted it in the first place. The result is a 'democracy without democrats'[76]—one that is marked by the incompatibility between the peculiar political culture espoused by the country's ruling elites, on the one hand, and, on the other, the provisions of a new liberal constitution premised on institution building and the exercise of the rule of law, voted in 2014 by many of the players that continue to dominate the political scene.

Importantly, the prevalence of such political culture undermines the work of the HAICA but also interferes with the ability of the various other IAAs to function as true institutional counter-powers. This is reflected in the incompleteness of the institutional design of the 2014 Constitution, particularly in the absence of the Constitutional Court, a keystone of the newly established political system. The delay in completing the institutions that are requisite for the transitional process led to a constitutional void that has been acutely felt with recurrent institutional deadlocks and political stalemates, which can only be adjudicated by the yet unformed Constitutional Court. This was the case, for example, with the controversy surrounding the reformulation of the election calendar following Essebsi's passing away while still in office; during the preventive detention of a presidential election candidate, Karoui, who qualified for the second round of voting; and with the personal interpretations of the Constitution by the sitting president. Beyond these challenges, the absence of a Constitutional Court structurally undermined IAAs such as the HAICA, whose effectiveness depended on a wider institutional network through which these constitutional bodies could operate and evolve under the watch of an institutional counter-power. Effectively, the kind of resistance with which the HAICA has been met since its establishment has left it embroiled in several legal disputes, which, in turn, undermined its authority over the media and communication sector. Despite several rulings of the administrative court in favor of the HAICA, the presence of a Constitutional Court would help provide a better environment for the HAICA to accomplish its role.

Considering these limitations, it is hard to speculate on the role the HAICA is likely to play in the future. While the HAICA continues to operate beyond the transition period mandated by the Constitution, the polarization of the media scene with the transposition of the political struggle to the audiovisual sector has transformed the HAICA into a political tool in the hands of political players. During the official period of its mandate (2014–19), the political cost for doing away with such a regulatory body was too high, particularly with respect to the international community—hence the efforts of the dominant political actors in parliament to circumvent the HAICA. For other political players, especially those deprived of media outlets, the continued operation of the HAICA beyond its original mandate proved to be opportune. For example, HAICA going after Nessma TV in April 2019 was particularly convenient for Prime Minister Chahed, as the sanctions would undermine Karoui, his political rival in the bid to succeed Essebsi. In 2020, the HAICA was narrowly saved from attempts to reduce its powers, which reflects the high degree of media polarization and politicization in the country. If anything, the legislative initiative to alter the process for appointing the members of the HAICA and removing its authority to issue licenses gave it an added significance, making it emerge as a necessary, albeit imperfect, transitional body. At the same time, the unprecedented political tension that ensued from the developments of July 25, 2021 drew critical attention anew to the dangers of instrumentalizing the HAICA by various political actors. The ardor with which the president's opponents sought to short-circuit the HAICA has obviously made it preponderant in the eyes of the president, particularly when considering its ability to either sanction or close down noncompliant media outlets in the hands of the president's political opponents.

The foregoing analysis explains the fate of the HAICA compared to other post-2011 transitional and constitutional bodies, some of which never came to light while others remained at the stage of an empty shell. Since 2011, Ennahda opted for a politics of 'consensus' that could yield a smooth transition. Yet, as its choices in the early phases of the transition show, compromise does not necessarily mean concessions. While Ennahda has always been a central player in the parliamentary system it had defended during the drafting of the Constitution, it had no interest in setting up the counter-powers of the transitional (and then constitutional) bodies that could theoretically limit the legislative and executive powers it commanded for the first time in its history.. This is all the more so because Ennahda did not manage to be adequately represented in these transitional institutions, which often called for special expertise—hence, the sluggish pace in setting up these institutions and the vigor with which they have sought to limit their power. The dynamics point to the limits of pacted transitions and,[77] even more so, to the deleterious limits of prescriptive democratization as promoted by international organizations, whereby institutional reform is enmeshed with what may be termed after Rosanvallon as 'unfulfilled political forms.'[78]

Ten years after the 'revolution' what lessons can be drawn for the Tunisian political regime from the failure of the HAICA? After all, the Tunisian experience is not the only one that falls short of success, which does not necessarily call into question the democratic nature of regimes that have failed to integrate audiovisual regulation into their institutional environment and media landscape.[79] What makes the case of Tunisia peculiar is the aversion to the independent nature of an authority such as the HAICA.

Indeed, since the adoption of the 2014 Constitution, most of the transitional bodies were meant to be replaced by 'independent constitutional bodies' (under the form of IAAs). Seven of these were to be the democratic guarantee of the regime, considering the policies they were supposed to oversee: elections, audiovisual, human rights, sustainable development, and the fight against corruption.[80] Seven years after the adoption of the Constitution, none of them has seen the light of day in its constitutionalized form. This delay can only be explained by a lack of political will. The fact is that democracy is far from being the only game for the 'new' elites. This rejection of the democratic game places Tunisia in a state of permanent institutional instability, as was the case with the 2019 elections and the political developments the country witnessed throughout 2020 and 2021. From a political standpoint, the constitutionalization of provisions, which are certainly promising but which have not been updated for years, places Tunisia into the catch-all category of 'hybrid regimes,' which combine 'democratic and authoritarian elements.'[81] However, this combination is to the detriment of the optimistic hypothesis of a democratic Tunisia: if the democratic elements are latent, the authoritarian elements are still in force. From this point of view, there is a great risk of seeing the HAICA and the other constitutional authorities as the result of a change in authoritarianism, understood as a 'renovation of authoritarianism towards more institutional dimensions.'[82]

4

POST-ISLAMISM POLITICS IN TUNISIA
ENNAHDA'S EVOLUTION SINCE THE REVOLUTION

Fabio Merone

Tunisia's Ennahda represents a paradigmatic example of a democratic, formerly Islamist, party.[1] It resisted domestic and regional political turbulence and succeeded in integrating into democratic institutions. It ruled from 2011 to 2013 within the frame of the National Constitutional Assembly (NCA) as the main partner in a three-party government coalition (the so-called Troika) and participated in a national union coalition with Nidaa Tounes—a party that brought together left wing politicians and former Bourguibians—which was hastily formed to counter Ennahda's perceived hegemony. Rachid Ghannouchi's party was also ahead of other parties in the municipal elections of 2018 and the legislative elections of 2019, and participated again in a new coalition government in 2020.

This outcome is partly the consequence of the party's dramatic transformation from 'Islamist' to 'Muslim democratic,' a change the party emphasized in its official documents, reflecting the important decision taken at its party conference in 2016.[2] In the words of Ali Larayedh, a prominent member of Ennahda, 'Ennahda has … overcome all those issues that still made some people instrumentally think of the party as belonging to so-called "political Islam." This common label no longer expresses the real identity of the party or the content of what its future projects are.'[3] Many of the party leaders' declarations to the international press throughout 2016 emphasized this point and highlighted the need for specialization (*takhassus*) and the importance of separating traditional social and preaching activities from institutional politics.[4] Abandoning *da'wa* activities and focusing on secular, liberal politics would, the party thought, make it 'democratic.'

Da'wa is the essence of Islamist political praxis and ideology. Preaching must not be seen as simply proselytizing or calling people to Islam; *da'wa* in Islamist intellectual thinking is the application of the fundamental principle of 'commanding good and forbidding wrong,' which implies the activation of a militant spirit of implementing the Islamic order.[5] It is in fact argued that it is the duty of Muslims to act wherever and whenever they see wrongdoing.[6] This principle implies an active consciousness of the faithful who feel personally engaged in realizing the word of God and a just society.

Separating *da'wa* activity from political activity is not merely a process of secularization, as it may seem on the surface; it is also necessarily about de-ideologization. By declaring that Ennahda 'moved beyond its origins as an Islamist party,'[7] Ghannouchi affirms the intention of the party to be a conservative democratic political player whose religious references are only a moral framework (as in the case of Christian democratic parties in Europe).[8]

Da'wa is central to Islamism and its ideology of social and political transformation. Here, 'ideology' is conceptualized in the way Antonio Gramsci and Ali Shariati understood it. Going beyond the traditional Marxist definition, the two intellectual activists thought of ideology as an overall vision of the world through which the marginalized social strata of the population—the subalterns for Gramsci, the *mustada'fin* for Shariati—would emancipate themselves. They thought that the political party was the instrument through which to convey the demands of the disenfranchised—Communist for Gramsci, Islamist for Shariati—and should have an ideology to make people aware of their sociopolitical condition in order to transform society.[9] By embracing the label 'Muslim democratic,' the Tunisian Ennahda sought to become a 'post-Islamist' and, in fact, post-ideological party that rests on a more secular conception of politics. Thus, Ennahda positioned itself as a democratic liberal party whereby the significance of political activism changes from ideological (social and political transformation) to post-ideological (technocratic management of public affairs). In this chapter, the focus is on Ennahda's ideological transformation and its political practice.

Post-Islamism as Post-Ideology

Specialists of Islamic politics use the category of 'post-Islamism' to describe an Islamist party's transformation from having a total social and political ideology based on the application of shari'a to accepting pluralism and advocating democracy.[10] Starting in the late 1990s, most Islamist political parties and organizations changed their discourse and implemented a strategy of integration into the political institutions of the state. In Egypt and Tunisia, Islamist parties joined democratic platforms with secular opposition parties and contested elections when allowed.[11] After 2011, Muslim Brotherhood-inspired parties in Morocco, Tunisia, and Egypt were elected to government against the backdrop of democratizing political institutions.[12] According to some post-Islamism scholars, 'Islamism' was a political ideology that—much like Communism—was defeated and ceased to exist.[13] The end of Islamism meant its transformation withered into 'neo-fundamentalism,'[14] or into a postmodern intellectual framework that integrates religiosity and civil rights.[15] While the first outcome implies the transformation of political activism into individual puritanism,[16] the second looks at this transformation as an attempt to look for an 'alternative modernity,' or as a democratization of Islam that is less a secularization than a way to 'couple Islam to the individual right for choice and freedom, democracy and modernity.'[17]

In both cases, the category of post-Islamism implies the idea of Islamism as ideology where the latter means a specific worldview (a weltanschauung).[18] In a post-ideological politics, political parties renounce the transformation of society and become a 'policing organism.'[19] According to Gramsci, ideology is a thought system that "'organise[s]" human masses ... create the terrain on which men move, acquire consciousness of their position, struggle, etc.'[20] It is both awareness of the social condition and a program of social transformation.[21] This way of understanding ideology applies to Islamism. In the 1970s and 1980s in the Muslim world, Islamism became an ideology the purpose of which was to radically transform the social and political order of post-independence nation-states. Islamism was a sort of revolutionary 'political theology.'[22]

Defined in this way, Islamism is a 'philosophy of praxis,' where Islam is not simply a system of ritual practices ('ibadat), but a practical way of transforming reality.[23] Post-Islamism can be conceived of as being opposed to this conception of ideology, and, in this sense, is post-ideological.[24] Islamism as ideology must be analyzed both as a political project and as a certain practical conception of political activity. This chapter postulates that the Islamist project is based on three tenets: an Islamic state, shari'a, and umma. It also defines Islamist political activity as based on da'wa.

A final point is worth making before developing the argument further. The category of post-Islamism is useful only insofar as it applies to Islamist parties originating in the different national branches of the Muslim Brotherhood. The transformation of Islamism into post-ideological politics does not reflect the whole reality if we consider Islamism in its broader definition, which includes Salafism and Salafi-Jihadism.[25] In this chapter, the category of post-Islamism, as described above, is applied to the Tunisian Ennahda party. In particular, the chapter analyzes the implications and consequences of the party's declaration 'to have overcome Islamism.'[26] The chapter unfolds along two sections: the first looks at ideological transformation and the second focuses on practical political activity.

Ennahda's Post-Islamist Ideology

In an interview published by *Middle East Eye* in 2016, Ghannouchi noted:

> The political field is not sacred nor immutable. It's civic, human. It's free for ijtihad or independent human reasoning.... We

consider few texts as fixed or immutable. Many Muslims …
consider all texts as sacred and untouchable and only capable
of bearing one meaning. The Islamic text concerning politics is
open to interpretation, and this is the field in which we now act.
We consider ourselves observant Muslims. We believe in Islam,
that Islam came to Earth to liberate mankind, and to define the
free person.[27]

These proclamations are in line with Asef Bayat's interpretation of
post-Islamism, whereby 'historicity rather than fixed scriptures'
is emphasized.[28] However, while this intellectual process outlines
the theoretical justification for the creation of a political space free
from religion, 'independent' from the immutable creed and 'open to
interpretation' and therefore reformist rather than revolutionary, in
practice it indicates the loss of the Islamist potential for radical social
and political transformation. The Islamic reference is maintained—
'we believe in Islam, [and] that Islam came to earth to liberate
mankind'[29]—but it remains simply as a matter of identity.

Investigating the ideological evolution of the party calls for
a critical enquiry into the notions of shariʿa, an Islamic state, and
umma, which, as previously noted, constitute the basic tenets of
the Islamist ideology. This entails analyzing the transformation of
the 'Islamic state' into the 'civic state'; of shariʿa (Islamic law) into
maqasid al-shariʿa (finality of the law); and of tunisianité in place of
umma. Particular attention will be paid to the period between 2012
and 2014, when the most critical issues were raised against the
backdrop of the constitutional debate.

The discussion on shariʿa and that of the nature of the state
was the consequence of the debate around the modification of
Article 1 of the 1959 Constitution, which states that 'Tunisia is a
free, independent, sovereign state; its religion is Islam, its language
Arabic, and its system is republican.'[30] The debate was about how
people understand the expression 'its religion is Islam.' While for
the secularists, this constitutional statement meant that Islam is
'Tunisian people's religion,' for Islamists, it implied that Islam is the
'Tunisian state's religion.' For some NCA Ennahda members, this
logically led to the conclusion that the Constitution as a whole should

reflect the Islamic nature of the state,[31] and that the party should ask for an amendment with a clear reference to shari'a as a source of legislation.[32] A discussion ensued within the party's shura council (its executive committee) and culminated in a majority vote against mentioning shari'a in the Constitution.[33] Commenting on the issue, Ghannouchi noted that 'Islam is a philosophy, not rules. It deals with *niyat* [intentions] and *maqasid* [higher objectives]—it is abstract and flexible. Sharia is not just about *hudud* [punishments] . . . people must understand that first. . . . They are scared of the word sharia because they do not understand it.'[34] As will become clear, what facilitated this ideological change was the way shari'a came to be understood.

The affirmation of the 'civic' (i.e., secular) nature of the state, a slogan of Muslim Brotherhood-derived parties after 2011, was also an intricate matter for Ghannouchi's party.[35] The issue came to fore during the drafting of the new constitution, particularly in the midst of heated debates bearing on the 'protection of the sacred' and the criminalization of blasphemy among other 'offences' to religion.[36] Defining the line between 'protecting the sacred' and 'criminalizing the freedom of conscience' was important as it could draw the boundary between a religious and a secular state. This issue was first dealt with in a constitutional draft (Article 2.3), which stated that 'The state shall guarantee the freedom of belief and the exercise of religious rites. The state shall also incriminate all acts of violation against any religious sanctuaries.'[37] The final version in the Constitution (Article 6), though, had a different wording: 'The state is the guardian of religion. It guarantees freedom of conscience and belief and the free exercise of religious practices. It is the protector of the sacred and guarantees the neutrality of mosques and places of worship from all partisan instrumentalization.'[38] By renouncing the principle of 'criminalization,' Ennahda accepted hearing out national and international experts on constitutional law who argued that including such a principle in the constitutional text would have grave consequences for individual freedoms.[39] Moreover, the final version of Article 6 and Article 2 of the Constitution affirms the principle of freedom of conscience and of the civic state, respectively.[40]

The issues of shari'a and an Islamic state are strictly interrelated. The essence of an Islamic state is the application of shari'a, while the very definition of state, in an Islamist ideological framework, is the protection of religion, where the community (the nation) is perceived as being Muslim.[41] This is why beyond an Islamic state, there is a shari'a law system and beyond both, Islamic state and shari'a, there is an Islamic community, the *umma*.

The concept of *umma* in Islamist ideology makes reference to a 'universalistic' concept to describe the Muslim community all over the world, which cannot be limited to national boundaries. Notwithstanding the fact that Muslim Brotherhood (MB) ideology was born within a nationalist environment and was developed along with the nation-state, there has always been tension between the affirmation of the national and cultural specificity of the latter and the internationalist *élan* of the *umma islamiyya*. The evolution of Ennahda's ideology toward a national(ist) perspective is clear in the way it dealt with the specific Tunisian heritage, which became part of the party's ideological *aggiornamento*.

The post-Islamist Ennahda party constructed a narrative of a specific Tunisian (and Maghrebi) Islamic tradition. The references are numerous, and they can be synthetized as referring to *tunisianité*, a reformist concept once associated with the modernist Bourguibian political vision.[42] The latter can also be seen as the party's reconciliation with the country's Islamic heritage, which is now associated with Islamic reformism. This evolution was explicitly expressed in the conclusive statement of the 2012 party conference: the Ennahda party 'believes it is a continuation of the Arab-Islamic reform movement from Khaireddine Ettounisi, Mohamed Ali Pasha, through Afghani, 'Abduh, Tha'alibi, al-Banna, Ben 'Achour and generations of reformers.'[43] In the Constitution's preamble, most of its concepts were reinforced where *tunisianité* appears as a banalization of the concept of Islamic community (*umma*). The national community's reference to Islam is in fact purely identitarian—'the foundations of our Islamic–Arab identity'—and is reduced to the 'heritage of our civilization' and part of the 'gains of human civilization.'[44]

Underpinning Ennahda's overall ideological transformation is the application of the principles of *maqasid al-shari'a*. This discipline, which looks at Islamic law from the viewpoint of its ultimate goals (*maqasid* means 'finality'), developed within the tradition of the Maliki law school.[45] Central to the Maliki / *maqasid* tradition is the concept of *masalaha* (general interest), which Abdelmajid al-Najjar, one of Ennahda's ideologues, asserts is 'shari'a's superior principle,' meaning that 'shari'a must be applied in practice to a proper historical reality, in time and space.'[46] On this basis, Ennahda leaders justified the most controversial issues that emerged during the constitutional debates and the difficult decisions taken. Salma Salsut, an Ennahda NCA member of the reconciliation commission, noted that 'the constitution has been approved by keeping in mind the spirit of *maqasid al-shari'a*,' which means 'the application of the Qur'anic principles from the view point of their finality, i.e., the defense of the person, justice and liberty.' Moreover, this discipline is evoked to justify a total change in the vision of the relationship between religion and politics more broadly. It is an instrument to eliminate the Islamist conception of an all-comprehensive vision of *din* (religion). Commenting on the party's orientation toward religion, Salma Sarsut noted that 'we are in favor of *ijtihad* [interpretation of the law]; the religious discourse must always evolve.' Advocating 'a politics of the practical,' Sarsut added that 'we are convinced that Tunisian society has its own specificity. It is not our job to change it.'[47] The whole reinterpretation of shari'a implies the formation of a de facto secular space where politics 'applies to the practical' and where ruling a country implies 'solving concrete problems.'[48] As a consequence, the state is no longer the instrument through which Islamic society should be realized. Where the word '*laïc*' (secular) is still a taboo for the party, 'civic state' *(dawla madaniyya)* takes its place.

All of this is a radical change in terms of reconfiguring Islamist ideology. The foundational principle of Islamism that Sayyed Qutb developed is in fact the theological / political idea of *hakimiyya*, or government of God,[49] in which God has appointed the human being as his representative on earth, '*khilafat- al-ard*.'[50] In this conception, God has given human beings a way (shari'a) and a perfect model of society to follow, historically realized in the *medina* (city) of the Prophet.[51] Ennahda's acceptance of the civic state is a post-Islamist transformation as it implies a secularized version of Islam—a modernist view—according to which the Qur'an does not provide any political recommendation nor offers a frame for a specific political system to be put in place.[52]

Ennahda's Post-Islamist Politics

In an article published in *Foreign Affairs* following Ennahda's 2016 conference, Ghannouchi argued that because the party was now 'Muslim democratic,' its practical activities would change, focusing 'only on politics' while separating the 'political party' from the 'social movement.' He argued that 'Ennahda has moved beyond its origins as an Islamist party and has embraced a new identity as a party of "Muslim democrats". The organization ... ceased to be both a political party and a social movement. It has ended all its cultural and religious activities and now focuses only on politics.'[53] This transformation seems to be the consequence of the specialization/ separation between political and religious activities. Because the latter are associated with the 'social movement,' abandoning religious activities meant that the party abandoned the perspective of changing society through social activities and solely focused on electoral campaigns and governing. This transformation implies a 'professionalization' of the party, which is now asked to provide technical solutions to governing of the country. Those in favor of politicization argued that Ennahda 'needed to present itself as a modern, technocratic political party with policies that appealed to both Islamist and non-Islamist voters.'[54]

Understanding the nature of this transformation calls for attention to the evolution of the movement's social activities (i.e., *da'wa*) before the party's 2016 conference and the party's professionalization of political activism since the conference.

Politics as da'wa

The party's predecessor (the Islamic group or *al-Jama'a*) began its activities in the early 1970s and focused on preaching.[55] The aim was to 'conquer' the existing spaces of religious activities. First by dominating the praying premises on university (or school) campuses and second by gaining access to religious studies through the Association for the Preservation of the Qur'an, a league of religious schools Bourguiba had created in the late 1960s.[56] While the Islamic group looked like a *tablighi* (or missionary) movement during its early years,[57] following its success, it evolved into an organization similar to the Egyptian MB and therefore closer to Hassan al-Banna and Sayyed Qutb's understanding of a *jama'a*.[58] The movement evolved in 1981 into a party, the Movement of Islamic Tendency (MTI), but the militant activities in the popular neighborhoods and on university campuses were still based on the principle of commanding good and forbidding wrong.[59] Between the end of the 1980s and the beginning of the 1990s, as a consequence of the failure of the political liberalization on the part of the newly established Ben Ali regime, Islamists within and outside Ennahda pursued a revolutionary solution that provoked a fierce repressive campaign.[60]

'Revolutionary' Islamist politics is retrospectively explained as a consequence of the repressive nature of the regime as much as its transformation after 2011 is justified through democratization:

> In this new democratic stage of Tunisian history, the question is no longer one of secularism versus religion: the state no longer imposes secularism through repression, and so there is no longer a need for Ennahda ... to defend or protect religion as a core part of its political activity.[61]

After the legalization of the party in 2011 and at the beginning of the transition to democracy, many of the grassroots militants still wanted the party to keep its Islamist character—that is, holding on to preaching and social activities.[62] However, the dramatic changes in the Tunisian political scene between 2011 and 2014 forced the leadership to focus on institutional politics and, specifically, on constitutional debates. This led to a divergence between 'Islamist' activists and 'politicians.' The former tried to reimagine *da'wa* activism under the new circumstances, while the latter wanted to succeed in institutionalizing the party and integrating it into the new democratic and liberal environment to ensure its organizational survival.[63] Tensions existed between the two constituencies of the party as well as within each one. While party figures like Habib Ellouz and Sadok Shouru tried to steer the Ennahda back toward its Islamist roots by remaining in parliament, other party members advocated properly 'secularized' militancy. The development of da'wa-oriented activism was due in large part to the creation in September 2011 of a new favorable legal system that created the conditions for channeling social activities into formal charity or preaching organizations.[64] This new Islamist public linked its social activities to religious-political campaigns, especially in the period between 2012 and 2013.[65] In 2012, around forty religion-inspired associations created a network called the Tunisian Front of Islamic Associations (al-jabha al-tunisiyya lil-jami'iat al-islamiyya), whose objective was to bring together Tunisian Islamic forces to fight for the inclusion of shari'a in the Constitution. In order to attain this goal, the front organized a demonstration outside the National Constituent Assembly headquarters on March 16, 2012. On September 14, the front organized another march from the Al-Fath Mosque to the US embassy and supported a sit-in outside the premises to express the organization's objection to the screening of a film that allegedly insulted the Prophet. Finally, the front also participated in the petition in support of Ennahda and against the strike the UGTT (Tunisian General Labor Union) called to protest against the government of the Troika on December 13, 2012.[66]

Between 2011 and 2014, the party struggled when caught between resisting the two-fold pressure of the seculars and its activist base. The former was pushing Ennahda to completely give up its Islamist heritage, while the latter was putting pressure on the party to hold onto its grassroots da'wa-oriented politics. The pressure from the base was particularly intense because Salafis were gaining ground in the social and religious space.

In the aftermath of the ninth party conference, a new organization was founded in Sfax on September 2012 to resolve this issue. The da'wa leaders of the party created Da'wa wa Islah (DWI), which translates to preaching and reform, with the primary objective of coordinating the activities of the religious associations created after the revolution. However, its implicit objective was to build a bridge between the hizb (party) and the haraka (movement) in light of the ongoing specialization process. In other words, the organization allowed Ennahda's leaders to keep functional ties with *da'wa*-oriented activists engaged outside party politics.[67]

This strategy did not succeed because Salafis already occupied the Islamist social movement space.[68] The radicalization of Islamist contention reached its peak with the assassination of two leftwing leaders and put an end to any Islamist experiment. The Ennahda leadership took advantage of the political juncture and, in July 2013, the Ennahda interior minister declared the Salafi Ansar al-Shari'a a terrorist organization.[69] In 2014, the technocratic Mehdi Jomaa government continued the campaign against Islamist activities, imposing stricter controls on the Islamic-oriented associations.[70] The Islamic space of contestation was therefore severely limited, but Ennahda remained a legitimate political force thanks to its participation in the national dialogue with the secular parties and civil society organizations. This political juncture represented the turning point for Ennahda. At the 2016 congress, the party could emphatically and with great confidence declare the end of 'Islamism.'

Politics as Technocratic Professionalization

Writing in 2016, Ghannouchi noted that 'Tunisia is finally a democracy rather than a dictatorship; that means that Ennahda can be a political party focusing on its practical agenda and economic vision rather than a social movement fighting against repression and dictatorship.'[71] Such a declaration reflects the changed political climate in Tunisia and within the party. The liberal political forces prevailed over Islamism with the help of the repressive apparatus and the Ennahda leadership finally achieved its transformation. In abandoning social movement activism and *da'wa*, its politics became post-Islamist. This is most evident in institutional politics. Since 2011, Ennahda ruled the country in coalition with secular parties,[72] and was the largest party in the 2018 municipal elections.[73] The party came to dominate political institutions. While it initially struggled to gain credibility as a democratic party, it managed to become a prominent political force that regularly participated in national unity governments.[74] From 2014 onwards, it started a policy of 'professionalization,' which meant inviting non-ideological personnel to the party, along with efforts to 'compete with professionalism for the government and the administration of the public affairs.'[75] Voices for the professionalization of the party were raised from within when party members, with a retrospective look at its performance in government, raised the issue of the scarce professionalism of the party's leadership in running the country.[76]

The main consequence of the division between party (*hizb*) and social movement (*haraka*) activities was the separation of careers between party members and *da'wa* activists engaged in civil society.[77] Thus, several preachers left the *majlis al-shura* (or shura council; the party's general council) to devote themselves to religious associations.[78] At the same time, the focus on electoral competition led the party to include people from civil society in its electoral lists. Since the 2014 legislative elections, Ennahda has consistently targeted the business and professional class and encouraged them to join the party.[79] At the 2016 party conference, Ennahda's rule of a two-year *ad interim* period before being granted full membership was lifted, precisely to make membership more attractive.[80]

This easing of procedures eventually facilitated the entry of new members and, ultimately, the de-ideologization of the party. This renewal of the party's membership has led to a reshuffling of its composition, welcoming new political personnel with a more 'technocratic' mindset and with a less ideological interpretation of politics. Ennahda's current focus on electoral competition and the exercise of power implies the professionalization of the party as a goal in itself, while 'for careerists, affiliation with Ennahda … is a vehicle for building professional expertise, personal skills, technocratic know-how, and social connections.'[81] The impact of this new policy was evident during the 2018 municipal elections in which Ennahda trailed the independent candidate lists. After four years of national unity government and few economic and social improvements, the legitimacy of the whole political class was at its lowest—Ennahda's included. Half of the 2,139 municipal positions Ennahda won belonged to independent members included in the party's lists, but without an official affiliation to the party.[82] The former Islamist party no longer had a large public and many local notables were accepted into the party in an attempt to gain consensus and to change its ideological nature.[83] During the October 2019 legislative elections, Ennahda emerged again as the largest party in the country, despite the loss of seats in parliament.[84] Rachid Ghannouchi reached a symbolic institutional role with his election as speaker of the parliament. This can be understood as a success in terms the former Islamist party's integration into Tunisia's institutional and political system. It can be also argued that the party has lost its ideological character in becoming similar to the rest of the political parties—it has become just like any other post-Islamist party.

Conclusion

Against the backdrop of an unprecedented economic crisis and the COVID-19 pandemic, on July 25, 2021 President Kais Saied imposed exceptional measures on the country. He dismissed the government, suspended the parliament, and waived MPs' immunity.[85] This evolution was the consequence of a wave of public outrage and social unrest against political parties. Ennahda, along with the rest of the ruling elite, was accused of corruption and being self-serving.[86] The former Islamist party could hardly react to this new situation and found itself almost isolated.[87]

On September 25, a 'group of one hundred' abandoned the party, following some of the leaders' resignation from office a month before. Long before September, important leaders such as Samir Dilou, Abdellatif Mekki, and Mohammed Salem had called for a new electoral conference, demanding internal democracy and a change of the historical leadership.[88] This highlights that the party has entered a new phase in its history and the end has not yet been written. Aside from that, Ennahda stands out as an example of an Islamist party that disengaged itself from its ideological character to evolve into a post-Islamist party. Both Islamism and post-Islamism are categories that scholars have devised in order to make sense of the phenomenon of Islamic revivalism since the Iranian revolution. The foregoing analysis of post-Islamism highlights the evolution of Islamism. While such an analytical frame is only applicable to Islamist parties and movements originating from the MB, it is useful for ideologically scrutinizing this evolution. Many authors focusing on the transformation of

Islamist parties have explained this ideological evolution as one from Islamism to conservative democracy.[89] Others have insisted that this transformation is a process of secularization.[90] This chapter looks at 'Islamism' as a transformative, potentially revolutionary ideology that offers an alternative model of society. The abandonment of such an ideology is considered here as a radical transformation in the politics of formerly Islamist movements. Instead of changing society, they evolved into technocratic politics, with a focus on managing government and contesting elections. This change implies both a new ideological framing and a change in practical political activities. The concepts of shariʿa, an Islamic state, and *umma* were translated into *maqasid al-shariʿa*, civic state, and *tunisianité*—that is, a nationalist narrative detached from Islamist universalism. In this sense, post-Islamism is the acceptance of liberal democracy and the normalization of Islamist politics.

5

TUNISIA'S RE-INVIGORATED CIVIL SOCIETY
CHANGES AND CHALLENGES

Zuzana Hudáková

Tunisia's re-invigorated civil society represents one of the most important achievements of the 2011 popular uprising. Facilitated by the changed legal and political context, as well as the availability of foreign funding, the unprecedented boom in civil society activity was engendered by the desire for change and self-actualization among a large number of previously demobilized, apolitical individuals who were spurred to action by the revolutionary experience. Driven largely by those marginalized during the authoritarian period— including youth, minorities, and religious groups—the newly created civil society organizations (CSOs) not only injected a new life into the associational sphere, but also added a much-needed diversity and bottom-up involvement of citizens in the social, cultural, economic, and political life of the country. Although not all of the post-revolutionary associations survived, many continue to thrive in the democratized environment and hundreds of associations continue to be created every year.

Tunisia's vibrant civil society is also widely credited with playing a crucial role in the country's successful democratization.

103

Established CSOs not only actively participated in the initial post-revolutionary governance of the country, but also played an important role in formulating new legislation and shaping the country's first democratic constitution. Most notably, a quartet of prominent CSOs launched a national dialogue that helped steer the country out of a political crisis that threatened to derail the democratic transition in 2013.[1] The National Dialogue Quartet's mediation efforts were recognized by awarding the four organizations involved in the initiative the 2015 Nobel Peace Prize. However, the prize was also 'intended as an encouragement to the Tunisian people' and as a more general acknowledgement that 'civil society institutions and organizations can play a crucial role in a country's democratization, and that such a process, even under difficult circumstances, can lead to free elections and the peaceful transfer of power.'[2]

Indeed, civil society is widely believed to have a significant democratizing potential to either help strengthen existing democracies or bring down authoritarian regimes.[3] In democracies, an active civil society is seen as crucial for democratic consolidation as well as the day-to-day practice of democracy,[4] while the experience with the democratization in Latin America and Eastern Europe had led some to view civil society in authoritarian settings as a potential 'counterweight' to the state, helping to resist the regime and democratize the society from below.[5] However, CSOs, including in the Middle East and North Africa (MENA), are routinely observed to reinforce and perpetuate rather than democratize authoritarian regimes.[6] In particular, instead of challenging the regime, CSOs often muffle their criticism in favor of a 'symbiotic' relationship with the state,[7] enhance the regime's social control,[8] or increase its legitimacy by helping it perpetuate an illusion of pluralism both at home and abroad.[9] Similarly, studies of civil society in a range of democratic settings demonstrate that an active associational life need not lead to democratization,[10] guarantee democratic consolidation,[11] or protect against autocratic backsliding, but can actually help facilitate the rise of authoritarianism.[12] Given the multiple, and often contradictory, findings regarding civil society's role in the democratization and transitology literatures, this chapter adopts a view of civil society, as well as its role and dynamics, that is not normatively driven but rooted in the specific sociopolitical and historical context under study.[13]

As a sphere of social and political action in which citizens pursue their common interests, civil society is located between the private and the political sphere.[14] As such, it is separate from political parties, as well as the contentious actions of social movements and various informal, temporary, and horizontally organized groupings (examined in Chapter 6 of this volume by Irene Weipert-Fenner).[15] Civil society, as a collection of organized, voluntary citizen activities, is comprised of a broad range of actors with diverse roles, organization, membership, and approaches to civil society activism, from advocacy nongovernmental organizations (NGOs), labor unions, professional associations, and a variety of charitable, sports, cultural, environmental, youth, or educational organizations, to local neighborhood associations. Examining a full range of CSOs—including illiberal, pro-regime, internally undemocratic, or otherwise 'uncivil' actors,[16] which are often excluded from studies of civil society—provides a more accurate picture of the role of civil society at any given moment, as well as its fluctuation, ambiguity, and heterogeneity.

In order to analyze the transformation, functions, and diversity of civil society in Tunisia, I will first explore its historical development under the authoritarian rule of Habib Bourguiba and Zine El Abidine Ben Ali. I will then highlight the general trends in the development of post-2011 Tunisian civil society before examining the particular composition and role of old, established, more institutionalized CSOs that trace their roots to the authoritarian period, and new, diverse, and often less professionalized CSOs created after the revolution. While the former have played an important role in the country's democratization, the latter have significantly diversified Tunisian civil society, broadening representation by enabling new actors and issues to come to the fore. The conclusion highlights both the complex landscape of civil society in the post-revolutionary period as well as its limits in facilitating change and participation in Tunisia's nascent democracy.

Historical Background

Civil society has played a prominent role in Tunisian social and political life since before the country's independence. However, prior to 2011, only a handful of CSOs, many of them unrecognized, were able to escape the regime's control and act as more critical and autonomous poles to the largely subdued CSOs, which characterized Tunisian civil society during the authoritarian period.[17] Representing some of the main sources of anti-regime opposition,[18] they were nonetheless limited in the degree of criticism and autonomy they were able to maintain vis-à-vis the regime for fear of personal and professional repercussions.

During Bourguiba's rule, Tunisian civil society was deeply intertwined with the ruling party. The relationship had already begun during the French colonial period, when an alliance between the Tunisian General Labor Union (Union générale tunisienne du travail, UGTT) and the Neo-Destour party, led by Bourguiba, helped bring about the country's independence in 1956. Presenting 'more than a classical labor union and something other than a party,'[19] the UGTT played an important political role in both opposing and supporting the regime throughout the country's modern history. Oscillating between dependency and autonomy,[20] the UGTT resisted political control most prominently in 1978, 1984, and 2008, when disagreements over the increasing liberalization of the country's economy brought it into open confrontation with the regime.[21] However, its more militant lower cadres continued to oppose the regime even when the union's leadership was closely aligned with it, leading some to speak of 'two UGTTs.'[22]

Adopting a highly personalistic and paternalistic approach to leading the country,[23] Bourguiba sought to eliminate both political opposition and the emergence of independent centers of power throughout his rule.[24] Limiting pluralism under the guise of national unity,[25] he sought to impose a secular, modernist vision of Tunisia in an authoritative, top-down fashion. To this end, Bourguiba not only established a monopoly over the political power in the country,[26] but also promoted 'a corporatist strategy of interest group organization' whereby all major groups in the society were organized into 'monolithic, monopolistic, state-controlled organizations, geared to rally citizens in support of the president's programs as well as provide the means for social control.'[27] Such national organizations would then act as 'transmission belts' for state policies.[28] For instance, while during the colonial period women were variously organized in the modernist-Islamic Muslim Women's Union of Tunisia, the socialist-communist Union of Tunisian Women, or the future ruling party-affiliated Group of Destourian Women, at independence Bourguiba moved to establish a monopoly over women's issues, just like other aspects of national life.[29] To this end, he not only granted women more rights via a progressive Code of Personal Status but also continued to exercise control over women's issues through the mass, pro-regime National Union of Tunisian Women (Union national de la femme tunisienne, UNFT), which took charge of disseminating the state-sponsored version of feminism around the country. Other such organizations included unions of farmers, youth, or mothers.

Although a number of smaller associations coexisted with the large, national, corporatist CSOs, they did not pose a significant challenge to the regime.[30] Not only was an approval by the Ministry of Interior required for an association to be formally established,[31] but the state was the main source of funding for associational work, loyal party members often led CSOs, and all forms of collective activity were subject to substantial regime surveillance.[32] As a result, Tunisian civil society under Bourguiba remained 'residual and unorganised,'[33] with few CSOs able or willing to vie for autonomy. A notable exception was the Tunisian League for Human Rights (Ligue tunisienne des droits de l'homme, LTDH), the Arab world's oldest human rights league, which was legalized in 1977. Comprising of a number of individuals who were part of the limited political opposition during the 1980s, the organization represented one of the few critical voices during the Bourguiba period.

Following the November 7, 1987 bloodless coup d'état by Bourguiba-era Prime Minister Ben Ali, Tunisia experienced an unprecedented period of liberalization. The Associations Law was amended, reducing the waiting period for the legal establishment of an association, requiring the Ministry of Interior to explain its decision if it refused an authorization, and introducing the possibility of recourse to legal action. [34] The effect was immediate. Almost 3,500 new associations were created in the first two years after the regime change, [35] increasing the total number of CSOs almost two-and-a-half-fold. Most new organizations were related to the education sector, [36] but a number of more critical CSOs were also legalized. Chief among them was the Tunisian Association of Democratic Women (Association tunisienne des femmes démocrates, ATFD), which presented a small, independent alternative to the mass-membership, regime-controlled UNFT.

However, the political opening was short-lived. In 1991, Ben Ali outlawed the Islamist Ennahda party as well as the Islamist student association General Tunisian Union of Students (Union générale tunisienne des étudiants, UGTE). [37] The subsequent crackdown decimated the Islamist movement in Tunisia. With virtually all prominent Islamists imprisoned or in exile, the regime moved against other political and civil society actors. In 1992, the Associations Law was amended to restrict the CSOs' sphere of operation by introducing a mandatory classification scheme that allocated associations to one of eight categories to which they were to limit their activities: women; sports; scientific; cultural and artistic; charitable, relief and social; development; friendship; and general character associations. [38] General character associations were also prohibited from having political party leaders in key positions within the organization and from refusing membership to anyone who agreed with the organization's principles. [39] This provision specifically targeted the outspoken LTDH, which was temporarily disbanded to avoid being flooded with pro-regime supporters. [40] At the same time as it was suppressing critical CSOs, the regime also encouraged the emergence of various loyal, apolitical, and government-organized NGOs (GONGOs), including a pro-regime alternative to the LTDH, the Higher Committee on Human Rights and Fundamental Freedoms, the existence of which was mostly formal. The dual strategy pursued by the Ben Ali regime not only limited civil society's democratization potential, [41] but also indicated that the formal liberalization that characterized Tunisia in the late 1980s mirrored the trend in other countries in the MENA region, in which the proliferation of civil society organizations was the result of a controlled top-down process rather than a genuine democratizing pressure from below.[42]

Indeed, a decade after Ben Ali's takeover of power, civil society criticism was muted and the country slid into 'deeper authoritarianism.'[43] The LTDH was reconstituted following domestic and international pressure, but, like the ATFD, it adopted a lower, less contentious profile. This was the result of the legal restrictions on the day-to-day operation of CSOs, as well as a variety of extra-legal methods—including harassment, violence, and arbitrary arrests—used to intimidate their members from speaking out against the regime. Ben Ali, who spent his career in the military and Tunisian intelligence services, relied on repression rather than co-optation to a much higher degree than his predecessor.[44]

Despite the repression, critical voices within Tunisian civil society began to reappear in the late 1990s and early 2000s.[45] Frustrated with the subdued LTDH, some of its members and several prominent regime opponents across the political spectrum formed the National Council for Liberties in Tunisia (Conseil national pour les libertés en Tunisie, CNLT) in 1998. More openly critical of the regime than the LTDH, the organization was denied legal recognition. This was also the fate of many other more independent CSOs that were created around the same time, such as the anti-globalization Rally for an International Development Alternative (Rassemblement pour une alternative international du développement, RAID), the Islamist-leaning International Association for the Support of Political Prisoners (Association internationale de soutien aux prisonniers politiques, AISPP), and the left-leaning Association for the Fight against Torture in Tunisia (Association de lutte contre la torture en Tunisie, ALTT). The two recognized oppositional CSOs, LTDH and ATFD, also became more critical of the regime in the early 2000s. However, as they were often forced to moderate their positions to continue their operations, a 'division of labor' emerged between the recognized and unrecognized CSOs, with the latter adopting a more critical stance.[46]

The last decade of Ben Ali's rule was also characterized by a search for greater organizational autonomy amongst professional associations. The Tunisian Bar Association (Ordre national des avocats de Tunisie, ONAT) undertook several general strikes in the early 2000s in response to police aggressions against lawyers and voted for more independent candidates for Bar president, bringing the organization increasingly at odds with the regime.[47] In 2004, a group of journalists tried to create a more independent Union of Tunisian Journalists (Syndicat des journalistes tunisiens, SJT) to counter the pro-regime Association of Tunisian Journalists (Association des journalistes tunisiens, AJT). The resulting schism was not resolved until four years later, when a new National Union of Tunisian Journalists (Syndicat national des journalistes tunisiens, SNJT) was established to replace the AJT. The SJT subsequently joined the newly created SNJT, steering it toward a more critical direction. However, the regime was able to regain control over the organization in 2009. The search for greater professional freedom was also thwarted within the Association of Tunisian Judges (Association des magistrats tunisiens, AMT) in 2005, when pro-regime judges helped the regime to muffle anti-regime voices within the organization.

Overall, while the different types of more critical, autonomous CSOs opposed the Ben Ali regime, they were in the minority and did not have the power to push it to democratize or counter-balance it, nor to mobilize sufficient support to bring it to heels.[48] That is not to say that they did not play a role in the popular struggle that erupted following the self-immolation of Mohamed Bouazizi in the central Tunisian city of Sidi Bouzid. Between December 17, 2010 and the departure of Ben Ali on January 14, 2011, members of CSOs supported Bouazizi's family, provided slogans and logistical support to the anti-regime movement, helped spread information, organize and coordinate protest actions, as well as negotiate with regime representatives. Notably, the decision of the UGTT national leadership to allow lower echelons to call for general strikes in the last days of the revolution significantly contributed to swelling the ranks of protesters in the main coastal cities, the traditional power-base of the regime. However, the handful of CSOs that maintained a more critical relationship to the regime were not the main driving force behind the protests.[49] The popular revolution, which engulfed the country and inspired people across the MENA region in early 2011, was propelled instead by thousands of previously politically inactive citizens who joined in the protests calling for Ben Ali's departure in a hope for freer, more prosperous, and just future.

Trends in Post-2011 Civil Society

Following the departure of Ben Ali in January 2011, Tunisian civil society witnessed a profound transformation in both the number of CSOs and their activities. Driven by increased citizen activism, almost five thousand new associations were created in the first two years after the revolution, presenting a 50 percent increase since the end of 2010 and a growth rate in new CSOs that was thirteen times faster than during the 2000s.[50] Most of the newly created CSOs were related to social, charitable, and relief work, as well as culture and arts, and development assistance.[51] The former trend reflects an increase in the activity of associations with religious affiliations, which were previously almost nonexistent in Tunisia due to the legal and extra-legal restrictions imposed by both Bourguiba and Ben Ali. The latter two trends indicate greater civil society participation of youth and individuals from the marginalized interior regions. Indeed, although a sizable number of CSOs remained located in the large coastal cities, and especially the capital, there was a significant increase in civil society activism in the south and the interior of the country, which had long been neglected and socioeconomically marginalized (for the origins of the prevailing regional disparity, see Chapter 9, by Alexandra Domike Blackman, in this volume). Scientific, environmental, and human rights organizations in the form of citizenship, rights, and women's associations also increased in number. However, as before the revolution, these organizations continued to concentrate overwhelmingly in the greater Tunis region.[52] For an overview of the development of the number of legally established CSOs in Tunisia over time, see Figure 5.1 below.

The re-invigorated civil society activity in the post-revolutionary period was facilitated by the new legal framework governing associations, which is 'among the most enabling in the MENA

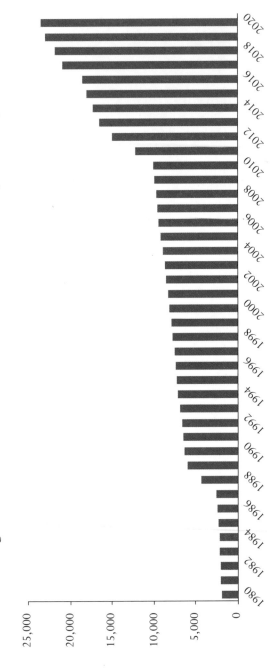

Figure 5.1: The Evolution of the Number of CSOs in Tunisia (1980–2020)[53]

region.'[54] Drafted with significant input from prominent CSOs during the first phase of the Tunisian political transition, the Law of Associations, introduced in 2011, removes the Ministry of Interior control over the creation of new CSOs and specifically prohibits public authorities from directly or indirectly hindering the activity of associations.[55] It also explicitly states that, in addition to organizing various types of associational activities, CSOs have the right to access information, evaluate the role of the state institutions, submit proposals to improve their performance, publish reports and information, print leaflets, conduct opinion polls, and file law suits. Particularly indicative of the radical break from the past, virtually all Tunisian CSOs now report feeling free to openly discuss their opinions in public and most describe their relationship with national authorities as collaborative and are confident about their ability to influence policy and legislative process.[56]

The initial boom in the creation of new CSOs had slowed down in 2013, with some observers noting that 'civic space has shrunk considerably' since then.[57] This was the result of the suspension or forced dissolution of CSOs suspected of terrorism or financial irregularities,[58] as well as a lack of long-term vision and resources among many of the new CSOs.[59] However, Tunisian civil society as a whole has become 'more mature and "professionalized,"'[60] and the rate of growth of new CSOs increased again in 2017 (see Figure 5.1 above), suggesting endogenous rather than exogenous drivers of Tunisian civil society developments. While not all formally registered associations are necessarily active, the sustained increase in new CSOs in the post-revolutionary period, which is significantly higher than during the rule of both Bourguiba and Ben Ali, indicates the continued vitality of the civil society sector.

Almost a decade after the revolution, more than twenty-three thousand CSOs are formally registered in Tunisia, with a little over one fifth of them operating in the capital.[61] The biggest increase in CSOs in the post-revolutionary period took place among the cultural and artistic associations, which doubled in number between 2012 and 2020, from 2,306 to 4,632. Their overall share increased from 13 percent immediately prior to the revolution to 20 percent of all CSOs in 2020. In the same time period, the share of development organizations doubled from 5 to 10 percent and that of charitable and social organizations increased from 7 to over 11 percent. The number of sports, friendship, and environmental associations, which are often youth-driven, also continued to increase in the post-revolutionary period, more than doubling since 2012. Meanwhile, the number of organizations within the historically largest category of CSOs, associations linked to the development of schools, remained virtually unchanged. As a result, their overall share decreased from 46 percent at the end of 2010 to just 20 percent in 2020. An overview of the changed composition of Tunisian CSOs between 2010 and 2020 is illustrated in Table 5.1 below.

Table 5.1: The Changing Composition of Tunisian CSOs by Area of Activity[62]

Type of CSO	2010	2012	2014	2016	2018	2020
Scientific	504	998	1,251	1,376	1,640	1,755
Women's	70	138	167	152	183	206
Sports	1,074	1,356	1,618	1,797	2,476	2,816
Friendship	334	602	767	919	1,226	1,307
Cultural and artistic	1,288	2,306	2,846	3,223	4,104	4,632
Social, charitable, and relief	696	1,826	2,211	2,230	2,439	2,615
Development	529	1,464	1,663	1,848	2,243	2,436
Micro-credit	330	330	288	288	291	302
Schools	4,595	4,624	4,642	4,603	4,587	4,592
Environment	102	269	364	422	548	588
Rights	18	208	292	315	359	391
Citizenship	11	321	472	565	741	815
Youth	211	274	324	337	384	404
Childhood	203	246	280	280	305	312
Network	.	.	48	62	69	75
Coordination	.	.	12	12	14	14
Foreign	.	.	.	129	167	196
Total number of CSOs	**9,969**	**14,966**	**17,245**	**18,558**	**21,776**	**23,456**

The initial boom, as well as the slight decrease in civil society growth since 2013, was partly a reflection of the availability of foreign funding. Many actors already involved in the country significantly increased their financial aid after the revolution, flooding Tunisia with money earmarked for civil society capacity building. For example, the German political foundations tripled their budget,[63] while the EU provided support to civil society actors through various sources, including the Programme to Support Civil Society (Programme d'appui à la société civile, PASC), which allocated € 7 million to civil society support between 2012 and 2016.[64] Not all civil society actors enjoyed the same access to foreign funds, however. While the German foundations tended to support a relatively broad cross-section of CSOs,[65] the EU has been focused predominantly on liberal, secular groups and the development of associational networks,[66] and the Gulf states concentrated on funding religious-based associations.[67] Overall, established, more professional organizations with experience in grant writing and project management tend to receive more of the available funds,[68] even if their representativeness of the broader population is more limited.[69] Specific donor priorities have also shaped the development of Tunisian civil society, leading, for example, to the proliferation of electoral monitoring associations prior to elections or the formation of civil society networks, for which there is generally little grassroots push or enthusiasm.[70]

However, the role of foreign aid in civil society development should not be overstated. Despite the importance of foreign support for certain types of civil society actors, a recent survey of Tunisian civil society found that less than two-fifths of CSOs received any foreign funding, and that only about a quarter of Tunisian CSOs relied on it as their primary source of funding, with most civil society activity financed through domestic sources like local individual donations, government funding, or membership fees.[71] While many Tunisian CSOs have been hit by the decreased availability of foreign support for civil society since the mid-2010s, a significant portion managed to refocus their activities, diversify their sources of income, or continue to operate on a largely voluntary basis. This is true especially of those CSOs with younger members or those located outside of the greater Tunis area, where funding is scarce. Finally, civil society support is often used by donors as a means to achieve other policy objectives, rather than as a goal in its own right, meaning that the availability of funds themselves are neither a guarantee, nor a necessary condition, for the development of a vibrant, autonomous civil society sphere.[72]

Established CSOs: Driving Change and Steering the Democratic Transition

While many of the formerly pro-regime CSOs, like UNFT, struggled for survival and relevance in the changed political environment,[73] established CSOs that were critical of the Bourguiba and Ben Ali regimes adopted a significantly more active role after the revolution. Further politicized during the revolution, many stepped up their political role to help steer the democratic transition. The UGTT was initially included in the first interim government announced on January 17, 2011, and a group of oppositional CSOs, including the UGTT and ONAT, helped form the National Council for the Protection of the Revolution (Conseil national pour la protection de la revolution, CNPR), which sought to oversee the work of the interim government.[74] The directly political role of civil society during the first phase of the transition was further expanded on March 15, 2011, when the CNPR was merged with the Higher Commission for Political Reform (Commission supérieure pour la réforme politique) to form the Higher Authority for the Realization of the Objectives of the Revolution, Political Reform, and Democratic Transition (Haute instance pour la réalisation des objectifs de la révolution, de la réforme politique et de la transition démocratique, HIROR).[75] The inclusive but unrepresentative HIROR was subsequently expanded to include national figures, political parties, CSOs, under-represented regions, as well as families of 'martyrs' and the Tunisian diaspora.[76] Split into a Council of Experts, which was composed of lawyers preparing draft legislations, and a Higher Authority, where the various groups, including CSOs, reviewed and voted on the laws for adoption by the executive power,[77] the institution steered the country until the October 2011 National Constituent Assembly elections. Among others, HIROR adopted a new Electoral Law, created an independent commission to oversee the elections, and prepared the new legislation governing political parties and CSOs.[78]

During the second phase of the transition, which began following the election of the National Constituent Assembly (NCA), established oppositional CSOs adopted watchdog and consultative functions. Following the work of the NCA, they were actively involved in the main debates surrounding the constitution drafting process of the Ennahda-led government. These included the highly controversial issues of the role of Islamic law, the prohibition of blasphemy, and the status of women. Although all three ultimately ended with Ennahda withdrawing their original propositions, it was not without a significant pushback from the country's secular political and civil society forces. The most heated of these debates surrounded Article 28 of the draft constitution released in August 2012, which defined women as 'complementary' rather than 'equal' to men (the other two debates are covered by Fabio Merone in Chapter 4 of this volume).[79] The negative reaction to the proposed formulation was particularly strong among secular women's organizations like ATFD and AFTURD, but the issue also mobilized large numbers of unaffiliated women from all walks of the society. Protests and counter-protests led by secular and Islamist parties and CSOs ensued and the subsequent drafts of the Constitution omitted the controversial term.[80] The various constitutional debates signaled the rising importance of identity politics as well as the increasing secular-Islamist polarization of the Tunisian society that unfolded within the political sphere, civil society, and the media as a struggle over national self-identity.[81]

The societal divisions played out against rising Salafi violence.[82] The political situation in the country reached a low on February 6, 2013, when Chokri Belaïd, a vocal, leftist critic of Ennahda, was assassinated. Protests erupted the following day, fueled by the UGTT calling for a general strike. The already tense situation further deteriorated at the end of July when a second leftist politician, Mohamed Brahmi, was murdered. Spontaneous protests erupted in the center of Tunis on July 25, 2013, followed by a UGTT general strike, sustained mobilization of protesters at the Bardo Square, and a withdrawal from the assembly by a group of NCA members.

Although the perpetrators of the two political assassinations came from radical Salafi ranks, many blamed Ennahda for helping to create an atmosphere of tolerance for religious extremism and demanded that the Islamist-led government resign. The situation also raised concerns about a 'counterrevolution' among government supporters, who had watched the concurrent forced removal of President Mohamed Morsi and the violent repression of Muslim Brotherhood supporters in Egypt. With the NCA at a standstill and both secular and Islamist groups mobilizing in the streets, many feared that the Tunisian political transition had reached a dead end and that the country might be on a verge of a civil war.

It is during this period of heightened crisis that established CSOs shifted from contributing to the increased polarization in the country to adopting a more 'conservative, consensus-oriented culture.'[83] To this end, the UGTT, together with ONAT, the LTDH, and the employers' Tunisian Union of Industry, Trade, and Handicrafts (Union tunisienne de l'industrie, du commerce et de l'artisanat, UTICA),[84] began negotiating a possible way out of the crisis with the different political stakeholders, including the extra-parliamentary Nidaa Tounes party.[85] The National Dialogue Quartet's 'roadmap,' which sought to diffuse tensions and keep the country on a democratic path, was signed by twenty-one political parties.[86] Taking place between October 2013 and January 2014, the National Dialogue Quartet led to the formation of a new technocratic government, finalization of the Constitution, and the holding of legislative and presidential elections. The work of the quartet, which defined the third phase of the Tunisian political transition, was later recognized by the 2015 Nobel Peace Prize.

Following the successful completion of the second competitive elections at the end of 2014, Tunisia was reclassified as the first Arab democracy in forty years,[87] and was lauded as the only successful case to emerge from the Arab Spring uprisings. In the 'post-transition' period, politics became more routinized and most of the established CSOs scaled back their directly political roles. Professional associations as well as the UGTT, which continues to be actively involved in political issues by mobilizing its base through strikes and anti-austerity protests, have faced significant pressure from parts of their membership to focus more strictly on associational concerns.[88] Established advocacy, human rights, and women's rights organizations, like the LTDH or the ATFD, continue to intervene in public debates in the areas of their expertise. Previously illegal organizations, like ALTT or the Union of Unemployed Graduates (Union des diplômés chômeurs, UDC), were able to obtain legal status and start reaching a fuller potential. In particular, although the latter continues to be fairly decentralized and weakly institutionalized, with only limited financial resources at its disposal, its membership, communication, geographical scope, and protest activities have significantly expanded in the post-revolutionary period.[89] Overall, whether directly or indirectly political, the more oppositional established CSOs continue to mobilize their networks to defend both the interests of their members and their larger organizational objectives, actively steering the country along a more democratic course.

New CSOs: Increasing Diversity and Bringing New Issues to the Public Domain

In the post-revolutionary period, hope, enthusiasm, and the drive for self-actualization—backed by a significant injection of foreign financial support earmarked for democracy promotion and civil society capacity building—helped breathe new life into civic activism. Religious charities and other associations with religious character, which were severely restricted under both Bourguiba and Ben Ali, mushroomed, as did youth-driven cultural and artistic associations, including in the heavily marginalized interior regions. The associational life of minorities has also increased significantly since 2011.

However, many of the new CSOs differ in their composition and approach to civil society work and organization. Rather than adopt the small, tightly-knit community model with professionalized leadership, partly overlapping membership base, strong international networks, and weak domestic roots (which characterized many of the oppositional CSOs during the Ben Ali period), many of the newly created organizations are loosely institutionalized, decentralized, run by volunteers, and rooted in the community. Similarly, while most of the established CSOs that had represented rare oppositional voices during the authoritarian period saw themselves as having a responsibility to continue to play a political role, a large number of the new CSOs have been happy to play an 'apolitical' role or to influence politics from the 'outside' rather than directly. That is not to say that all newly created CSOs fit this pattern. On the contrary, as before the revolution, a full spectrum—from the more elitist, politically oriented CSOs to more community-based, apolitical CSOs—coexists, with internal divisions based on multiple, often contradictory positions and preferences, reflecting the diversity of the Tunisian society.

The old established human rights organizations with a political standing and anti-regime experience have been joined by a plethora of new political watchdog organizations created by younger, tech-savvy activists. The 'generational divide' between the two sets of secular, politically oriented CSOs is characterized not only by limited contact and interaction, but also lack of respect and understanding for each other's work, mutual distrust, and large differences in communication styles and approaches to civil society activism.[90] Where the old organizations prefer to keep their membership small and focus largely on press conferences, reports, and communiques, the new organizations often make extensive use of new networks, volunteers, as well as the internet.[91]

Among the visible new CSOs is the Mourakiboun (Observers) network, formed in 2011 by a number of newly created CSOs, which has successfully dispatched its more than four thousand volunteers to monitor Tunisian legislative, presidential, and municipal elections in the post-revolutionary period. Equally noteworthy is Al-Bawsala (Compass), an organization created by young, returning Tunisians to promote greater transparency by observing the work of the legislative assembly (the Masrad Majles project). Since 2011, it made available on its website not only the list of elected representatives, together with their biographies, political affiliations, and contact information, but also their voting record and attendance, as well as summary information on the work of the assembly, voting outcomes, related briefs, draft proposals, and meeting minutes. Its political watchdog function has been so successful that members of the parliament often approach them to provide an explanation for absences.[92] Since 2014, the organization expanded its work to also monitor political activity at the municipal level (the Masrad Baladia project) and public spending (the Masrad Budget project).[93] Another successful example of a new, youth-led CSO is the anti-corruption watchdog I-Watch, which has become the official partner of Transparency International in Tunisia in 2013. Subject to intimidation, defamation lawsuits, and smear campaigns, the organization has undertaken a number of high-profile naming-and-shaming campaigns, played an instrumental role in drafting a ground-breaking February 2017 law protecting whistleblowers, and filed a complaint against several prominent politicians, including former Prime Minister Youssef Chahed. I-Watch also runs 'I Assist,' an e-learning platform offering a range of courses intended specifically for civil society,[94] and accountability 'meters' that keep track of the fulfillment of the president and prime minister's political promises.[95]

Greater diversity in the post-revolutionary period is also visible among the Tunisian women's associations, where the defining cleavage reflects the country's secular–Islamist polarization. For religious-based organizations, including women's associations, the revolution presented an unprecedented opportunity for self-actualization, resulting in a genuine boom of religious civil society activity. Rather than joining the existing CSOs, many took the opportunity to create their own associations. Islamist women's organizations—like the Tunisian Women Association (Association femmes tunisiennes), which is close to Ennahda and works on transitional justice issues—focus specifically on the experiences of women persecuted by the former regime for their religious beliefs. Indeed, although Islamists were frequently targeted during the authoritarian period, they have generally received little sympathy from most secular CSOs, which are deeply skeptical of the Islamist agenda.[96] In the same vein, while the two main established secular women's organizations—the formerly anti-regime ATFD and pro-regime UNFT—vary in terms of their approach to membership, they have both aimed to exclude Islamist women from their ranks for fear of diluting their missions. The ATFD has remained intentionally small, limited to a trusted circle of individuals predominantly within the urban coastal areas, while the UNFT has refrained from imposing membership fees, despite a significant loss of members and funding that have endangered its operation and national outreach.[97] Radically opposed to each other on virtually all gender-related issues, the two groups have continued to mobilize and counter-mobilize throughout the post-revolutionary period. Among others, religious and secular women's associations clashed around the status of women in the Constitution in 2012, took part in the 2013 Bardo sit-in, and mobilized in response to the equal inheritance legislation proposed by President Beji Caïd Essebsi, which failed to win parliamentary approval in 2018. Overall, while the ATFD as well as religious women's organizations have thrived in post-2011 Tunisia, the UNFT faced repeated calls for dissolution by both Islamist and secular women's organizations and experienced not only an internal crisis but also physical attacks on its members and offices by Islamists, especially in the first two years after the revolution.

The post-revolutionary period also opened new avenues for minority rights, which were previously virtually absent from the public sphere. Chief among them are the issue of race and LGBTQ rights. Although black Tunisians and sub-Saharan residents represent an estimated 10–15 percent of the Tunisian population, they are mostly invisible in the political, cultural, and social spheres. Faced with persistent racism, widespread stereotypes, and both systemic and everyday discrimination, they are not only frequently economically exploited but also socially not accepted. The Association for Equality and Development (ADAM pour l'égalité et le développement, ADAM), established in 2012, was the first CSO to defend the rights of black people in Tunisia. It has since been joined by a number of others, including M'nemty (My dream), an anti-discrimination association created in 2013. Vocal about the racism experienced by black Tunisians, who are frequently referred to as 'slaves' and other pejoratives, these organizations have been focused primarily on making race-based discrimination illegal. In large part thanks to pressure by CSOs, in October 2018 Tunisia finally adopted a law against racial discrimination—the first of its kind in the Arab world—with offenses punishable by fines up to 3,000 dinars (around

1,000 euros) and one to three years in prison. A number of anti-racism CSOs were subsequently included in the law's monitoring in partnership with a ministry committee.

Another vocal and highly controversial minority rights group is Shams (Shams: Pour la dépénalisation de l'homosexualité en Tunisie), founded in 2015 to defend LGBTQ rights. In Tunisia, homosexuality is prohibited by Article 230 of the Penal Code and punishable by up to three years in prison. The association has been advocating most prominently for the abolition of the sodomy provisions and an end to forced anal examinations to which suspected offenders are often forcefully subjected by the police. The state has repeatedly tried to dissolve the association on charges of sexual-based discrimination and its mission running counter to 'the Islamic values of Tunisian society,' but the judiciary has upheld the organization's claim, most recently in February 2020,[98] making it the only officially recognized LGBTQ association in North Africa. The organization was most prominently in the public view in 2019, when Mounir Baatour, its head, launched an unsuccessful bid for the presidency. Although important milestones have been reached on both issues, meaningful change has been slow in practice. The issue of racial discrimination gained prominence again in December 2019 after Jamila Ksiksi, a black Ennahda deputy and the only black representative in the Tunisian parliament, was attacked on social media by a fellow representative from another party who compared her to a monkey. Similarly, while Baatour's rejected candidacy for the presidential elections attracted public attention to the association's cause, it also resulted in a series of death threats that led to his decision to leave Tunisia. While there is still long way to go on the road to tolerance and equality, both types of CSOs have nonetheless managed to successfully open a public dialogue on their respective issues.

Other groups have organized around single-issue campaigns (like outlawing Tunisia's harsh anti-drug law, responsible for a significant share of youth incarcerations) or sought to provide youth in marginalized regions with a space to foster creativity and civic engagement. One such example is the Mash'hed (scene) association, established in 2011 by a group of youth in Gafsa, one of Tunisia's interior cities, with the objective of creating a cultural space. The association, which is run almost exclusively by volunteers, organizes various youth training programs as well as cultural festivals, cinema screenings, theater, painting, plastic arts, graffiti, games, and other cultural and artistic activities. Advocating for decentralization, Mash'hed not only has an established network of partners in other regions in Tunisia, but also international partners in France and Morocco, with whom the association conducts exchanges.[99] Although not all cultural and artistic associations have been as successful, especially in attracting funding, many continue to be deeply embedded in their cities and neighborhoods, providing the youth with a creative outlet for their frustrations and an opportunity for self-realization.

Conclusion

In the decade since the revolution, Tunisia has developed a strong, vibrant civil society that reflects the diversity of its society and mobilizes in response to political developments in the country. This contrasts sharply with the situation before the revolution, when Tunisian civil society was largely an instrument of regime control, limiting political opposition, and helping to execute government policies.[100] Its expansion, transformation, and development since 2011 is thus rightly celebrated as a success story and as one of the most important achievements of the revolution. CSOs were not only actively involved in the constitution drafting process and in orchestrating a compromise that helped the country's political forces to continue on a path of peaceful, democratic transition, but they also regularly contribute to public debates, weigh in on legislation, provide training and opportunities to their members, and mobilize segments of society in support of their organizational causes.

However, civil society is not a panacea for all problems. CSOs are no substitute for political parties. They can articulate citizens' positions and grievances, provide public services, or specialized expertise, but they cannot be relied on to resolve deep structural issues that require government intervention and political, social, and economic reforms. Indeed, corruption, nepotism, the deteriorating economic situation, and other pressing issues facing Tunisia in the post-revolutionary period cannot be addressed exclusively by CSOs, although they do have a role to play, including as watchdogs and secondary service providers for the most vulnerable populations. Offering alternative activities to excluded, unemployed, or frustrated youth also goes only so far in the absence of future prospects for employment and self-actualization.

Furthermore, CSOs cannot be expected to articulate and channel all citizen activities. In fact, despite the importance of civil society in the post-revolutionary democratization of the country, many Tunisians remain skeptical of CSOs. The Arab Barometer surveys show that only around a third of Tunisians have a medium or high trust in CSOs, while about one in two respondents said they did not trust CSOs or had only limited trust in them.[101] Further, many, especially younger, Tunisians have opted to pursue their political agenda and interests by temporarily coming together in loose, horizontally organized networks or informal local groups mobilizing around a single issue (studied by Irene Weipert-Fenner in Chapter 6 of this volume), rather than by creating or joining formal CSOs. As a result, protests have increasingly taken the form of localized, spontaneous social movements, strikes, and road-blocks, as well as collective and individual hunger strikes, public threats of suicide, and illegal emigration. This trend has become visible especially since 2015, exacerbated by the worsening socioeconomic situation and decreasing trust in institutionalized channels of social and political change. In this respect, CSOs, like political parties, have often been viewed as part of the problem, contributing to the vilification, marginalization, and criminalization of social movements in Tunisia.

The turn away from traditional politics and organized civil society toward populism, on the one hand, and more disruptive, informal, and individual acts of protest, on the other hand, is a clear sign that Tunisia still has a long way to go to address the various grievances of the population. It does not, however, mean that civil society has failed. Located in between the political and the private sphere, the country's various CSOs have an important function both as mediators and actors in their own right. Mature and diverse, the Tunisian civil society landscape stretches from elite CSOs that are close to political power to local associations that are deeply entrenched in their communities, horizontal, decentralized, and volunteer-run. The activities, forms of mobilization, and topics of concern of CSOs partly overlap with those of political parties, on the one hand, and those of more spontaneous protests and social movements, on the other, without dissolving into either. Despite their inherent limitations and practical challenges, Tunisia's CSOs—like political parties and social movements—fulfill crucial functions in articulating and organizing a wide spectrum of societal interests and concerns. As such, although civil society is neither inherently pro-democratic nor a guarantee of successful democratization, Tunisian CSOs have been crucial in both building and maintaining democracy in the post-revolutionary period.

6

MOBILIZATION IN TUNISIA POST-2011
FROM POLITICAL PROTESTS TO NATIONAL
CAMPAIGN MOVEMENTS

Irene Weipert-Fenner

Interest in studying protests in Tunisia increased dramatically after the mass uprising of 2010–11. However, contentious actions are not new to Tunisia: milestones in the history of popular protests include mobilization against the French during the struggle for independence, the general strike of 1978, and the bread riots of 1983–84. Student activism from the 1970s to the 1990s turned universities into sites of public protest. The most important instance of contention prior to 2011 was the six-month regional uprising of 2008 in the Gafsa mining region.[1] While the history of popular protests in Tunisia is far more extensive than the major events listed here, it would be fair to say that what we witnessed in 2011, and ever since, has been unprecedented. Although there is ample research that looks into particular aspects of these events, an overview of how protests have developed in the first decade after the end of dictatorship and an understanding of what they mean for the transition process is still lacking.

This chapter explores the development of popular protests in Tunisia from the fall of Zine El Abidine Ben Ali in 2011 until the end of 2019. It focuses on non-routinized contentious collective actions, which encompass various forms of protests and collective action but do not include strikes staged by the national labor union federation as part of wage negotiations. A close examination of nearly a decade of contentious popular action uncovers trends that can be grouped into three phases. The first phase revolved around political protests that were associated with the re-institutionalization of the political system (2011–13) and were intertwined with an identity conflict between Islamist and secular forces. The second phase was characterized by the prevalence of socioeconomic protests, mainly at the local level, that remained isolated from each other, primarily focused on single issues, and unfolded independently of formal organizations. While occasional regional waves of protest did occur, they were rather short-lived outbursts of discontent. Gradually, attempts toward creating national campaigns became more and more important. This happened while at the political level, under President Béji Caïd Essebsi, a broad intra-elite consensus was formed as a grand coalition between Nidaa Tounes and Ennahda and in cooperation with various oppositional and social actors, including the Tunisian General Labor Union (UGTT), and was formalized in what came to be known as the Carthage agreement.[2] In the third phase, protesters also took to the streets to express socioeconomic grievances but these protests grew bigger and were pointedly political, as in the case of the protests against the Finance Laws of 2018 and 2019, which ushered in austerity measures prescribed by the International Monetary Fund (IMF) as part of a 2016 loan agreement. The third phase saw the expanding role of campaigns as a form of greater coalition-building along with the re-emergence of the Tunisian Trade Union Federation at the national level, functioning as a protest actor for non-routinized contentious actions in the form of general strikes. During these years, Nidaa Tounes, which emerged victorious in the 2014 parliamentary and presidential elections, fell apart because political infighting and the unpopular politics of austerity evaporated general support for the then-ruling parties, resulting in the sweeping victory of an independent politician as president and the success of populist parties in the parliamentary elections in late 2019.

The aforementioned three phases were built on two characteristics of protests: protest actors and protest demands. Protest actors can be described as falling on a scale between formally organized actors, such as a trade unions, on one end and protesters that were independent of any formal organization on the other. It is important to note that there is a wide range of possibilities in between, and that the phases are defined by a *dominant* protest actor, not a sole actor. In this sense, phase one reflected a mix of actors who were linked to political camps; phase two was marked by a clear dominance of protests outside formal organizations; and phase three was characterized by a return of the role of organizations and of national campaign movements. Again, these phases should not be understood as rigid distinctions between various forms of activism but more as representing predominant trends. For instance, though campaigns could be found throughout the period under consideration, they increased in importance with the end of phase two and beginning of phase three.

The second defining characteristic of these three phases were protest demands. For instance, during phase one, political demands were paired with an ideological conflict over the relation of Islam and the state. Phases two and three were mostly about socioeconomic demands, though each of these phases had distinct characteristics. While in phase two demands were either very specific (for personal employment, for instance) or very broad and vague (such as the call for regional development), phase three marked a shift to the politicization of socioeconomic grievances in an explicit criticism of neoliberal policies.

The notable increase in protests in Tunisia post 2011 raises the question of what these developments mean for the transition process. In classic transitology literature, mobilization is generally treated as an enabling factor for pushing dictators out of office; but, as soon as negotiations regarding transitions took place between soft-liners of the old regime and 'modest' opposition, protests came to be seen as a threat.[3] Demands for the redistribution of wealth and power were regarded as a risk to the willingness of former elites to support a new system. Yet, empirical evidence tells us that polarization and mobilization will continue when we consider revolutions as a process rather than an event. Jack Goldstone considered 'further polarization' as one of the components of revolutions.[4] Chantel Berman further developed this category by putting greater emphasis on vertical polarization going beyond the original focus on elite-centered polarization, looking at the case of Tunisia between 2011 and 2013.[5]

This chapter further broadens this scope and includes protests in the consolidation phase of democracy. After the political re-institutionalization that ended in 2014, socioeconomic protests increased, demonstrating that political liberties alone did not suffice and that social justice was a crucial part of expectations from democracy. The rise of explicit anti-austerity protests from 2018 onwards made collective contentious actions more political and, as I argue here, paved the way for the landslide victory by populist forces in 2019.

In order to develop a general understanding of contestation in Tunisia and what it means, I build on previous studies on protests (including my own) and my ongoing research addressing contention against IMF reforms. I also draw on various sources, including secondary literature, press reports, and primary data from fieldwork, comprising interviews with protest actors between 2014 and 2016, as well as statements made by actors on social media and protest event datasets.

Protests in Tunisia in Numbers

Looking at the quantitative development of protests, I refer to data from the Armed Conflict Location and Event Data Project (ACLED), a widely used dataset that covers many world regions and has tracked protests in Tunisia since 1997.[6] Based mainly on media reports, it codes different types of events. Of interest here are 'demonstrations' that include non-violent events coded as 'protests' and violent forms coded as 'riots.'[7] It encompasses comparable data on actors, dates, and geographical locations down to the city level. The dataset mainly relies on local, national, regional, and international media.[8]

Looking at the quantitative development of protests and riots, there is a slight increase in 2008, mostly in relation to the events

Figure 6.1: Number of Annual Protests in Tunisia
January 1, 1998–December 31, 2019[9]

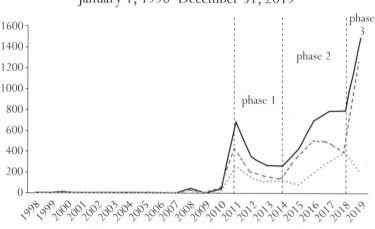

in the Gafsa mining region, and a sharp increase in 2011 followed by a decrease during the time of political transition and re-institutionalization. Since 2015, the number of protests and riots has constantly remained higher than during the revolution itself— with a massive increase in 2018 for riots and in 2019 for non-violent protests. Peaceful protests have always greatly outnumbered violent protests. The type of protest actor, however, has changed over time: the share of protests carried out by associations and organizations has oscillated between 30–40 percent (30 percent in 2011, 40 percent in 2012–13, 25–30 percent in 2014–17) and sharply increased in 2018 and 2019 to 60 percent.

Prisca Jöst and Jan-Philipp Vatthauer recoded ACLED data for the period extending from 2011 until the end of 2016.[10] They constructed the variable 'demands,' which is not included in the original dataset, using information from the one-sentence summary of the protest event in the dataset ('notes') and additional media research. They differentiated between socioeconomic and non-socioeconomic demands and found that, from 2015 on, socioeconomic protests outnumbered other protests, including political protests. Given the sheer number of protest and riot events from 2017 on, particularly in 2018 (631) and 2019 (1394), I was only able to gain a general idea about the protest events, allowing me to conclude that this trend has continued and that most protests and riots raised socioeconomic claims.

Although the ACLED numbers support the qualitative findings, a few potential caveats should be kept in mind, as relying on traditional media creates 'significant coverage biases associated with event size and proximity to media sources,'[11] leading to overreporting of urban and large protests. The quality of data also greatly depends on the quality of the media itself. Although the quality of Tunisian media has certainly improved since 2011, it is still in a stage of transition, torn between ideological, socioeconomic, and geographical biases but also suffer from institutional lacunae.[12] I also found that Arabic sources were used only from 2018 onwards. On the one hand, this is a significant development, as other available data sets rely solely on English and French news reporting.[13] At the same time, it raises questions regarding the comparability of ACLED data before and after 2018, particularly given the sharp increase in the number of protests since 2018 (Figure 6.1). In sum, ACLED data nevertheless is a useful representation of the general trends I identified in the qualitative analysis of secondary and primary data. In particular, the changing composition of protest actors correlates with the three phases of protest development I identify and explain in the next sections.

The Evolution of Protest in Tunisia Since the Revolution

Protests can never be understood as isolated phenomena; in fact, they are a part of complex interplays with other actors, prominently but not solely with state actors. The following analysis therefore is closely linked to the development of elite politics, from polarization (2011–13) over consensus politics (2014–17) to the rise of populism (2018–19). While the overlap between protest and political phases is no coincidence, it should not be misunderstood as the result of direct causal effects between elite politics and contentious collective actions. Rather, it shows the interrelatedness of the two spheres that mutually shape each other. While Chapter 2, Marina Ottaway's contribution to this volume, elaborates on the complex developments of politics from above, this chapter takes up the challenge of doing so for politics from below. One of the driving factors for the protest development is the persisting of socioeconomic grievances, particularly for young people, many of whom feel frustrated with unfulfilled expectations and angry for being ignored or betrayed, as Alyssa Miller vividly depicts in Chapter 7 of this volume.

Phase One: From Revolutionary Mobilization to Polarized Political Protests

The most important characteristic of protests in this phase is the shift from anti-regime protests to contention between two ideological camps—Islamists and secularists. Regarding the first category, it is important to highlight that for many activists in Tunisia, particularly those from the interior regions, the revolution did not come to an end with the ousting of Ben Ali. All political institutions remained in place, as the old elites did, most visible in the figure of Mohamed Ghannouchi, who had been prime minister since 1999. Although he did integrate some opposition party members and UGTT members into his cabinet, these changes were less than the protesters expected. The severing of ties with the old regime was brought about by the 'Kasbah I' and 'Kasbah II' protests, which was seen by the participants as the second phase of the revolution of 2010–11.

The so-called Kasbah I protests took place on January 23–28, 2011, mobilizing tens of thousands of people from all over the country who had come to Tunis in 'caravans of freedom.' Demonstrations against the continuity of the former regime in the form of political institutions and government personnel were staged in front of the cabinet's building at Kasbah Square in Tunis. One month later, Kasbah II brought one hundred thousand people to the square. Together with trade unionists, Islamists, and opposition parties, protesters demanded a new constitution.[14] This goal was realized when Ghannouchi gave in under popular pressure. Upon his resignation on February 27, 2011, Essebsi, who was brought in to serve as the new prime minster despite having filled posts under Ben Ali, announced elections for a National Constituent Assembly.

Looking at the conflict lines, these protests were still characterized by multi-sectoral cooperation,[15] and can be seen as the continuation of revolutionary mobilization from December 10, 2010 to January 14, 2011.[16] However, one conflict line—a marginalized interior versus the prosperous coastal region—was consciously suppressed, as can be observed in the development of the form and framing of the Kasbah protests. During the Kasbah I mobilization, popular action coalesced around caravans—as a form of collective action in which people walk or drive to the capital— thereby connecting the local with the national. Caravans had previously been used in the 2000s mainly in solidarity and support for the Palestinian cause. In 2011, people from the marginalized interior initiated the caravans with a dual intention: to overcome their marginalization, symbolized by regionalism, as well as to gain control over the state as a provider of resources by abolishing the old system entirely.[17] However, the conflict between the marginalized interior and the coastal regions was suppressed during the Kasbah II events in order to make protest seem less threatening, especially since the interior regions evoked perceptions of the movement being 'chaotic, violent and "tribal."'[18] This conflict line, visible in the Kasbah protests, remained suppressed for a few years but resurfaced later in 2015.

The early transition phase is more complex than can be portrayed here.[19] Different bodies tasked with defining the rules for changing the game—mainly how to elect the National Constituent Assembly— were formed, merged, contested, and modified. This is the case with the Higher Commission for the Fulfilment of Revolutionary Goals, Political Reform, and Democratic Transition (Haute instance pour la réalisation des objectifs de la revolution, des réformes politiques et de la transition démocratique, HIROR), which laid the groundwork for the National Constituent Assembly (NCA) elections that took place in October 2011. At the same time, the NCA served as the legislature for the transitional phase. During this period, the Troika government headed by the majority party (the Islamist Ennahda party) also took the lead in the constitutional process, and, after a profound crisis in the summer of 2013, this process was successfully completed with the enactment of a new constitution in January

2014. The parliamentary and presidential elections of the same year marked the beginning of a new political system.

This period was defined by a major cleavage, structured along the question of the role of religion in politics. This first became visible immediately after the announcement of the elections, 'when opposing demonstration groups stood on either side of Avenue Habib Bourguiba and chanted "the people want a secular state" and "the people want an Islamist state" respectively.'[20] This line of division deepened and polarized Tunisian society into two political camps: one representing the Islamist movement and political party Ennahda and the other representing a more diverse anti-Islamist camp, including liberals and leftists, trade unionists, and former members of the Ben Ali regime. From 2012 on, Nidaa Tounes became a political alliance for all anti-Islamist political actors, rallying around Essebsi, who later became president. This alignment replaced the original dividing line between revolutionaries and the old regime.[21] The identity conflict, however, was carried out in struggles over political issues, the new Constitution, elections, and attaining formal state power. It was also intertwined with questions of national identity, unity, and security.[22] Both camps relied on street politics, although the mobilization potential of the secular camp mainly came from the UGTT. At the same time, some social movement organizations, including the Tunisian Association of Democratic Women and the Union of Unemployed Graduates, were included in formal transitional institutions like the HIROR. They achieved some success by integrating their causes with the agendas of these transitional bodies and, in the case of women's rights, even helped endorse the equality clause in the final constitutional text. Still feeling frustrated by the lack of responsiveness, these social movement organizations also resorted to street politics, which, in the case of unemployed activists, meant facing state repression.[23]

The most important mobilization during this phase (after Kasbah I and II) was certainly the so-called Bardo protests—named after the Bardo Museum, which is situated next to the parliamentary building where the protests were staged. These protests of around one hundred thousand people marked the peak of polarization and a shift to elite consensus politics immediately afterward.[24] In 2013, the transition process almost came to a standstill when two politicians from the secular camp, the leftist Chokri Belaïd and the Nasserist Mohamed Brahmi, were assassinated in February and July, respectively. Anti-government protests erupted and were followed by pro-government demonstrations. The conflict reached its peak in August 2013. Leftist members of the NCA joined the anti-government protests, followed by Ettakatol, a former coalition partner of Ennahda. The National Constituent Assembly was suspended by its own president, Mustapha Ben Jafaar.

Chantel Berman conducted surveys with members of both protest camps and found striking similarities: protesters from both sides had already participated in the early-to-mid-January 2011 mobilization, revealing the break-up of the old revolutionary coalition against the authoritarian regime. At the same time, the individual camps were heterogeneous internally, particularly with regard to socioeconomic questions, reflecting the cross-class character of the 2011 protests. Trade unionists from the UGTT were also found in both camps in equal measure, supporting the oft-cited umbrella function that the UGTT used to have under the dictatorship that brought together oppositional forces from different backgrounds.[25] This observation is important as it highlights that the UGTT as an organization was clearly positioned within the anti-Islamist coalition. Yet, less surprisingly, the two protest camps differed in terms of the degree of personal religiosity among their members as well as attitudes toward the government dominated by the Islamist Ennahda.[26]

Despite its members participating in both protest camps, the national UGTT leadership took on the role of chief mediator that, together with the country's businessmen association (Union Tunisienne de l'industrie, du commerce et de l'artisanat, UTICA), the Tunisian League for Human Rights (Ligue tunisienne des droits de l'homme, LTDH), and the National Bar Association, helped find a compromise that led to the finalization of the Constitution. This was in combination with Ennahda's withdrawal from executive power, the installment of a technocratic interim government, and the announcement of new elections in October 2014.[27] Despite the legendary role of the quartet that won the Nobel Peace Prize in 2015, one must acknowledge that the crucial during this sensitive period was the willingness of the leadership of Ennahda and the head of Nidaa Tounes to engage in behind-the-scenes negotiations while their supporters stirred up public sentiment on the streets.[28] It is fair to say that, in the end, the number of dialogues taking place at that time—directly between the competing political actors as well as through the mediation of social actors—paved the way for a consensus at the political level, which became characteristic of phase two. Moreover, diffusion effects from Egypt contributed to a willingness to compromise. The Egyptian protests against a democratically elected president, which called for early elections and mobilized along the same anti-Islamist lines as in Tunisia, were usurped by the military, leading to massive human rights violations and the complete loss of democracy—an outcome that also demonstrated the potentially disappointing results of street politics. In addition, the external influence of the United States, the Gulf countries, and international financial institutions in favor of a successful transition process played a role in Ennahda giving in and the leaders of both camps shifting toward consensus. Ultimately, the country's key political forces realized that there was more to win from cooperation and more to lose from continuing to rely on street politics.[29]

Phase Two: A Shift to Fragmented Socioeconomic Protests

In 2014, the new Constitution was enacted, Nidaa Tounes won the parliamentary elections, and its leader Essebsi was elected president. The government that took office in 2015, headed by Habib Essid and replaced by Youssif Chahed in 2016, represented a grand coalition with Ennahda and two junior partners, the Free Patriotic Union and Afek Tounes. Furthermore, the Carthage agreement of 2016 integrated five opposition parties as well as three civil society actors (including the UGTT) into the elite consensus.[30] Nidaa Tounes, which originally emerged as a front against a common enemy (political Islam), soon fell apart. Many members of parliament left Nidaa in protest of the president's son, Hafedh Caïd Essebsi, and his allies of former RCD members assuming leadership of the party.[31] Young Ennahda members felt betrayed by religion's downgraded role in the politics of the Ennahda leadership, some subsequently joining the Salafi scene that had been flourishing in Tunisia since 2011.[32]

Also within the UGTT at the local level and in some sectoral unions, a huge sense of disappointment emerged with the realization of the fact that the national UGTT office had mainly played a political and intermediary role and was perceived as having sacrificed its socioeconomic goals.[33] At the same time, openness toward street politics among political actors decreased. Some showed solidarity but tried to calm protesters and asked them for patience, as the UGTT did with unemployed protesters,[34] while others, including the president, openly delegitimized public contention.[35] In the meantime, terrorists targeting visitors of the Bardo Museum in March 2015 and tourists in Sousse in June of the same year shocked the nation. These factors had an effect on contention: 'in the context of the multiplication of terrorist attacks and the weakening of security at the borders, notions of national unity, stability, and consensus took precedence over ideas of dissent, contestation, and pluralism.'[36]

These observations are in line with analyses of protests during this time period: as the national level for political and societal actors was closing and becoming more hostile toward public contention, mobilization around national goals decreased.[37] In its place, protests generally became more fragmented, localized, and staged outside of formal organizations. Occasionally, individual local protest events turned into regional waves of protests—or even into a national one, as was the case in 2016.[38] However, they quickly fell apart. These protests mostly promoted socioeconomic demands and were held in marginalized interior regions, bringing to the fore the cleavage that had largely been suppressed since the Kasbah II protests in February 2011.

There were certain hotspots for these fragmented protests, and most of these consisted of local conflict in regions that were subjected to natural resource extraction for decades but left poor in development.[39] In particular, contention in regions rich in natural resources focused mainly on employment and local development as well as on the distribution of state rents. Extractivisim was a central issue that mobilized people, be it in the phosphate mining region of Gafsa,[40] on the island of Kerkennah near the Chergui gas field,[41] or in Kamour in the oil-rich south in Tataouine.[42] The main actor group was comprised of unemployed people and, depending on the local context, many were organized within the union of unemployed graduates (Union des diplômés chômeurs, UDC). However, as I have argued elsewhere, a large part of their mobilization dynamics is best understood in the local context. At the local level, the UDC was autonomous and, even though local protests drew support at the national level, this consisted mainly of raising national awareness and express solidarity with their cause.[43]

The central demands were for secure employment (mostly understood as public sector jobs) and regional development. The primary forms of protest were sit-ins, riots, roadblocks, and hunger strikes, while the main source of leverage protesters had was to disturb the production or transport of natural resources. Nationally owned enterprises, such as the Compagnie phosphate de Gafsa (CPG), and multinational companies, such as Petrofac on Kerkennah, were likely targets. These protests enjoyed a great deal of local support, as the majority of the population had close personal ties to unemployed people, generating a strong feeling of local solidarity. This created tensions within the UGTT: on the one hand, trade unionists needed to protect workers' interests that were often undermined by the protests, but, given the local ties, even workers sympathized with the unemployed activists. The result was often that the local unit of the UGTT supported the protesters while the regional and national levels turned to a more balanced approach, expressing solidarity and calling for negotiations but at the same delegitimizing disruptive modes of protest.[44]

When demands were fulfilled (e.g., employment for the protest actors themselves), contentious actions ceased. They would, however, resume when those who were promised a job were ultimately not hired, when their employment remained insecure, or when new jobs were distributed in an opaque way, again raising allegations of clientelist modes of distribution. These protests could last a very long time and remain at a very low level of intensity. Just how much influence these mostly fragmented protests could amass became visible during waves of contention, when a single trigger would suffice for the numerous small-scale ongoing sit-ins and blockages to join forces—as was the case for the regional wave in Gafsa in 2015, or even the national wave of contention starting in Kasserine in January 2016.[45] The latter lasted only ten days but quickly spread and mobilized people in other marginalized regions, even reaching the capital.[46] Protests around the anniversary of the revolution happened regularly, but 2016 was marked by the first massive demonstrations that brought interior and coastal regions together in contentious actions—as had happened in 2011. In spite of the time conjuncture, these waves of contention did not lead to deeper networks between unemployed activists.

In contrast to the isolated protests described above, phase two also shows the beginnings of direct cooperation in the form of campaigns—a mode of mobilization that became ever more important in phase three. The two major campaigns during these years built upon the perception that old informal networks were still present in the distribution of the country's wealth. The first, rather short-lived, campaign took on the question of extractivism and distribution of wealth: 'winou el pétrole?' (where is the country's oil?). After training sessions with the international nongovernmental organization (NGO) Natural Resource Governance Institute, six Tunisian NGOs from different regions shared their knowledge on transparency in extractive industries through numerous workshops across the country in February 2015. They started a successful signature campaign for greater transparency and for the distribution of a fair share of the gains among the resource-rich regions. More specifically, they requested that Tunisia join the international transparency index Extractive Industries Transparency Initiative (EITI).[47] A social media campaign and protests in the capital as well as in the oil-rich south in Kébili in May 2015 placed pressure on the government. The protests in the south escalated, leading to days of clashes between security forces and protesters. In June 2015, ministers responded by sharing some information about Tunisia's oil with the parliament.[48] This move triggered a counter campaign designed to shift the focus away from the call for transparency by questioning the motivation of the protesters.[49] The campaign was framed as scaring away investors and destabilizing the country.[50] In August 2015, the campaign came to an end but the call for a fair share of gains from natural resources to be given to the resource-rich regions themselves remained part of local and regional protests and was also applied to phosphate (Gafsa).

The other and—as I will argue—more influential nationwide campaign was called Manich Msameh (MM, which translates as 'I will not forgive'), and was particularly important as a major source of inspiration and a precedent for subsequent campaigns in phase three. It started when Essebsi, the president at the time, announced the introduction of a so-called Economic and Financial Reconciliation Law in 2015. The basic idea was to offer businesspeople and civil servants who had committed economic crimes before the revolution the chance to give back stolen funds, pay a compensation fine, and avoid legal prosecution and public blaming; i.e., amnesty in combination with anonymity.[51] The official explanation from the government and the president was to find a quick way to achieve a stable investment climate, allowing businesspeople to invest in the country instead of worrying about prosecution for old crimes.[52] Many people outside of elite circles, however, read this law as an attempt by the old regime elites to protect themselves and avoid any punishment or even public blaming by the transitional justice process. The Truth and Dignity Commission, the transitional justice body installed in 2014 after a long political process,[53] had much more legitimacy in the view of the activists to deal with cases of past economic crimes and should have dealt with them as with other cases: openly and publicly. After two years of recurrent mobilization against the bill, it was finally passed in September 2017 and renamed the Law on Administrative Reconciliation, granting amnesty only to civil servants who, as it was argued, had not had any other choice but to obey to orders from superiors as part of the authoritarian bureaucracy.[54]

As Laryssa Chomiak notes, mobilization against the law tried 'to block a coalescence of political consensus around "turning the page" by forgiving economic crimes.'[55] The elite consensus involved the UGTT, which did not throw its weight behind attempts to block the law, instead using the opportunity to push for salary increases in the public sector. Cracks within the Ennahda party became visible when the party's shura council voted to support the bill, pending its amendment, thereby opposing Ennahda's executive leadership.[56]

MM mobilized to oppose the very idea of forgetting and forgiving crimes of the past. It was an umbrella campaign for over twenty Tunisian NGOs and independent activists who staged protests all over the country, particularly in Tunis. Mobilization came in waves and oppositional parties, mainly the Popular Front, supported the campaign. First, in September 2015, street protests against the draft law created a great deal of momentum in Tunis and across the country, both in the interior regions and the Sahel.[57] The next wave of contention was caused by Ben Ali's son and businessman Slim Chiboub, who became the first member of the former ruling elite to sign a reconciliation and arbitration agreement with the Truth and Dignity Commission and avoid legal prosecution for past economic crimes, all within the framework of the Transitional Justice Law 2013–53. At the same time, members of parliament were about to resume the discussion of the draft reconciliation law before the summer recess.[58] Nationwide demonstrations and posters reading 'WANTED' (using American-style Wild West posters) called for corruption trials against former regime members. In May 2017, thousands of activists gathered in Tunis as a reminder that there was still resistance to the law and, on July 27, 2017, the campaign launched protests against the amended version of the law in front of parliament. The High Judicial Council, a newly created organ, decided to delay the vote in order to have more time to study the draft.[59] Ultimately, however, protests in September could not prevent the amended version of the law from passing in parliament.[60]

MM was outstanding in many regards. It was a sustained mobilization of over two years. It was partially successful in its political aim of stopping a specific law from passing, which led to a substantially modified version. Although many activists were disappointed, others thought of it as a valuable compromise.[61] MM also created a horizontal nationwide network of activists within and outside of formal NGOs, and practiced collective, consensual decision-making and built on youth culture, including aesthetics and music.[62]

In a reflective piece, one of the founding members of the campaign, Laila Riahi, laid out its achievements and challenges.[63] On the one hand, she argued, the heterogeneity of MM was part of its richness, bringing together people from different regions and social backgrounds, mostly young people who had participated in the 2011 revolution. On the other hand, this diversity created tensions due to conflicts within the campaign concerning, for instance, the stance on the official transitional justice process and particularly the role of the Truth and Dignity Commission. Moreover, support for other social movements, such as the one mentioned above in Kamour, was contested within MM as well. Many activists saw extractivism as a problem and did not intend to support a movement that aimed at precarious employment and subsequently greater integration into the exploitative extractivist system. Nevertheless, when repression by security forces increased, solidarity from MM for the Kamour protests was no longer questioned.

Additionally, relations with political parties remained difficult. As Riahi elaborates, while there was a constant fear of being instrumentalized by parties, at the same time, it was obvious that cooperation was the only channel for parties and street activism to become strong enough to stop the law from being enacted. As an unintended consequence of this alliance, Riahi argues that MM helped the fragmented partisan landscape to reunite and rally for a common cause. Finally, the focus on a single issue served as the smallest common denominator that fostered regional and ideological autonomy. In the opinion of its members, however, the campaign did not manage to connect the law to its overarching context, such as the role of international financial institutions. Writing in early 2018, Riahi herself implied that the style adopted by MM seemed to serve as an inspiration for another campaign, Fech Nestanaou, which the next section closely examines.

In sum, the years 2014 to 2017 were largely marked by local, fragmented, single-issue socioeconomic protests, mainly in the marginalized interior regions and often centered in those rich in natural resources. At the same time, this period saw the development of campaigns that comprised a loose network of independent activists and NGO members. They started to rally for broader causes beyond personal grievances while also merging socioeconomic and political issues, be it the call for transparency in resource management with the redistribution of resource wealth or the demand for the prosecution of economic crimes. As the following section shows, this trend continued, but was met by the collapse of consensus politics.

Phase Three: Mobilizing against Austerity

The year 2018 marked the end of consensus politics between Nidaa Tounes and Ennahda. The former broke up into different factions, one of which coalesced around Prime Minister Youssef Chahed and was considered as having the support of Ennahda. In 2018, cooperation among the major societal actors, including that between the UGTT with the political leadership, ended. This was most clearly visible in the failure of the Carthage II agreement—another attempt by then-president Essebsi to align all major stakeholders.[64] One major controversy at the center of these conflicts involved the neoliberal reforms that Chahed implemented as part of the 2.9-billion-dollar loan the IMF granted Tunisia in June 2016. This deal came with strings attached; namely, demands to float the dinar, which lost 40 percent of its value compared to the dollar,[65] as well as austerity measures, including subsidy cuts and a freeze on public salaries.

In 2017, Chahed implemented some of these conditions in the Finance Law of 2018. The annual budget is put into force every January, which means that social cuts and tax increases coincided with the anniversary of the revolution on January 14. Over the years, protests, particularly in the marginalized interior regions, have erupted around this time of year, driven by people expressing disappointment with the revolutionary socioeconomic outcome. Yet, 2018 was different in that massive protests against austerity politics were partly driven by a joint campaign, Fech Nestanaou (FN), which translates as 'what are we waiting for?'. This was described as a mix of people with party and NGO backgrounds on the one side, and activists outside of formal organizations on the other, many of whom were former activists from the MM campaign—and, in that sense, had many of the same characteristics of the horizontal, leaderless campaigning that were also visible in MM.[66]

Those involved in the campaign engaged in raising awareness about the hardship imposed by the new Budget Law. The mobilization of FN in Tunis, Ben Arous, Sfax, and Sousse coincided with protests in the interior regions, some headed by local UGTT offices, some by the Popular Front party alliance, and others without any organization.[67] A lack of responsiveness from the government as well as harsh measures from the security forces led to an escalation of events, including the death of a man who allegedly suffocated from tear gas. Riots broke out in the disadvantaged neighborhoods of Tunis, including the looting of banks and shops. Protesters faced police repression and were portrayed as spreading chaos and anarchy, mainly by coalition parties.[68] The blame was placed on leftist opposition parties for fueling anger on purpose and instrumentalizing popular discontent.

Given that the opposition parties, mainly the Popular Front, suffered tremendous losses in the 2019 elections, it is safe to say that the accusations of instrumentalization by third parties was a typical delegitimation strategy. The distrust between societal actors and political actors that was created and fostered under authoritarian rule still persists, as I show in the case of the mobilization of unemployed people.[69] The fact that parties were more involved in the FN campaign does not mean that protest actors—within the framework of FN or outside of it—were mere puppets of politicians. The same held true for MM, according to activist Riahi. Instead, I argue that what was witnessed in January 2018 was a new step in the transformation of fragmented socioeconomic protests into networked forms of protest. The campaign, as a form of protest, developed into a strategy that seemed to offer sufficient structures to channel discontent and to voice political demands—rather than be limited to personal calls for employment, for instance—while still leaving the activists sufficiently independent and autonomous. The fear of instrumentalization was thus curbed and cooperation fostered. This finding also supports available research on coalitions and alliances in the MENA that found that mobilization for a single cause or a campaign can still 'influence social structures, shape norms, representations and discourses, and challenge the boundaries between coalitions and social movements,'[70] challenging the predominant view of coalitions as only successful when transforming into a social movement with a common identity. The Tunisian case demonstrated how campaigns themselves create some kind of shared identity and how consecutive campaigns increasingly influenced public and political discourse. However, the next attempt for a nationwide campaign, Basta, in 2019, which was similar in organization and appearance to MM and FN, did not generate the same degree of attention. This shows that the success of social movements does not depend on internal factors alone. One major obstacle could have been the shifting role of the UGTT into a protest actor itself. This was another major development arising from anti-austerity protests. In 2019, the UGTT held a general strike for the first time since 2011 to push for salary increases, contrary to the demands of the IMF. It clearly marks a shift in the trade union federation from prioritizing political aims—mainly stability and the success of the political transformation process—toward socioeconomic aims.

This development arose in response to a notable increase in internal tensions, with certain sectoral unions having previously staged massive strikes, posing a threat to the unity of the UGTT. Internal fragmentation, however, is a danger for the federation—particularly as new trade union federations have started to emerge—mainly because its power stems from public sector employees. The plans for restructuring public sector companies, yet another condition of the IMF loan, were seen as backdoor privatization, threatening the UGTT's representative power and thereby its bargaining strength vis-à-vis political actors and its counterpart, the UTICA, the business association.

The general strike in January 2019 to demand salary increases must be understood against this background. Months prior to the strike, the UGTT had been pushing for higher wages and was against the government's plan to implement one of the central IMF loan conditions. The UGTT leadership felt betrayed by the government, especially since trade union leaders had joined the Carthage agreement on the condition of regular salary increases.[71] As part of the negotiations involving the 2019 Budget Law, the Chahed government too quickly gave in to IMF demands to freeze salaries. Resorting to a general strike for an economic demand had not happened since 2011; before that, the UGTT only used its most powerful lever in the context of the political transformation process. On January 17, 2019, the UGTT showed its mobilization potential when workers went on strike nationwide, paralyzing nearly all vital sectors, including public transportation, education, and large parts of the healthcare system.[72] The strike was successful in the end and salary increases for public sector workers and government officials were achieved.[73]

Some sectors, education in particular, had been especially contentious earlier on. Demands for higher wages in higher education and criticism of the privatization trend in this sector have been voiced through increasingly non-routinized contentious actions since 2018.[74] Even more attention was raised during a struggle by high school teachers to attain better working conditions that started in 2017 and continued despite calls from the UGTT national executive board to put an end to the protests.[75] These protests also created a great deal of pressure on the UGTT leadership to resist further cuts and withdraw support for the government.

Anti-austerity protests, in the form of campaigns in 2018 and massive labor union mobilization in 2019, contributed to a loss of legitimacy on the part of the government and the entire party landscape that had developed since 2011. The single measures implemented by the Chahed cabinet, such as an increase of social protection for the unemployed (the so-called AMEN program), did not have any substantial positive effects. At the same time, pressure from the IMF to decrease public spending became critical and ultimately visible when the transfer of the sixth loan installment was halted in summer 2019, allegedly because the IMF wanted to wait for a new government to be formed after the elections in the fall of the same year.[76] However, the established parties lost the 2019 parliamentary and presidential elections, with massive socioeconomic discontent creating support for populist parties and political players from both the left and right.[77] The new president, Kais Saied, directly addressed the disenfranchised people with his own humble appearance and made direct calls for employment and development. At the same time, he openly called for a complete overhaul of the constitutional order, including the abolishment of the representative parliamentary system. On July 25, 2021, Saied put his demand into action, making use of the widespread discontent with the government's dealing with the COVID-19 pandemic and its massive economic fallout. He froze parliamentary activities, stripped members of their immunity, and dissolved the cabinet. At the time of writing, it remains open whether and how Saied will restore democratic order and improve the socioeconomic situation. He still enjoys public support, often expressed in the form of protests, but also increasingly sees public contention,[78] a process eventually leading to the return of a polarized political street as witnessed in the first years after the revolution.

Contentious Politics and Democratization

I write these lines in the midst of a global pandemic crisis. Although one can only speculate about its mid- to long-term consequences, the economic situation will certainly further deteriorate. Countries are currently rushing to the IMF for quick financial aid. Tunisia was granted 745 million US dollars in emergency funding, which was tied to promises of public sector reform.[79] We should therefore expect the conflicts analyzed here to gain in intensity. We should also closely observe further development of protest structures and characteristics, as networks between activists of all kinds have just started to emerge. While still too early to tell, it seems that mobilization in Tunisia is following a pattern identified in the context of political transformation processes in Latin America during 'the long 1980s.' In Latin America, as well, immediately after the end of dictatorships, protests became more and more fragmented until, roughly a decade later, they transformed into networks of local associations and social movements—with marginalized populations playing an important role. From this base of mobilization, large-scale anti-neoliberal protests developed, helping to bring about the leftist turn in the 2000s. Without arguing for any deterministic parallel, Jonas Wolff and I have suggested keeping this pattern in mind when thinking about the future development of protests in Tunisia.[80] Fragmentation might be just one step in the formation of networks between different cells, as we saw with the campaigns of MM and FN. This power of the masses created political pressure that has led to electoral gains by populists, clearly demonstrating that Tunisia's political system allows for responsiveness—in this case, for voicing a deep frustration with certain socioeconomic policies, but also for paving the way for anti-democratic forces into the political system.

When engaging in further comparative analyses of the impact of protests on the consolidation phases of democratization, certain important context variables should be kept in mind. First, the constellation of different cleavages can vary and matter for the overall mobilization and political dynamics. For instance, socioeconomic cleavages in Tunisia were cross-cutting with ideological conflicts— secular versus Islamist actors—at the political level. The secular camp was composed of both left and right forces, and also within the Islamist movement one can find a rather business-friendly national leadership in the party and a more socioeconomically focused grassroots level engaged in charity work, for instance. Secondly, the existence and degrees of cooperation between protest actors and political parties can vary in different contexts as well as over time. Before the revolution, protest actors were willing to join forces with opposition parties, as was case with the Gafsa protests in 2008. After 2011, however, these actors mistrusted political parties altogether, including credible ones that were active during the Ben Ali era. Over the years, mistrust toward political parties has increased and was one of the factors President Saied exploited when he froze parliamentary life in 2021. Similarly, the relation between activists outside formal organizations and trade unions can vary as well. Although the role of organized labor has decreased with the pursuit of neoliberal reforms, trade unions are still an important societal actor that, as the UGTT example shows, can be a cooperation partner, a mediator, but also an adversary to other forms of social activism. The latter is related to the fact that organized labor, particularly in the public sector, represents a lower middle class with social protection. This class is relatively privileged compared to informal workers, who have become the new subaltern in the age of neoliberalism.

Thirdly, political economy perspectives should be integrated more strongly into the study of transition processes. It is not only macroeconomic data that will tell us about the satisfaction with and potential consolidation of democracy but also how different stakeholders perceive the developments and what they expect as an outcome of economic policies. One central issue observed here was the role of the state and the degree of its involvement in the national economy. The neoliberal policies pushed for by the IMF and the Chahed government aimed at reducing state spending, while the trade unions fought for a constantly growing share of the state budget by defending public sector salary increases and unemployed activists called for the expansion of the role of the state, particularly in investing in employment and development. While external actors kept on pushing for a slim, neoliberal vision of the state, voters showed their discontent with this vision and voted for politicians who promised a radically different vision, vague as it may be.

Last but not least, the Tunisian transition teaches us once more that social contention needs to be understood as part of a longer process. Experiences made over time shape the evaluation of the present. While protest actors tolerated the suppression of the socioeconomic cleavage after the Kasbah II protests, patience ended when the newly institutionalized political system did not produce the expected outcomes. In this sense, the three phases identified here built upon each other. A lot will depend on how the Tunisians people will perceive the new political elite's approach to dealing with the COVID-19 crisis and its aftermath and whether this will produce a little more patience in the face of difficult conditions or whether the new leaders will again bring about disappointment and even more waves of contention.

7

THE VIOLENCE OF ENDURANCE
YOUTH PRECARITY AND SOCIAL JUSTICE IN INNER TUNISIA

Alyssa Miller

Those who have followed the media coverage of Tunisia over the past decade will have noticed the repetition of a particular story: a journalist revisits one of the major theaters of the Dignity Revolution—places like Redeyef, Sidi Bouzid, or Kasserine—to gauge the magnitude of social change, and finds it wanting. The sources of popular discontent that fueled the protests of winter 2010–11, such as unemployment, corruption, environmental degradation, and infrastructural neglect, clearly persist in the interior regions today.

Tunisian national development is often described as proceeding 'à deux vitesses' (at two speeds). This depiction evokes the spatiotemporal rift wrought by uneven development, separating Tunisia's wealthier coastal regions from its underdeveloped interior. This geography of exclusion stands, in part, as the legacy of an extractive colonial economy and the indirect administration of peripheral regions under Ottoman and French rule.[1] Yet, these disparities accelerated greatly under the neoliberal policies of Zine El Abidine Ben Ali. Abandoning equitable development as even a

151

guiding ideal, the state concentrated investment in Tunis and the Sahel, while treating the hinterlands as mere warehouses for raw materials and cheap migratory labor.[2] With its slogan of 'work, freedom, and national dignity,' the revolution sounded a full-throated demand for economic citizenship from the dispossessed interior.

Until recently, Tunisia was hailed as the great success story of the Arab Spring. The 2014 Constitution enshrined many of the revolution's social justice ideals: equitable regional development, the right to work for a fair wage, and a commitment to nurture the potential of youth. Yet, each successive government has failed to bring these ideals to fruition. Amid urgent calls for job creation and the return of the welfare state, Tunisia instead renewed its dependence on International Monetary Fund (IMF) loans, increasing its sovereign debt and shackling the nation to continued austerity. As a result, economic hardships have only deepened for ordinary Tunisians during the political transition. Meanwhile, electoral politics fostered a new alliance between the political class and old-regime economic elites, who not only survived the transition to democracy, but substantially increased their fortunes.[3] Although outrage over the Ben Ali kleptocracy was a major driver of the revolution, those complicit in structural and explicit state violence have largely evaded accountability.

Widespread dissatisfaction with an ineffectual party system led to the election of political outsider Kais Saied to the presidency in 2019.[4] His decision to invoke emergency powers in the 2014 Constitution to dismiss the prime minister and dissolve parliament on July 25, 2021, appears to have ended Tunisia's experiment in representative democracy. While Saied's ideas about decentralized direct democracy and his anti-corruption crusade promise to re-enfranchise a forgotten majority, early signs suggest that he too may disappoint the marginalized subjects who brought him to power. Recently, Saied reneged on his commitment to implement Law 38 of 2020, which would facilitate the public sector recruitment of university graduates who have been unemployed for more than a decade. Bowing to pressure from international lenders, Saied commented that the law was 'a tool for ruling, controlling anger, and selling dreams' rather than serious legislation.[5] In response to this news, a fresh round of protests broke out in the usual places (namely, Gafsa, Sidi Bouzid, and Kasserine).

This continued cycle of revolt emanating from the interior regions, with endlessly renewed demands for 'jobs, services, adequate health facilities, schools, and clean water,' makes visible the enduring structural violence of uneven development in transitional Tunisia.[6] Structural violence refers to the myriad, avoidable injuries caused by institutionalized inequality, which systematically prevents certain people from attaining a full quality of life.[7] Unlike more spectacular forms of violence, structural violence often passes unnoticed due to its embeddedness in ordinary social structures, yet it is just as effective in distributing harm, up to and including death.[8] Attuned to these multiple registers of violence, this chapter investigates the political endurance of youth in inner Tunisia. Rejecting their devaluation as merely a surplus population, young people wagered their lives in the 2011 revolution for dignity and a better future. More than a decade later, the vast majority have yet to see a return on their courage. Cycling through a limited repertoire of grueling possibilities, including informal labor, migration, hyper-exploitation, and protest, I show how precarious youth negotiate the violence of endurance in their quest for secure employment.

Precarity and the Social Roots of the Tunisian Revolution

The popular uprisings that swept Tunisia in the winter of 2010–11 (as well as the Arab uprisings more broadly) participated in a world-wide revolt against precarity in the wake of the 2008 financial crisis.[9] Precarity refers to the pervasive condition of socioeconomic insecurity brought on by the end of life-long labor and the retreat of the welfare state. First theorized in the Western European social movements of the 1990s, the precarity concept has been criticized for taking twentieth-century Fordism, as experienced in advanced industrial societies, as the norm against which it measures injustice.[10] Since, from a broader geographical perspective, such protections have always been the exception rather than the rule, experiences of precarity in the Global South must be grasped from within their own historical specificities.[11]

Social protection has long been the lynchpin of the Tunisian social contract, key to securing legitimacy for the postcolonial state. Following independence, Tunisia pursued 'peripheral Keynesianism' to stimulate national development, while a power-sharing relationship between the Tunisian General Labor Union (UGTT) and the Neo-Destour party gave labor a determinant role in economic policy until the mid-1980s.[12] However, President Habib Bourguiba's adoption of a structural adjustment program in 1986 marked a decisive shift toward flexible accumulation.

Neoliberal reforms proceeded apace under President Ben Ali, whose moderate success was greatly exaggerated as an 'economic miracle.' Pro-capital revisions to the labor code gave enterprises greater control over hiring and firing, and allowed for the extension of short-term contracts (CDD).[13] Privatization and technological upgrading at state-owned enterprises gutted the industrial workforce, defusing the fiercest bastions of labor militancy.[14] Meanwhile, the 'democratization' of the university, coupled with a decline in educational quality, led to a breakdown in education as a reliable motor of social mobility, giving rise to the *chômeur-diplômé* (unemployed graduate) as an emergent category of the dispossessed.[15] According to Lorenzo Feltrin, the limited extent of Tunisia's industrialization has meant that populations disembedded from agricultural lifeways were thrown back onto an exploitative service sector, forced to accept work that is irregular, insecure, low paying, and often 'informal and/or self-employed.'[16] Though some may dream of immigrating to Europe, rural youth more commonly engage in 'footloose labour,'[17] seeking daily wages or semi-permanent work on the eastern coast, or smuggling goods across the Libyan or Algerian border.[18] Keenly aware of their generation's exclusion from an erstwhile social contract, economically disenfranchised youth became the major protagonists of the revolution.

Béatrice Hibou has cautioned against any reading of 2011 as a clean break with the moral economy that prevailed before.[19] While Ben Ali unquestionably employed brutality against political opponents, Hibou maintains that domination operated primarily through consent, describing a 'security pact' in which the authoritarian state ensured access to consumer modernity.[20] The notion of a 'security pact' underscores how securitization became inseparable from social protection under Ben Ali, in a system where the state conjures up dangers and positions itself to neutralize them. In contrast to rights-based entitlements, Ben Ali's signature social programs, such as the Banque Tunisienne de Solidarité or the Fonds de Solidarité Nationale (Caisse 26/26), targeted 'at-risk' regions and populations, such that identifying beneficiaries of the state's largesse simultaneously framed them as a potential security threats.[21]

While the revolution exposed the cracks in Tunisia's over-hyped 'economic miracle,' its demands for inclusion also testified to the security pact's enduring force.[22] Hamza Meddeb describes how the former ruling party, the Democratic Constitutional Rally (RCD), had distributed social protection, leaving behind an ambiguous legacy of clientelism and corruption.[23] Using its network of allied businessmen, the RCD was able to grant 'favors' as a means of smoothing over social crises, ranging from formal employment and registration in a welfare program to access to the informal economy, free medical treatment, and other supports to survival. Following the RCD's dissolution in 2011, local officials were left with a meager toolbox to respond to urgent demands for assistance. They have therefore played on the variable of time, urging patience and 'waiting' as a means of governing the unruly poor.[24]

This 'governmentality through waiting' presents a thorny predicament for youth locked out of formal employment. Many young Tunisians, particularly university graduates, view public sector positions, with their stability and generous benefits, as the only acceptable form of employment.[25] While in an earlier era, a university degree virtually guaranteed employment, today a surplus of graduates means that each must wait their turn, thrusting youth into a limbo of 'waithood,' where full adulthood is put on hold.[26] Meanwhile, rumors frequently circulate about candidates with family connections who are mysteriously recruited despite hiring freezes. In these circumstances, unemployed youth understand that they must take action.[27] While Irene Weipert-Fenner has read these fractured protest movements as primarily depoliticized fora for negotiating jobs and welfare benefits—sometimes even on an individual basis—Sami Zemni detects a latent possibility for solidarity across struggles, positioning the marginalized to redefine 'the contours of the political itself.'[28]

Nevertheless, exiting the posture of the patient, virtuous poor carries inherent risk. Immediately after the revolution, when Mohammed Bouazizi was apotheosized as a national martyr, the figure of the *zawali* (the miserable) was widely celebrated as a hero in Tunisian popular culture.[29] Since that time, ever-deepening economic and security crises have hastened the return of familiar securitization discourses. These often construe contentious social movements as a form of terrorism, allied with the likes of the Islamic State in targeting—and destabilizing—Tunisia's nascent democracy.[30] Moreover, the limited repertoire of tactics available to marginal protesters, including the roadblock, the riot, the sit-in, the hunger-strike, and the public suicide, often draw on explicit techniques of self-harm, leaving protesters vulnerable to accusations of violence and disorder.

Toward an Ethnography of Marginalized Youth

In the following sections, I hone in on this space of tension between waiting and revolt through an ethnography of marginalized youth following the January 2016 uprising in Kasserine. Similar to other protest movements that have erupted in Tunisia since 2008, the riots in Kasserine were inspired by a scandal in public sector recruitment. Upon discovering that his name had been excluded from a list of youth slated for employment, a young man named Ridha Yahyaoui climbed atop a utility pole outside the *wilaya* (governorate) building in Kasserine and was electrocuted in an apparent suicide-protest.[31] Following Yahyaoui's death, hundreds of protesters occupied the *wilaya* complex and conducted a sit-in, reclaiming the right of youth to 'work and a decent life,' as well as 'the region's right to fair and long-term development.'[32] In a few short days, the demonstrations in Kasserine spread across the national territory in a pattern that eerily echoed the revolution five years earlier. As the protesters sustained their sit-in well into the month of February, exasperated local officials urged them to meet with the ministers of development and employment in Tunis. When this meeting produced no positive resolution, the Kasserine delegates resumed their sit-in outside the Ministry of Employment building in Tunis.

In her appraisal of precarity's uptake in anthropological writing, Clara Han has criticized an overemphasis on revolutionary potential and resistance, due to the way in which these concerns unwittingly reproduce the optics of the state.[33] Rather than harnessing ethnography in the service of any master theory of revolutionary-becoming, Han advocates for theorizing from within ethnography itself, to lend 'a specific texture to the ways in which the larger forces of the reorganization of labor and state violence interpenetrate everyday life.'[34] Rather than describe the exuberant outbreak of the January uprising, my narrative begins six months later, as the Kasserine sit-inners maintained their position, steadfast on the pavement. This untimely vantage point shifts our analytic focus from revolt to endurance, which Elizabeth Povinelli describes as the 'ability to suffer and yet persist.'[35] Even if we accept Zemni's optimistic thesis on the emergence of a 'counter-power' from the margins, this remains a fledgling project, struggling for actualization.[36] In the meantime, marginalized subjects muddle through 'in ways that are ordinary, chronic, and cruddy rather than catastrophic, crisis-laden, and sublime.'[37]

Young people in Kasserine describe the condition of unemployment as akin to suffocation or social death.[38] Yet, the minimal material requirements for subsistence are available to most in the family home, where they are fed, housed, and perhaps receive pocket money for coffee or cigarettes. What was at stake for the Kasserine sit-inners is not quite the good life, but what Ghassan Hage refers to as a 'viable life,' a life worth living within the receding horizon of expectations for the precarious under contemporary capitalism.[39] In the absence of a social safety net, the family often serves as a welfare institution of last resort.[40] Yet, as families absorb the brute force of socioeconomic precarity, they also redistribute its violence along gender and generational lines. I therefore look beyond the individual dimension of youth aspirations for self-actualization, to reveal their entanglement in the messy moral economy of kinship.

From Shadow Zone to City of Martyrs

Kasserine governorate is situated on the arid western–central steppe, where the sovereign territory of Tunisia abuts the Algerian border. Abandoned by the development state due to its fractious history, Kasserine bears the dubious distinction of being Tunisia's most underdeveloped region, a paradigmatic 'shadow zone' in Ben Ali's development discourse. Despite its marginal position in the national cartography, Kasserine played a central role in the 2011 revolution. Over the course of a single week, from January 8–12, Kasserine suffered greater casualties than any other governorate.[41] Despite concerted efforts by the regime to denounce the protesters as criminals and terrorists, digital images of massacred Kassernois youth outraged the Tunisian public, thus nationalizing an uprising that had been largely confined to the interior. Two days later, in the face of a general strike and massive protests in Tunis, President Ben Ali and his family fled the country to seek asylum in Saudi Arabia.

In the immediate wake of revolution, the inhabitants of Kasserine hoped that their sacrifice would be rewarded with a development dividend, bringing new vitality to the region. They longed for the transformative presence of the state to harness Kasserine's natural riches and bring them into productive relation with an inoperative workforce. Unfortunately, due to a convergence of factors, none of this came to pass. The revolution sent the national economy into free fall, causing a trend of stagflation, worker layoffs, and increased unemployment numbers. While some found meagre relief in *chantier* workfare jobs designed to stabilize the region, by and large, Kasserine youth remained stuck in pre-revolutionary patterns of wageless life.[42]

Making matters worse, Kasserine's symbolic capital as a province of martyrs was spoiled through an emergent association with terrorism. Beginning in 2013, Kasserine became the theater of armed confrontations between security agents and Islamist militants, who crossed the Algerian border and took cover on the mountainous frontier. After a gruesome attack claimed the lives of eight Tunisian soldiers in July 2013, the army declared the mountain a closed military zone, and began aerial bombardments to flush the militants out of their places of concealment. Although a 2015 initiative sought recognition for Kasserine as a victim of underdevelopment at the Truth and Dignity Commission, many residents feared that the window for restorative justice had already closed.[43] Reflecting on these misfortunes, one civil society activist lamented:

> What Tunisia needs—and Kasserine in particular—is a welfare state (*état providence*). We need state support as Kasserine navigates a crisis that is deep, ancient, structural, and traumatic. Unfortunately, there was no effort to capitalize on the role we played [in the revolution] at any level. Now, it's as if we had committed a crime, rather than a revolution!

In frontier regions like Kasserine, where opportunities for formal employment are scarce, livelihoods are sustained by *kuntra*, a smuggling economy based on traffic in subsidized commodities from Algeria and Libya. Living in the shadow of underdevelopment, many consider smuggling a regional right, a marginal form of accumulation that ensures community survival.[44] However, in the wake of the Arab uprisings, security concerns have drawn intense scrutiny to Tunisia's porous land borders. Informal labor—and smuggling, in particular—has been characterized as a vector of arms trafficking and financial assistance to terrorists, prompting the installation of berms to disrupt cross-border mobility.[45] These shifting boundaries between the licit and the illicit run through the bodies and livelihoods of small-time smugglers in Kasserine, exposing them to new sources of risk and depredation.

When Youth Live off Risk

I met Mehdi through friends from Kasserine who participated in the sit-in outside the Ministry of Employment in Tunis.[46] At twenty-six, he has already worked for ten years in the smuggling economy. Mehdi grew up in the working-class neighborhood of Hay Zuhour with a network of brothers, cousins, and friends involved in smuggling, and it was easy for him to make pocket money unloading goods while he was in high school. Although he attended university in Kairouan,

Mehdi encountered what he called *zuruf* (adverse life conditions) that forced him to quit his studies. Since then, he has sought out a number of paths to economic viability, some of which—like activism and irregular migration (*harga*)—were intimately linked to the revolution. Whenever these initiatives came to a dead-end, Mehdi always fell back on smuggling. 'Tunis[ia] is a poor country,' he told me, 'it cannot provide for us all. *Kuntra* is the only thing that can provide a livelihood for all of Kasserine.'

Prior to 2011, the state was deeply imbricated in the practice of smuggling.[47] Participation was governed by a human infrastructure of kinship, state agents, and business organizations, run by wholesale bosses who employed a network of drivers and lookouts. With the withdrawal of security forces in the wake of revolution, the border regime has been reconfigured, democratizing smuggling and allowing new players to enter the game.[48] Unfortunately, this increase in practitioners has meant declining returns for all. As Mehdi explained: 'Before the revolution, we used to make money, but it was more difficult to bring in the goods. If customs caught you, they had no mercy. They would confiscate your car and your merchandise. Now that's no longer the case; you pay a bribe and they let you go.'

Illicit materials, such as weapons, vodka, and *zatla* (hashish), required more capital and connections than small players like Mehdi could muster. Familiar with areas in his neighborhood where alcohol and *zatla* were openly sold on the street, Mehdi found the idea of trafficking in these materials morally repugnant. Whereas poor Kasserine neighborhoods like Hay Zuhour were routinely demonized in the press as 'factories of jihad,' Mehdi assured me that it was businessmen from the Sahel who profited from the trade in weapons and drugs. They alone had the power to 'purchase the road,' clearing their path of security personnel. 'Take alcohol, for instance,' Mehdi said.

> When hard alcohol is brought in from Algeria, it goes to the touristic areas, where there is a great demand for liquor. So how does that work? The big smugglers are employed by hotel owners, who call the police and ask them to open the road so

their merchandise can pass through. These days, it often happens that all of *my* profits are eaten up in bribes. Yet, when a cartel boss is moving merchandise, everyone disappears. You are left wondering: where is the state?

Mehdi criticized the uneven application of the state's regulatory power as an indictment of corruption throughout the political system, which had hardly been reformed seven years after the revolution. Invoking kinship as a metaphor, Mehdi described the moral economy of the nation as a family: 'If the father of a family is correct and he looks after his kids, then everyone is well-behaved. The state is exactly like that. If the president is clean, then the whole state will be clean. Now, in our country, the president, ministers, and parliamentarians are all thieves.'

Mehdi had lived through the revolution in Hay Zuhour. Extending his palm out toward me during our interview, he reveals the scar where a bullet had passed through his hand. 'During the revolution,' he said, 'many of my friends died, right before my eyes. Most of the shots were deliberately fatal, targeting the heart or the head. I was lucky; it's rare to find someone with a bullet wound in his hand.' When he returned to university after the revolution, Mehdi joined the Unemployed Graduates' Union (UCD) and participated in sit-ins demanding expanded job opportunities in the public sector. With time, Mehdi grew weary of activism and decided to migrate to Europe instead. The temporary retreat of the security apparatus prompted a massive spike in irregular migration in 2011.[49] Departing from Djerba with perhaps eighty people in a tiny fishing boat, Mehdi arrived safely in Lampedusa, but was later apprehended by the Italian authorities and deported back to Tunisia. When I pointed out how risky and potentially lethal this trip might have been, Mehdi replied: 'When you engage in irregular migration, death is before your eyes. In fact, you expect death more than you expect to survive. But it is the same in smuggling. You take your soul in your hand and go forward.' For Mehdi, this dimension of risk, the chance encounter with violence, was woven into the fabric of everyday life in Kasserine.

Revolution Redux and the Labor of Endurance

On January 16, 2016, news of Ridha Yahyaoui's death spread like wildfire in Kasserine. Hundreds of protesters took to the streets, clashing with police and barricading the roads with burning tires. Long after the satellite protests throughout Tunisia had been quelled by a nationwide curfew, protesters in Kasserine continued to occupy the *wilaya* complex and regional municipality buildings. Aware of their vulnerability to accusations of terrorism, protesters struggled to calm the unruly elements among them, as some protesters stitched their mouths shut in declaration of a 'savage' hunger strike, or climbed to the roof of the *wilaya* building and threatened to jump.

Participants at the Kasserine sit-in included both women and men. For women in particular, joining the protest meant transgressing gender norms that are enforced more strictly in the interior regions.[50] At a coffee shop with a group of women protesters in July 2016, each recounted their decision to join the struggle, which would consume their lives for the better part of a year.

Radhia grew up in a family of girls, supported by their father who worked in construction. However, after her father was diagnosed with kidney disease and had to undergo surgery, he could no longer sustain strenuous labor. As the family grappled with medical expenses, Radhia quit her MA program in business English in the Cap Bon region and returned home to support her parents and a younger, unmarried sister. Due to her father's illness, Radhia felt confident that she would qualify as a 'social case' with priority for state assistance. Yet her family's misfortune unfolded immediately after the revolution, when government offices in Kasserine were inundated with applications to join new workfare schemes. 'Normally, they should have accepted me immediately, due to my situation,' Radhia said, adding,

> But when I went to sign up for the *hada'ir* (workfare program) they told me no, it was impossible. So, I went to the office of regional training, thinking even if they don't hire me, they'll still offer some kind of compensation. But when I arrived, they wouldn't even speak with me. They said there was nothing available.

Frustrated in her bid for state assistance, Radhia turned to the private sector, where she cycled through a series of low-end service positions. Her first job was at a local supermarket, engaged without formal contract. 'The legal workday in Tunisia is eight hours long, but they had me working from 7 am to 9 or 10 at night,' Radhia complained. 'They made me do all kinds of tasks: cashier, stock manager, cleaning lady, whatever.' Despite the long hours, her pay never surpassed TND 300 per month (less than minimum wage), and any money missing from the register at the end of the day was docked from her paycheck. After one year at the supermarket, Radhia thought she might do better in Tunis: 'I got fed up in Kasserine because this work is beneath my diploma. My father wore himself out, working in the sun, in the rain, and everything to provide for my education. After all that, it's unacceptable for me to be exploited this way.'

Once in Tunis, however, Radhia discovered that 'you need connections to accomplish the simplest task.' She was prepared to accept any job, even outside of her specialization, but each time she found herself saddled with tasks beyond her job description. Working incessantly, but unable to save any money once rent and utilities were paid, Radhia finally quit her job and returned to Kasserine to clear her head. She had planned to stay only a few weeks, when the January uprising began. 'I heard about the sit-in. Everybody rushed to the *wilaya* to submit their files, and I decided to join them. That's how, on January 19, 2016, I went from the misery of work, to the misery of the sit-in!'

It took tremendous bravery for Radhia to venture out to the *wilaya* complex. As she described it:

> There was tear gas and burning tires everywhere in the streets. Taxis had vanished, even the roads were closed. I tied a scarf around my face to protect against the gas and went to the *wilaya* on foot. I spent every day there for a little over a month. When I returned home at night, others would take my place. We worked this way together, in shifts.

Despite rumors of impropriety targeting female protesters, many young women stayed the night in mixed company at the *wilaya*.[51] Miriam was a 35-year-old law school graduate, unmarried and unemployed since she obtained her diploma in 2006. Her widower father had recently died, leaving Miriam to care for her younger sister. Like Radhia, Miriam had sought assistance from the Office of Employment after the revolution and was admitted to a program offering university students TND 200 per month (nearly half the minimum wage) to volunteer at an association. However, it was incredibly difficult to run a household on such limited means. Miriam had known Ridha Yahyaoui personally, and immediately joined the sit-in upon news of his death. She described the scene at the *wilaya* as 'catastrophic': 'People were packed in. There was only one toilet for both boys and girls. You slept on a chair and table, like this [*folding her arms on the table and putting her head down*], with only your purse for a pillow.' At the end of the month, Miriam underwent surgery for hearing loss in one ear. 'That was due to the cold. You know what Kasserine is like in the winter!'

Near the end of February, the governor invited a delegation of two protesters from each district (*mu'tamdiya*) to negotiate an end to the sit-in. This meeting, however, failed to reach any mutually acceptable conclusion. Reasoning that only the central government had the power to grant a solution, a group of protesters traveled to Tunis, where they ultimately resumed their sit-in before the Ministry of Employment.

Strangers in the Capital City

The sidewalk outside the Ministry of Employment in Bab al-Khadhra is not a hospitable place. The street is congested and impatient drivers sound their horns incessantly to speed up traffic. Yet, it was here, nestled beneath the iron security grills covering the ministry's ground-level windows, that the delegation of Kasserine youth conducted their sit-in. Tents fashioned from *klim* rugs or heavy winter blankets were fastened to the recessed windows; foam mattresses, stacked in multicolored piles beneath the tents and on the side of the building, lent the protesters minimal comfort in an otherwise hostile environment. Amid a flurry of handwritten signs, bearing slogans in Arabic and French, there hung a giant banner, stating in English: 'Kasserine: we just need job.'

As an outside observer who frequented the sit-in in July 2016, I was struck by the temporal gap between the strident political claim-making on the handmade posters and the spectacle of weary bodies assembled on the pavement below. Protesters passed the time playing cards, smoking cigarettes, and taking long walks in the city, like foreign visitors. Leisurely conversations were occasionally interrupted by insults hurled from the windows of passing cars: '*barra, raowah!*' (go home!). These insults, however, were sometimes counterbalanced with gestures of solidarity. One afternoon, as I was leaving the encampment to get coffee with two of the sit-inners, a passerby suddenly stopped and looked at us in amazement. 'You're still here? *Ya Rasul Allah!*' he exclaimed. 'After all the money that flowed into this country after the revolution. The loans, the international assistance. Where did it go?' He remained for a moment, staring into space, then muttered: '*rabbina ya'ounik*' (may God help you).

Conducting a lengthy sit-in far from home meant embracing a temporary, yet open-ended, period of homelessness. Collective strategies had to be made to meet people's basic needs. Early on, a kind attendant at the neighborhood Agil gas station offered the sit-inners access to his bathroom to wash and use the toilet. With toiletries purchased from their pooled resources, sit-inners took showers at the gas station, a critical gesture of self-care in the merciless summer heat. Using the green space of nearby Belvedere Park, they washed laundry in a bucket, hanging the clothes out to dry on an iron security chain separating the sidewalk from the street.

Just as in Kasserine, the daily rhythms of the Tunis sit-in were structured by gender norms. Many of the men had prior experience working as day laborers, and could support themselves through odd jobs as waiters or painters. Yet, these forms of casual employment were largely unavailable to women. It was therefore difficult for them to participate in the sit-in without friends and relatives in Tunis to support them. During a *lamma* (gathering) with a group of women sit-inners, it emerged that they nearly all slept at the private residences of friends or kin. However, they emphasized their commitment to the sit-in's ethic of hardship, only briefly leaving the encampment each night to sleep. This was not only to protect themselves from rumors, but to shield their male comrades from harm. The Ministry of Employment is located across the street from an upscale hotel, which serves alcohol and hosts live cabaret music at night. The women told me that if an inebriated hotel patron insulted them, their male comrades would be compelled to fight in their defense. Women in patriarchal societies regularly police their own conduct to maintain their companions' masculinity while protecting them from violence.[52] By sleeping at a private residence, the women preempted any unnecessary brawls. Those without a support system in Tunis were generally unable to persevere and returned to Kasserine.

The Night Pharmacy

We are 35 young people from Kasserine. Our demands are not frivolous. If you examine each protester's story, you will see we are social cases who merit the care of the state. Among us are those without fathers to support them; there are those with chronic illness in the family. There are those with children at home, but who face such intolerable conditions that they willingly left them behind to remain at the sit-in these long months. We have nothing but the face of God (*wajh rabbi*).

Since our arrival in February, we have endured harsh physical conditions. Last month, we spent Ramadan on the street, exposed to sun and *sheheli* (heat wave) as we fasted. At sunset, we broke our fast on whatever we could. As difficult as it was during Ramadan, living on the street in winter was far worse. When the rains came, there was nowhere to take shelter. The water penetrated our coats and saturated our beds and belongings. Despite the pain of physical suffering, our mental state is more painful. This is the worst part of the sit-in. Not one person has shown us sympathy.

Those who work for the state have no decency (*la din la milla lihum*). The Minister of Employment enters and exits the building without even casting us a glance. The contempt (*hogra*) we receive from state officials is incomprehensible; it boggles the mind. When you see them on TV acting so pious—what God are you talking about when someone is starving? Are we citizens of Tunisia or Niger?[53]

Late one July evening, well past the hour of midnight, I received an urgent call from the Tunis sit-in. Picking up the phone, I was informed that one of the protesters had attempted suicide.

The incident occurred just after Eid al-Fitr. The Minister of Employment had requested to meet with two representatives from the sit-in—a departure from his usual policy of ignoring them and periodically dispatching the police to dismantle their shelters. During this meeting, the minister told them frankly that employment was off the table. He could, however, provide microloans to help each participant start a small business. While favored by the state, such market-based solutions were undesirable for the unemployed because the businesses rarely succeeded. Moreover, the representatives felt insulted by the minister's cavalier attitude. Many of the protesters held university diplomas and insisted on their right to dignified employment on that basis.[54] The minister, however, replied that the role of education is to impart culture; it does not constitute a guarantee of employment for anyone. When they argued that some of the protesters were approaching the age of forty and risked growing old in their unemployment, the minister joked that forty is still young. Of course, the representatives had been concerned about youth as an administrative category; at the age of forty, one is disqualified from entry-level positions in the public sector.

The failure of this meeting cast a mood of despair on the sit-in. One young man, named Majed, suspected that the minister had lied about his capacity to grant them jobs. Feeling defeated, he wandered off by himself to Bab al-Assal, where he purchased rat poison at a night pharmacy. He thought about his older comrades, approaching forty years old and still waiting to enter the workforce. 'I could see my future before me—one day I will end up like them. So, I decided that death is better,' Majed reflected, several days later. He took solace in the thought that, like Bouazizi, his death might help his friends to secure their rights.

Like any suicide attempt, a degree of inscrutability conceals Majed's motivations, obscuring them from the ethnographic gaze.[55] His mother and friends described him as sensitive and reserved; he took things hard and tended to bottle up his feelings. But this was not the first time that Majed had used self-harm to advance the cause of the sit-in. Several months earlier, Majed and another protester named Youssef attempted to enter the Ministry of Employment. Upon presenting their identity cards at the front desk, the receptionist called the police to have them removed. In recounting the incident, Youssef told me that young men from Kasserine often carry razor blades in the summer. When the head aches from the heat or becomes swollen with stress, they use the blade to make small incisions on the forehead, letting out some blood to release the pressure. When the police arrived to apprehend them, Majed and Youssef used the blades to strike deeply into their chests, spilling a lot of blood to create a scene of chaos. 'When the police arrived, they insulted and hit us,' Youssef explained. 'Of course, we cannot strike them back, so we harmed ourselves instead.'

These extreme acts had something of an impact. As emergency medics arrived on the scene, the media arrived with them. Several members of parliament later pledged to meet with the young men. In a similar fashion, the day after Majed attempted suicide, representatives from the Tunisian Organization Against Torture visited the sit-in, including the organization's renowned director, Radhia Nasroui.[56] After warm, boxed lunches were distributed to everyone present, the sit-inners gathered in a circle to offer their testimony, while Radhia listened intently. She was dismayed to hear about the attempted suicide and urged the protesters to use her organization's headquarters to give a press conference. 'Don't commit suicide,' she counseled. 'It won't accomplish anything.'

Early the next morning, Majed's parents traveled to Tunis, along with his two-year-old sister, Ayah, to visit their son in the hospital. Unable to afford a hotel, a group of protesters found them later, sitting under a stand of palm trees in the hospital's front garden. They coaxed them back to the sit-in, where they would be fed and given a soft mattress to sleep on. Arriving there the next day, I found Ayah laughing at play with some plastic toys while the sit-inners looked after her; her child-sized clothing had been washed and hung out to dry on the roadside iron barrier chain. Exhausted from travel and the emotional reunion with their son, Majed's parents hung back by the ministry walls—the father lounged on a mattress, while his wife sat silently on an adjacent chair. I hesitated to approach them, wishing not to intrude on their worries and sorrow. But a woman from the sit-in urged me to interview them. 'Don't worry,' she said, 'They wish to tell their story.'

Majed's father rose briefly to shake my hand, then returned to the mattress to stretch himself out. Majed's mother, Rahma, greeted me warmly with several kisses on the cheeks. Her face was browned from exposure to the sun, and, on this hot day, was covered with a fine layer of sweat. At several points in our conversation, Rahma was overcome with emotion and I felt certain that she would cry. Instead, she paused and passed a hand over her face, in a gesture of exhaustion.

Majed is the eldest son of five children who share a two-room home in Kasserine. With two younger boys in high school, Rahma described how the family struggled to cover school expenses. While public school is free and compulsory in Tunisia, the cost of clothing and supplies presents a significant burden for families. These days, in order to succeed, students must often pay for private tutoring. At the age of fifteen, Majed took up work as a painter, a job that required hauling heavy loads and was hard on his adolescent frame. 'When they begin to work at such a young age, they cannot manage, their bodies cannot take it,' Rahma said. Majed dropped out of school just before his baccalaureate year to help cover his younger brothers' expenses. Despite this sacrifice for the household budget, one of Majed's brothers, now sixteen, has also begun to work. Rahma fears that her younger sons will drop out of school, following Majed into a life of poverty.

'The youth of today want to live,' Rahma explained. 'They want to dress well, they want to have their own room where they can relax. But we are poor, we cannot provide that for them. Young people today are not like our generation. They are no longer satisfied to live in poor conditions, to go to bed hungry. They refuse to accept that they cannot wash their hair because we can't afford shampoo; they have to be clean. We accepted those conditions, but they do not. They are only satisfied with a good life ('*eicha behiya*').'

Throughout our conversation, Rahma described her family as 'tired,' indicating a state of deep exhaustion; pushed to the breaking point. Rahma's husband, a former day laborer himself, stopped work

after an injury ten years ago. With her husband inactive, Rahma began
seeking work in the agricultural sector. She described how, during
her pregnancy with Ayah, she would go to the fields to harvest olives
in winter, or stoop down low to dig in the summer heat. 'I have to
do it,' she explained, 'so that my sons can live.' This drive to provide
her sons with the lifestyle they expect and desire has exacted a
terrible toll. Rahma was recently diagnosed with cataracts, which
are aggravated by work in the powerful sun. Without treatment,
the pressure on her eyes increases and she may become blind. Yet,
each injection for her eyes represents a significant burden on the
household budget. Rahma often foregoes her cataracts injections in
order to spend on her children.

'eicha behiya *(A Good Life)*

I had a chance to spend time with Majed in Kasserine after his
discharge from the hospital. On a walking tour of the city, he
proudly showed me the murals he painted with friends during the
Streets Festival in 2013, when internationally renowned graffiti
artists led workshops for local youth. 'Arts of Revolution' were
heavily promoted in Kasserine after 2011, as development agencies
like USAID saw graffiti, breakdancing, and rap music as tools to
engage the youth population. Majed adored hip-hop and rap, and
his Facebook page revealed the care he invested in self-fashioning.
In online photos, he imagined himself participating in the lifestyles
portrayed in music videos, wearing blinged-out sunglasses and a
hardened facial expression, sometimes brandishing fake handguns.
Other times, he Photoshopped himself into the iconic sites of global
tourism: the Eiffel Tower or the Nile River's palm-lined banks.

Rahma's insight about the 'good life' strikes me as central to
the problem of dignity for Tunisian youth today, having authored
a revolution, yet still caught in the vortex of 'wageless life.'[57] At
his mother's house, Majed has access to the material necessities to
sustain survival. And yet it is the 'supplements'—athletic shoes,
gym classes, shampoo, stylish clothing—that render his existence in
Kasserine minimally bearable. For Majed, and so many of the other
protesters at the Tunis sit-in, there is real pathos in the balance of life

and labor in the household economy. To all evidence, Majed enjoys a close relationship with his mother. A tattoo on his forearm, reading 'Rahma's Wolf,' testifies to the value he places on the mother–son bond. Still, Majed knows that his mother courts blindness when she toils in the fields on his behalf. In providing a life for her sons, Rahma's own life was being diminished.

A decade after the revolution, the situation of Kasserine youth compels us to ask the question: 'what do you do when nothing you can do seems likely to have much effect?'[58] In the ethnographic vignettes above, I have sketched out some of the major avenues available to Tunisian youth to stay afloat, and make life more bearable in the absence of stable and dignified employment. Eschewing a reading of revolutionary-becoming, or heroic resistance against an unjust state, I have shown instead how the work of endurance, as practiced at the Kasserine sit-in, bleeds into other forms of precarious labor, such as low-end service work or smuggling. As older mechanisms of clientelism, undergirded by the infrastructure of the RCD, are no longer operative, spaces of contentious action like the sit-in have emerged as an arena of negotiation with the state, where youth use suffering as a currency to maximize access to welfare benefits. Amid an uncertain future and in the absence of an inclusive national development strategy, Tunisian youth in the marginal spaces of the nation have few tools left to combat the slow violence of precarity.

8

CHANGING SECURITY DYNAMICS IN TUNISIA
RECONSIDERING THE BATTLE FOR BEN GARDANE

Ruth Hanau Santini

On March 7, 2016, a group of armed Islamic State (IS) militants attacked Ben Gardane, a small Tunisian town on the southern border with Libya. The assault was warded off by the army and security forces with the support of local civilians following a fierce gun battle. Had the attack been successful, Ben Gardane would have become the first Tunisian IS base. This dramatic event was particularly significant for the country's stabilization trajectory not only because the terrorist attack failed, but because security forces successfully coordinated their operations and enjoyed support from the local community. The mutually reinforcing nature of these elements strengthened—an at least epiphenomenal—sense of national unity in those historically marginalized areas, curbed the threat of political violence, and was instrumental in stabilizing the country.

The politics of national commemoration of the battle's 'martyrs' took shape in a threefold way. First, visible reminders of the battle of Ben Gardane became permanent icons of the town, including erecting a new monument specifically designed for this purpose at the entrance of the town, dedicating a part of the town's cemetery for the martyrs' bodies, and establishing annual commemorations meant to honor the memory of those who died, remember personal sacrifices, and take stock of the town's evolution. The second element of the politics of memory revolved around the hagiographic construction of an epic battle, where 'us' versus 'them' neatly separated good Tunisian security forces and local residents against Tunisian and foreign terrorists attacking a town on the southern borders with the aim of infiltrating the country. This paved the way for the formulation of a discourse aimed at wiping the slate clean of long-held perceptions and previous negative connotations attributed to southern populations, historically considered disloyal to the post-independence statist project. Thirdly, the politics of memory articulated in the aftermath of the attack facilitated the implementation of new security practices at the local level, premised on the inauguration of allegedly new state–society relations. The bravery not just of security forces but of the local population has since then become a standard reference in the public discourse, partially aimed at reshaping the image of previously socially and culturally marginalized local residents now heralded as the symbol of national virtues and merits, and at symbolizing the ideal type of brave new Tunisians fiercely defending their homeland.

This chapter argues that the creation of a 'myth' surrounding the discrete episode of the attack on Ben Gardane, the moral standing attributed to the town and its residents, and the symbolic value widely attached to the event have partially altered the deep-seated mistrust between the southern border town and the capital. Second, the chapter explores how this event has enabled the experimentation of new forms of security cooperation and operational changes in the modalities and the *dispositifs* utilized by the security forces on the ground (as exemplified by the *police de proximité* tested in those areas), premised on more regular information exchanges with local residents on potential security risks and pending threats, especially arising from the unstable border with Libya at Ras Jedir. Third, the chapter elaborates on an underlying conceptual and incremental shift in post-revolutionary Tunisia in the prevailing understandings of security that the Ben Gardane battle attests to, from 'regime security' to 'state security,' often manifesting itself in an ad hoc way in societal security understandings and approaches.

The Moral Geography of the Tunisian Southern Border Region

During colonial times, a specific moral geography of Tunisia was articulated around a binary opposition between Tunisians, on the one hand, and French and Europeans, on the other. More often than not, with the exception of coopted local elites, who enjoyed an in-between status, locals tended to belong to lower classes and were stigmatized as 'others' and inferior to the colonizer. Far from being a purely descriptive category, the 'us' versus 'them' binary opposition carried within its fold a normative connotation of morality. In the colonial discourse, namely, French/European individuals were associated with 'cleanliness,' while Tunisians with 'dirtiness.'[1] The lack, or backward state, of sanitary infrastructures in much of the non-coastal areas of the country was tactically employed as a signifier for the moral state of these populations. The artificial creation of spatial boundaries—supposedly according to the existence of sanitary infrastructures—conflated with racialized and colonial demarcations and new processes of exclusion.

The usage of exclusionary linguistic devices was further developed after independence. After 1956, President Habib Bourguiba upheld an alleged modernist approach and discourse, which, by distinguishing between modern cities (*bedawi*) and rural areas (*baldi*), legitimized a reading of the latter as backward and archaic.[2] Political elites have since then looked down on rural populations, in particular poor rural populations from the center and south-east of the country. With the demands of these populations for recognition unfulfilled, the gap between these populations in the border regions and the ruling elite continued to widen. The under-development and under-investment in these areas further triggered discontent and resentment, with occasional outbursts of collective mobilization, which, in turn, led Tunisian elites to consider them a threat to their rule. Bourguiba—and Ben Ali after him—legitimized a discourse that stigmatized these regions, whose populations were not just deemed to be under-developed but also racially inferior, thereby legitimizing the old colonial rhetorical device of associating purity with an allegedly superior race; in this case, with an explicit sub-national socio-geographical connotation. Bourguiba, in particular, substantiated a hierarchical spatialization that associated center and southern 'dirty' rural areas with social disorder. This was hardly eliminated in the aftermath of the 2010–11 uprisings. During the protest outbreaks, key government figures depicted revolutionaries as *voyous* (rascals), by referring explicitly to Kasserine, one of the epicenters of mobilization and the site where more protesters lost their lives.[3]

This chapter makes the case that this old, colonial discourse only changed tune with the battle of Ben Gardane in March 2016. It does so by looking at national discourses and interviews with local residents divided by category: politicians, including the mayor of Ben Gardane; members of selected local associations born in the aftermath of the attacks aimed at remembering the battle; its martyrs and legacy; members of youth groups, including the *Union des Diplomés Chômeurs* (the union of unemployed graduates); and local residents.

For an outsider, investigating the changing security dynamics in Tunisia comes with field research challenges that are important to note. In terms of positionality, the identity of the scholar carrying out the research (female, European, conducting interviews in French and, only to a limited extent, in Arabic, with a decade of scholarly and fieldwork experience in Tunisia) was quickly singled out as that of an outsider entering a closely-knit community. As soon as I set foot outside the small hotel where I was staying with a colleague, the key interviewee I was supposed to meet—a resident whose presence on social media and activities related to the 2016 events was most visible—reported me and my colleague to the police and, soon enough, we ended up in the local police station. There we were asked to produce authorization or a permit from the Ministry of Interior to carry out research in the country. Oddly, such an ill-defined permit had no material existence: no template, no link, no form, and nobody, not even the European Embassy to which the author referred at the time, could confirm the existence of such a document. After being interrogated for a few hours, we were released from the police station. On the first day of meetings and interviews, two officers followed me around. From the second day, the situation somewhat stabilized and only random checks were carried out on my whereabouts and the agenda of my meetings.

It is important to acknowledge that these forms of micro-surveillance and tight social control played a role in the 'metadata' and its importance during interviews.[4] Namely, the expressions, tone of voice, ease with the interlocutor, and postural shifts when talking were, to some extent, influenced by the initial coercive approach experienced and by concerns about interviewees' safety and freedom of expression during interviews and informal chats.[5] Compared to almost every other site in Tunisia in which I carried out fieldwork since 2011, the Ben Gardane site requires exceptionally careful and repeated practices of confidence building and processes of gaining trust.[6] Despite these fieldwork difficulties, the research yielded new insights, both informative and complementary to the existing official accounts of the attack, its meaning, and its legacy, but also more critical insights, offered especially by members of youth organizations, on perceptions of the state and of state–society relations during the post-revolutionary period.

The Battle of Ben Gardane

The Unfolding of the Attack

In the early morning hours of March 7, 2016, the town of Ben Gardane, lying on the southeast border with Libya, some 550 km from the capital Tunis, was assaulted by a commando of over fifty jihadis that simultaneously stormed the police station, an army barracks, and a National Guard post. Casualties amounted to the deaths of seven civilians, twelve members of the security forces, thirty-six terrorists, and dozens of injuries.[7]

This was not the first time Tunisia suffered an attack from an armed group that infiltrated the country through its southern borders. Now a distant memory, the Gafsa attack of 1980 undoubtedly posed a serious national security threat to the then ailing President Bourguiba. On the morning of January 27, 1980, around sixty armed militants opened fire on the local police station and the military barracks, urging inhabitants to revolt against Bourguiba. Although the attackers' call was met with indifference by the local population, it still took several days for the Tunisian security forces to overwhelm the militants.

The events of Ben Gardane stand out in a different way. Historically, Ben Gardane has been associated with two images in Tunisia. The first is a clandestine marketplace for foreign currency exchange and merchandise of smuggled goods from Libya, especially fuel and cheap goods imported from East Asia, and the second is one of the sites of fiercest anti-colonial and later anti-Bourguibian resistance.[8] If one were to depict the key components of the national discourse that have framed this southern border enclave, these could be subsumed in two categories: informal economy and political activism.

Most of the terrorists who stormed Ben Gardane in 2016 were Tunisian and some were from Ben Gardane itself. They entered from Libya, where they had been regrouping and training in IS camps in the months preceding the attack. This is also where they amassed their arsenal of weapons. The group's goal was not just to disrupt life in the town and to destabilize the precarious political trajectory in the post-revolutionary polity, but to establish a new base for the IS caliphate in North Africa.

As reported in the media and in the accounts of local residents, the IS group were likely expecting a more welcoming attitude and were caught by surprise when local residents turned against them, siding with the security forces and denouncing the terrorists. This unprecedented armed operation was countered by an effective response by the security forces—army, police, and National Guard—and local citizens, who either shielded security forces personnel or facilitated the capture of terrorists. The improved coordination among security forces was epitomized by the quickly assembled joint operation of the Unité spéciale de la garde nationale (USGN), the Brigade anti-terrorisme de la police (BAT), and Groupe d'intervention militaire (GIM). The three units were based in different areas of the country when the attack unfolded, but quickly regrouped and united their forces in Ben Gardane, where they staged a successful counter-attack.

The 'battle of Ben Gardane' has come to symbolize a moral and social 'redemption'—as seen by the capital—of a border community often stigmatized as an outlier, blamed for its economically illicit practices of cross-border smuggling with Libya, and considered a potential hotbed for radicalization and political violence. Significantly, while these perceptions have been publicly expressed by mainstream media and political elites in Tunis, they have not been uniformly adopted. In fact, the Ben Gardane local community widely rejects this reading and the projected image of itself. Local perceptions, expressed in interviews I carried out in November 2019, pointed to a widely shared perception and feeling among local residents that there was nothing that required redemption, and insisted that the acts of the citizens of Ben Gardane were heroic and saved the country from a new wave of political violence.

Discourses and Testimonies

Those civilians and members of the security forces who lost their lives defending the town became, in the official state rhetoric, 'martyrs of the homeland' as former President Béji Caïd Essebsi put it.[9] In the same speech, Essebsi described the citizens of Ben Gardane in particular, and the south of the country in general, as 'pillars of the state' and a source of pride. Despite being a contingent declaratory acknowledgement of the sacrifice endured by these communities in successfully fighting against terrorists and aiding security forces, it is hard not to take note of a significant shift in public rhetoric. Namely, up until the 2010 uprisings, the political establishment did not refrain from referring to these populations in derogatory terms. In the post-independence era, these communities were described as 'filthy' and immoral southern communities. At the end of the Ben Ali era, when revolts broke out across the country from the center and the south toward the north and coastal regions, politicians talked of *voyous*, or thugs, conflating the decade-long historical experience of resisting the imposition of post-independence Bourguibian authority—i.e., their political activism and conscience—with the cross-border smuggling activities that kept afloat the economy of many of these areas.

Shortly after the Ben Gardane attacks, former President Essebsi reiterated that 'the state trusts the populations in the south, and that they are the real shield of the homeland.'[10] Ben Gardane became the country's last line of defense, a human shield so to speak, against foreign interferences messing with the complicated and often unstable post-revolutionary political trajectory of the country.

The positive annotation of trust testifies to the implicit lack of trust beforehand. The reference to local residents as 'shields' acknowledges the capacity of these populations, being on the territorial frontlines, dutifully protecting the homeland against external threats. It is noteworthy how threats are exogenous and how disenfranchised local populations become citizens merely through the act of self-sacrifice, falling in battle as martyrs. Moreover, Essebsi's social construction of danger crystallized a minimal understanding of statehood—intended as a monopoly on the use or threat of violence—and its territorial integrity and its sovereignty, which was intended as ability to control its borders and delineate its perimeter. The president made no reference to linkages between, let alone causes of, historical injustices suffered by socioeconomically and culturally marginal populations and emerging security threats. In this socially constructed notion, the Tunisian nationality of many of the assailants was not taken into account, as it would have annulled the neat inside–outside dichotomy that is premised on the existence of a menacing foreign 'Other,' rather than a more nuanced discourse requiring a critical, diachronic view of winner and loser of post-independence statist projects.

The president's speech, far from testifying to the end of the securitization of border communities and the legitimation of their smuggling-based moral economy,[11] expressed the suspension of the enduring Manichean geographically-premised culturally excluding paradigm. After the attacks against Ben Gardane, the new demarcation line was drawn between terrorists, depicted as 'barbarians' and 'rats,' and the noble citizens in arms, seen as defending the homeland for all Tunisians.

The battle of Ben Gardane was deemed—across the country and by the local population—the first time civilians had successfully repulsed a large-scale terrorist attack. Interviews with members of local cultural associations, schools and unions, as well as relatives of the town's martyrs in November 2019, revealed a shared narrative on the importance and legacy of the battle. Respondents depicted these events as an indisputable military and civilian victory against radicalism and violence as well as a key factor in accounting for the beginning of the end of IS. Many interviewees shared the view that this popular resistance movement against IS was not so much premised on a sense of defense of national homeland or of national belonging, but rather by the imperative of keeping Ben Gardane free from political violence and from radicalized individuals depicted as aliens threatening their way of life and interfering with their community. A second narrative that emerged focused on positively assessing the changes in citizens–security forces' relations. This was captured by discourses of an alleged post-2016 unity of *dawla* (comprising state institutions) and *watan* (homeland), two entities previously perceived at odds. The former was historically associated with the regime and tied to its interests, and readily identifiable in its brutal but omnipresent institution, i.e. the police. The latter, the homeland, was confined to the individual perception and attachment to an idea of what Tunisia is, navigating between a cultural affinity and an emotional understanding. Several of the interviewees seemed to conflate those two notions and referred to the collective response by security forces and civilians during the March attacks and the ensuing closer collaborative efforts to ensure the security of the area both as a testament to that and its very cause.

Public Trust and Security Practices

The post-2016 collaboration between security forces and local civil society has been sponsored by external actors engaged in security assistance through the Group of Seven (G7+).[12] This was the case with the G7+ working group on preventing and countering violent extremism (P/CVE), in collaboration with the United Nations. In particular, the UN interagency PVE engagement has adopted a holistic approach to mitigate risks and to enhance the local populations' resilience to violent extremism.[13]

One of the flagship programs is community policing (*Police de proximité*), focused on the capacity building of police officers and jointly led by the United Nations Development Program (UNDP) and the Tunisian Ministry of Interior. Disenfranchisement is not limited to the Medenine governorate, which includes Ben Gardane— it extends to other areas of the country where the government and the UNDP launched such initiatives (though with the end-goal of scaling them up across the national territory).[14]

Community-oriented policing is not a Tunisian invention. It is premised on positive, nonenforcement contact with the public and is aimed at enhancing public trust and police legitimacy. It has been practiced and implemented in a variety of settings across the globe. Recent studies have demonstrated how it can significantly contribute to improving attitudes toward police forces, especially in minority communities where distrust and longstanding conflict with the police are documented.[15]

The UNDP is also working indirectly on PVE with local police officers, civil society, and local authorities (delegations or municipalities) within their local security plan adopted under the framework of local security committees (*Comités locaux de sécurité*). These community activities are aimed at raising awareness within the local population on core issues, namely drugs and crime prevention. By opting for a micro-level approach and low-politics issues, community policing has a twofold goal. It aims at re-establishing the reputation of police through more grassroots activities (and the vertical relation between the state and society), while avoiding the risks connected to a culture of suspicion in a 'post-police state' like Tunisia.[16] These activities do not extend to or involve the army because the Tunisian military continues to enjoy very high legitimacy and is widely recognized as the single most respected institution, thereby not qualifying for similar efforts.[17]

During the meetings I conducted in Ben Gardane in November 2019, a select number of interviewees—school teachers, young university graduates, local activists engaged in commemoration activities of the March 2016 events, and trade unionists—expressed increased trust in security institutions since the terrorist attack in 2016 and shared a positive and constructive view of the experiment of the community policing as effectively reducing the distance and mistrust between police forces and the local community. Additionally, some pointed out how this was potentially a useful tool for sharing information about changes in the security landscape, should anything suspicious emerge and put at risk the safety of the town and its community. To consider these security practices as new practices, however, would be neglecting decades of authoritarian surveillance under Ben Ali, where *dispositifs* of micro-surveillance, social control, and tipping off were a tacit but standard way of operating by the government, especially in areas deemed potential hotbeds for revolts or turmoil.

What the in-depth, qualitative interviews suggest is that, rather than interpreting these forms of cooperation between security forces and local communities as an attempt at social control, since the 2016 attacks, they are seen as a sign of increased attention from state institutions on the security of border areas, a manifestation of care for these communities, and as an effort to enhance societal security. Whether respondents exercised a degree of concealment during these interviews, offering only constructive comments to the researcher—particularly given the attention by security forces in the tight-knit community of Ben Gardane—remains a viable possibility. What can be ascertained with more certainty is the hope that behind the efforts of government and external actors in southern governorates, the discourse and practices of fostering societal resilience through the more active engagement of youth could imply the implementation of the socioeconomic component of the social contract. Relations with local populations in the border areas with Libya also seem to be more constructive and dictated by an increased faith in the security forces and a sense of a shared mission, fostering a willingness among the general population to cooperate with the police—something that would have been unthinkable in the past.[18]

Security Configurations and Understandings

Mainstream, rationalist understandings of security have traditionally looked at state survival in the face of external threats. Threats were considered objective, external, and clearly identifiable and security was deemed to be a fragile accomplishment as it rested on the power and intentions of other states. These readings were predicated on two main assumptions: the existence of an observable independent reality and the given nature of states as foundational objects. Sovereignty, on the one hand, and territoriality, on the other, were the markers of statehood. With the end of the Cold War and the emergence of new security studies, not only was the agenda of security widened to encompass aspects of social life previously completely detached from security considerations (economic security, food security, environmental security, and societal security), but the targets of security changed. In a nutshell, the Copernican revolution involved the shift from states as ontological objects to states tasked with securing individuals.[19] The Copenhagen school followed by the Welsh and the Paris school elaborated on these understandings.[20] What is relevant to this chapter is the notion of societal security and of security issues in terms of identity. Ole Wæver refers to fear for the survival of culture, community, nation, and religion as examples of security understandings in terms of identity.[21] Identity security as collective or societal security therefore implies the defense of an identity or a community against a threat to its identity.

The argument developed in this chapter, through the illustration of the Ben Gardane terrorist attacks, makes the case that both the response to the attacks and emerging practices afterwards in terms of increased trust and cooperation between security forces and local population testify to a shift in prevailing security understandings. Ben Ali's Tunisia, as widely illustrated in the literature, endorsed a conception of security that revolved around regime security, a notion not encompassing state security but mainly focusing on the political elite's survival.[22] Any threat to the survival of the leader and his immediate circle was deemed a national security threat, without necessarily posing an existential threat to the country itself.

With the 2010–11 uprisings and the democratic trajectory Tunisia has embarked upon since then, security has come to be understood more pointedly as that of the state, a shift which was particularly evident when the country faced terrorist threats, both in 2013, with the two rounds of political assassinations, and in 2015, when IS-led attacks hit the tourist sector and risked derailing the political trajectory by plunging the country into fear and chaos.[23] At the forefront of this reading of security were territorial integrity, control over terrorist groups' activities, political neutrality in border countries' uprisings or conflicts (the transition in Algeria in 2019, the evolution of the civil war in neighboring Libya), and economic security, at least rhetorically.

The March 2016 attacks in Ben Gardane point to a partially innovative and qualitative change in security understandings and practices. In particular, the response to the attacks, with a direct involvement of local communities offering their help to the security forces defending the town, heralded a symbolically poignant change in state–society relations in this historically marginal area. The assault was internalized by the local population as an existential threat that could not just be left to state security forces but required an active role on the part of the townspeople. This signaled a contingent outburst of trust and *esprit de corps*, cutting across previously neatly separated bodies—security forces, on the one hand, and residents, on the other, with the latter often subjected to harassment, violence, arbitrary arrests and requests for bribes under the pretext of cross-border smuggling activities. The driver for these collective acts of self-sacrifice by local residents was not heroism or ideological proximity with the state or the security forces, but rather the need to preserve their community's ontological security.

As recounted by Weaver, society is about collective identity, i.e., the self-conception of community, which, far from being static or reification of individual identity, is processual, fluid, and constructed. The March 2016 attacks served as focal point exemplifying the dangers faced by the community's collective identity. In several interviews, there was a pointed reference to identity dimensions ('we are not like them, we have nothing to do with terrorists,' 'they would have changed how we live,' and 'they were alien, different from us, also the ones from Ben Gardane, came from Libya'). This narrative about an external threat—not only to physical survival but also to community values and way of life—points to an acknowledgement of a specific system of values that required dramatic action and active efforts to be defended. From the side of the community, in other words, it was ontological security that drove individual and collective responses:

acting as human shields for police agents; denouncing exact locations of terrorists; and refusing to embrace arms when asked by terrorists. In a way, that episode became a defining moment for the community to draw a line regarding what it stood for: the rejection of political violence and the use of arms. The manifestation of an awareness of collective identity in a second phase after the attack paved the way for improved relations with security forces, a diminished mistrust, and an enhanced willingness to cooperate to defend the area from terrorist infiltrations while providing for more opportunities for younger people (as part of the UN-funded programs in the area, requiring the joint implementation with grassroots and local organizations). From the side of the state, the prevailing perception and narrative were about the weak link represented by the southern region which bordered Libya and was prone to being more easily penetrated by foreign terrorists or Tunisian returnees from conflict zones in the region who may represent a security threat. In this context, the March 2016 counter-terrorism success was interpreted as a testament to the moral unity of the country facing the same existential threat—i.e., terrorism and political violence—with no distinction between Tunis and coastal regions and the south. In the official narrative, this epitomized a victory of a post-revolutionary statehood, which, far from being limited,[24] here pointed to the underdog town symbolically protecting the homeland.

The longer-term trajectory of the southern population's attitude vis-à-vis security forces will depend on the quality of governance the southern regions will experience in terms of services and economic growth, but also on the security forces' restraint when handling civil unrest and protests, which, given the continuing dire conditions of those areas, continue to manifest themselves. In other words, while the 2016 IS attack in Ben Gardane epitomized a moment of common goal and unity in the identification of shared ontological concerns between civilians and security forces, which paved the way for increased intelligence sharing and cooperation, in the absence of a socially oriented state presence in the area, this cooperation is unlikely to continue or to have a lasting effect.

9

WHAT CAN TUNISIA'S PAST TELL US ABOUT
ITS FUTURE?
CRITICAL JUNCTURES AND POLITICAL TRENDS

Alexandra Domike Blackman

In her seminal work on repression and autocracy in Tunisia, Béatrice
Hibou warned against overly relying on historical and culturalist
explanations to understand Tunisian politics, specifically cautioning
against the 'culturalist vision that turns the cult of the leader into an
eternal given in Tunisia.'[1] Indeed, a decade after the fall of Zine El
Abidine Ben Ali, it is safe to say that a highly personalist and autocratic
ruler is not an eternal given in Tunisia.[2] What, then, can history tell
us about Tunisia's future? How do historical legacies reverberate,
even after the significant political upheaval of the revolution? And
through what processes and mechanisms do these legacies operate?

In recent years, a growing literature has examined how historical
events, institutions, and individuals are important determinants
of contemporary political outcomes.[3] This work moves beyond
proximate antecedents as explanations for current politics, instead
locating contemporary outcomes within a longer time horizon and
linking them directly to factors and dynamics from the pre-colonial,
colonial, Bourguiba, or Ben Ali eras. In this chapter, I provide

an overview of how historical legacies are used to understand contemporary Tunisian politics. I then discuss the mechanisms of historical persistence between the more distant past and today.

To illustrate these dynamics, I discuss two case studies related to important political issues facing Tunisia today: regional inequality and the Islamist–secular cleavage. I demonstrate that these two phenomena—while gaining renewed focus after the revolution—have their roots in long-run historical processes. Disparities between the regions, I argue, can be viewed as an outgrowth of colonial policies that were exacerbated by regional favoritism under the Bourguiba and Ben Ali regimes. Similarly, in the case of the Islamist–secularist cleavage in Tunisia, I locate its origin in the colonial era and demonstrate that the cleavage persists today, both in terms of the political geography and the ideas and concerns raised by each side. These case studies illustrate the continuities and discontinuities between political issues of today and pre-revolutionary periods of Tunisian history.

Critical Junctures and Lasting Changes in Tunisian History

The first way to approach the study of historical legacies in Tunisia is through the examination of specific periods, looking closely at policy changes and critical junctures that may have had a lasting effect on Tunisia's long-run trajectory. In this section, I provide an overview of the literature on historical legacies in Tunisia, looking specifically at what era or events authors argue continue to have implications today. For each era, I only highlight a few of the more common historical legacies from that period, though this list is by no means exhaustive.

The Pre-Colonial Era

Research on the current historical legacies from the Ottoman period and earlier is fairly sparse in the Tunisian context, though work on the broader historical trends in the region suggests several significant critical junctures in Ottoman times.[4] For instance, Lisa Blaydes, in her review of research on state formation in Middle East, argues that the Ottoman Land Law of 1858 marked a significant change throughout the empire, facilitating private ownership of agricultural land and creating large landed elites.[5]

In Tunisia, the Ottoman legacy is often referenced to help explain three contemporary outcomes in the country's politics: centralized bureaucracy, inclusive politics, and social class structure. The period of Ottoman rule marked a clear shift in the centralization of the state bureaucracy. Prior to the nineteenth century, Ottoman control in Tunisia was primarily concentrated in the large coastal cities along the Mediterranean. While an Ottoman governor nominally controlled the entire state, the large interior regions were largely managed through local intermediaries. The arrival of the French in Algeria in 1830, however, put the Ottoman Empire on the defensive. In response, the Ottoman regime pushed for the rapid modernization and bureaucratization of its North African proto-states.[6] Thus, as I will discuss in the next section, the French colonial administration in Tunisia inherited a fairly centralized bureaucracy that it was able to further centralize through additional administrative reforms.

Additionally, researchers often reference the Ottoman period in discussing the long legacy of inclusionary politics in Tunisia. In his discussion of Tunisia's successful democratic transition, Alfred Stepan argues that Tunisia has adhered to a relationship between religion and politics, which he refers to as the 'twin tolerations.'[7] These twin tolerations consist of religious individuals recognizing the authority of elected officials to legislate and of elected officials recognizing the freedom of conscience of religious individuals. Stepan locates the historical roots of the twin tolerations in the legacy of fourteenth-century thinker Ibn Khaldun, as well as in the Ottoman political culture that supported Tunisia's abolition of slavery in 1846 and the country's 1861 Constitution, which guaranteed certain rights to all individuals regardless of religion.[8] Stepan writes: 'There is historical evidence that Tunisia was already becoming what we might call "twin tolerations-friendly" as long ago as the nineteenth century (and perhaps even earlier, if one wants to search back as far as Ottoman and medieval times for cultural roots of tolerance and openness).'[9]

Finally, the social class identities and class structure in place during the Ottoman period continue to be relevant in the post-independence period. In his 1939 study of Tunisian elites, Henri de

Montety found that the leadership of the Destour party, a nationalist party and predecessor to Habib Bourguiba's Neo-Destour, came primarily from old Mamluk families in Tunisia.[10] Many of these established families remain politically influential today. Famously, Tunisia's first elected president following the 2010 uprising, Béji Caïd Essebsi, was from a prominent Mamluk family with close ties to the Ottoman ruling family.[11]

While this literature on the Ottoman legacy highlights a number of important historical factors, there are several pre-colonial factors that demand further research. First, work on the Ottoman Empire should engage more with how the events and institutions from that period continue to have an effect on today's politics. In other words, what are the modes of reproduction that carry the Ottoman legacy through from the distant past until today? In a subsequent section in this chapter, I discuss mechanisms of persistence, but little of the research on the Ottoman period makes explicit how cultural institutions like religious tolerance are transmitted over the decades. Second, future research should examine the long-run legacies of the spread of Islam in Tunisia and the local legacies of Tunisia's various tribes. These are identified as important historical factors, but little work has connected these events and institutions to political outcomes today.

The Colonial Era

In 1881, the French invaded and occupied Tunisia, quickly establishing it as a protectorate. Seventy-five years later, in 1956, the French protectorate formally ended. At the beginning of the protectorate, the French population in Tunisia was only 708 French citizens and reached its peak right before decolonization with a French population of 180,440.

Tunisian society underwent radical transformation during that period as a result of changes to state power, land policy, labor markets, and educational institutions brought about by French settlement. The rapid arrival of French citizens also brought with it urbanization and new communication networks in many parts of Tunisia, as well as new settler politics.[12] Many researchers trace contemporary trends in Tunisia to this period in the country's history.

In this section, I examine the legacies of colonial bureaucratization and state centralization and participation in war, before turning to the implication colonization had on patterns of urbanization and educational opportunities across Tunisia.

In *State and Social Transformation in Tunisia and Libya*, Lisa Anderson argues that colonial policies had a lasting effect on political stability and state legitimacy that is still evident today. She writes: 'The critical difference in the historical experience of state formation in the two countries [Tunisia and Libya] is the differential impact of French and Italian colonial rule in sustaining or destroying the local bureaucratic administrations that developed during the nineteenth century.'[13] In Tunisia, the French extended the preexisting Ottoman state and further centralized power within the French colonial administration. This strengthened the state and undermined the influence of pre-colonial kinship networks and tribes.

In addition to political stability, Mounira Charrad posits that one of the most significant legacies of Tunisia's strong central state and disorganized tribes is the state's action in putting legal protections for women and gender equality in place. In contrast to Morocco and Algeria, Charrad argues that in post-independence Tunisia, partially as a result of its colonial experience, women's rights improved rapidly with the implementation of the personal status laws granting women the right to divorce and banning polygamous marriage at independence.[14]

Another long-term consequence of the growing centralized state was the transformation and bureaucratization of the land tenure and property ownership systems.[15] In the late 1880s and early 1890s, prior to the creation of an official Colonization Service in Tunisia,[16] many French citizens began to resettle in the country privately. This settlement process was accelerated by the creation of a French Colonization Service in Tunisia in 1898, precipitating important changes with long-run consequences. In that same year, the French administration also made 'habous,'[17] or religious endowment, lands available for lease or sale to French settlers.[18] By undermining a primary source of financial support, this move crippled the country's religious establishment as well as the network of schools and mosques supported by the *habous* system. The weakening of this system, which was affiliated with the Zeitouna Mosque and University, facilitated its complete elimination by President Bourguiba after independence. Moreover, Clement Henry Moore argues that French acquisition of *habous* properties was a key factor in the rise of the nationalist Destour party, which sought to prevent French expropriation of these lands.[19]

The centralization of Tunisian bureaucracy in the colonial era also continues to influence Tunisia's more recent efforts at decentralization and local governance. According to Assia Khellaf, the underdevelopment of local governments in the country can be traced to colonial policy, which was 'successful at breaking the existing tribal structure and at weakening the local social and political structure, but it deprived the country of any reliable form of subnational government.'[20] Local elections in post-revolution Tunisia were delayed several times, in part because the central government could not agree about the role for municipal councils. Even after Tunisia's first democratic municipal elections were held in 2018, the mandates of the municipal councils and local mayors remained unclear.

In addition to more incremental changes to Tunisian society brought on by colonial policies and centralization, World War I and World War II were critical junctures that influenced and continue to shape Tunisia today. Roughly sixty-five to seventy thousand Tunisians served in World War I and, of the Tunisian infantrymen, nearly ten thousand were killed.[21] Others were sent to France to work in factories. World War I marked the first time that Tunisians were conscripted in large numbers to serve in the French army, a move many colons had tried to avoid because they feared it would increase demands for equal rights.[22] Even today, these wars have important implications for human capital investments in North Africa, cross-Mediterranean migration, and diaspora politics.

World War II is also credited with accelerating the rise and success of anti-colonial movements in North Africa. Adria Lawrence argues that the rise of anti-colonial nationalism resulted from French colonial subjects' unfulfilled demands for equal citizenship and French participation in war.[23] She finds that nationalist protests increased when involvement in war disrupted imperial authority within the colonial territory and undermined France's ability to maintain local stability. These nationalist movements eventually formed the basis of the first postcolonial independent governments.

The Bourguiba Era

Habib Bourguiba, a lawyer and leader within the nationalist Neo-Destour party, became independent Tunisia's first president in 1957. He is often regarded as having had a significant individual impact on Tunisian political and social development, leaving a mark on the country's politics that is still apparent today. For instance, Intissar Kherigi argues that Bourguiba's territorial reforms—introduced right after independence—sought to eliminate any potential counterweights to the authority of the central state, such as local tribal or religious authority.[24] In many cases, these internal boundaries established by Bourguiba remain today. In this section, I discuss some of the historical legacies associated with the Bourguiba years, focusing on women's rights and Bourguiba's individual ideological commitments.

Both within the MENA region and globally, by most measures, Tunisia ranks highly on women's rights and gender equality metrics.[25] Many observers credit Bourguiba for leading a top-down, state-led push to enshrine women's rights in law directly after independence. Though women's movements have played a significant role in demands for women's rights, particularly more recently, the top-down approach of Bourguiba and Ben Ali largely overshadowed grassroots efforts.[26] Under Bourguiba, women secured a number of important reforms, including the 1956 Personal Status Code that gave women and men equal rights with regard to divorce, established a minimum age of marriage, and banned polygamy and verbal divorces. In addition to these legal changes, Bourguiba established the National Union of Tunisian Women (UNFT), increased educational opportunities, and expanded access to contraceptives for Tunisian women.[27]

To some extent, these relatively progressive top-down gender politics continued under Ben Ali. For instance, Ben Ali's autocratic party, the Rassemblement Constitutionnel Démocratique (RCD) or Democratic Constitutional Rally, adopted internal gender quotas for its local electoral lists.[28] And, more significantly, the push for further improvements to the situation of women and gender equality in Tunisia has continued since 2010. Following the 2010 uprising, Tunisia's new Electoral Law mandated that every electoral list have vertical parity between male and female candidates. This law guarantees that fifty percent of all electoral candidates are women—though, in the three parliamentary elections since 2011, women constituted roughly one-third of the winning members of parliament.[29]

Moreover, historical allies of Bourguiba, including President Essebsi, the first democratically elected president in a direct election, had pushed for additional reforms in 2011. In 2017, Essebsi overturned a decades-old decree in order to grant Tunisian women the right to marry non-Muslim men.[30] This move followed the Tunisian parliament's promulgation of a new law that put in place new protections against gender-based violence.[31] The early reforms of Tunisia's personal status laws under Bourguiba helped to elevate women's rights as a key focus of the regime and develop a constituency for such reforms. While the modes of reproduction of Bourguiba's influence on women's rights remains opaque in some cases, it seems evident that progress in that area may be supported through the mechanisms of institutional and behavioral path dependence discussed later in this chapter.

Another oft-referenced legacy of Bourguiba was his specific ideological commitments to political values such as inclusion and secularism. For example, Thomas Brady of the *New York Times* writes admiringly of Bourguiba's 'faith in liberal modernism,' and Lisa Anderson states that the 'ruling ideology of Bourguiba's Tunisia was inclusive, socially if not politically democratic.'[32] This inclusionary ideology, she argues, laid the groundwork for Ben Ali's National Pact in 1988. However, ultimately this legacy of his appears short-lived, much like the National Pact itself, and, importantly, this overlooks the waves of repression that Bourguiba himself pursued against his political opponents. Thus, the political value of inclusion was rarely reflected in Bourguiba and Ben Ali's policies, despite the portrayal of Bourguiba as inclusive in some accounts, in part because tangible institutional mechanisms were not established. Fittingly, not long after it was drafted, the inclusive National Pact gave way to the unforgiving repression of the regime's political opponents.[33]

However, this view of Bourguiba as having specific and strong ideological commitments that remain influential today is a persistent one. It comes in part from his work on women's rights as discussed above. It also comes from his secularist ideology.[34] After independence, Bourguiba undertook a number of legal reforms and public campaigns aimed directly at undermining the role of religion in society and subordinating religious institutions to his political power. These moves included nationalizing the public *habous* system, dissolving the private *habous* system, and placing the Zeitouna Mosque and University under the control of the Ministry of Education and transforming it into a single department within the University of Tunis.[35] Rachid Ghannouchi, the leader of the Islamist Ennahda movement, argues that Bourguiba's nationalization of the public *habous* lands was the most pernicious of his policies aimed at undercutting the independence of the country's religious institutions.[36] This example demonstrates the institutional changes that may have helped support the historical reproduction of the president's secularist orientation.

Bourguiba's secularist ideology was also reflected in several of his public campaigns. In the 1960s, he famously challenged one of the core tenets of Islam, the fast during Ramadan. He publicly drank orange juice during the hours of the fast in Ramadan, arguing that fasting had a negative effect on economic productivity. In an interview, he said: 'Eventually I hope to make Ramadan the most productive month of the year. For those who want to deny themselves, I suggest an extra hour of work rather than fasting. That will help our economic struggle.'[37] While at times Bourguiba displayed willingness to adopt more religious positions when it was politically expedient, broadly speaking, his tenure is associated with a strong secularist ideology.[38]

While this is suggestive of Bourguiba's ideological legacy, secularism in Tunisia is not his legacy alone. Later in this chapter, I discuss how the French Third Republic's colonial education program also played a historical role in inculcating secular ideas among a certain population of Tunisians.

The Ben Ali Era

The tenure of Ben Ali, who removed Bourguiba from power in November 1987, was a period of both continuity and change. For instance, in many ways, Ben Ali continued to enact policies in the name of gender equality, including further custody protections for women and internal party quotas. In other ways, he sought to distinguish himself from the politics of Bourguiba. While Ben Ali did not allow the Islamist movement, Ennahda, to form a political party, he initially made overtures to the movement, freeing its members and re-affirming Tunisia's commitment to an Arab–Muslim identity. Rather than focus on how Ben Ali built upon or disrupted the legacies of Bourguiba, I focus here on two historically significant political developments that came out of the Ben Ali period: economic liberalization and repression and extra-institutional contentious politics.

While policies aimed at economic liberalization began under Bourguiba, after taking power in a bloodless coup in 1987, Ben Ali pursued a series of economic reforms, ostensibly aimed at further integrating Tunisia into the global economy and reducing the role of the state in the economy.[39] The economic restructuring of the Ben Ali regime led to an improved international credit standing, budget deficit reductions, the liberalization of imports, the diversification of domestic production and exports, and a reduction in poverty.[40] These economic changes led, in turn, to a number of significant social changes, including higher literacy rates, further integration into the global economy, and increased access to technology. Francesco Cavatorta and Rikke Hostrup Haugbølle argue that some of these social developments contributed to anti-regime mobilization and the revitalization of trade unionism in the long run.[41]

Despite these economic successes, these policies also had significant costs. Unemployment remained a top concern, the elimination of certain labor protections led to the decline in real wages, and austerity measures squeezed some parts of the population. Importantly, the benefits of these economic policies were not evenly distributed, with certain individuals and regions benefitting more than others. As many critics have observed, the neoliberalism that was initiated in the 1980s led to further marginalization and frustration among Tunisia's youth. Bob Rijkers, Caroline Freund, and Antonio Nucifora show that firms connected to the Ben Ali family made up a disproportionate share of profits between 2006 and 2010.[42] Some also attribute patterns of regional inequality to a perceived regional favoritism in economic benefits.[43] Finally, Hibou argues that one important long-run legacy of this economic liberalization is that there remains an ideological commitment to neoliberal policies among the country's technocrats.[44] Overall, this period of economic liberalization represents a critical juncture in Tunisia because of the social changes associated with it, the reconfigured way in which the state controlled the economy, and the rise and dominance of technocratic ideas associated with liberalization.

Economic liberalization aside, one of the most widely discussed legacies of the Ben Ali regime was his aggressive use of repression to marginalize his political opponents. When Ben Ali first came to power, he made some overtures to the political opposition as embodied in the National Pact of 1988.[45] But this thaw in relations was short-lived. In the early 1990s, roughly eight thousand members of Ennahda were arrested and an estimated thirty thousand members were arrested over the course of the subsequent decade.[46]

Research on the legacy of this repression suggests that it had far-reaching effects that play a significant role in contemporary Tunisian politics. At the individual level, Hibou states that repression in the Ben Ali period can have long-run individual effects on those imprisoned or their families, as well as those who suffered economically under the former regime. Under the Ben Ali regime, those incarcerated experienced a form of 'social death' after their release from prison, the consequences of which are long-term.[47] This social ostracism included forms of exclusion from certain professions and from registering at Tunisian universities, which can continue to affect an individual's life even after the fall of the regime. Sharan Grewal finds that politicians' experiences with repression and exile also affects their current political beliefs: Islamist politicians who were in exile in the West are more likely to vote to defend freedom of conscience and against enshrining Islamic law into the Constitution than their counterparts who remained in Tunisia.[48]

At a societal level, Elizabeth Nugent argues that repression in the Ben Ali period has shaped the level of political polarization between the political elites today. In Tunisia, because the Ben Ali regime engaged in widespread repression of both Islamist and non-Islamist groups, such as the Tunisian Communist Workers' Party (PCOT), the polarization between competing opposition groups is lower than that in countries like Egypt, which engaged in targeted repression under former President Hosni Mubarak. This has important political implications as lower affective and preference polarization can facilitate elite compromise.[49]

Moreover, as Laryssa Chomiak points out, while Ben Ali's repression limited the avenues for oppositional political activity through formal and institutional structures, the Ben Ali period also witnessed a rise in informal and extra-institutional political activities. These activities included the 2008 protests against the state-run Compagnie Phosphate de Gafsa (Gafsa Phosphate Company, CPG) in Gafsa and Redeyef, two towns in Tunisia's mining basin, as well as political events and debates organized online.[50] These extra-institutional acts of contention remain an important mode of political expression today. Chantal Berman's research shows continuity in the demands and tactics of the social movements of Tunisia's mining region before and after the 2010 uprising. These movements continue to make similar demands for employment and eschew formal party politics in favor of working through unions and local protest movements.[51]

Mechanisms of Historical Persistence

The legacies outlined above are by no means exhaustive, but they illustrate the critical junctures and political trends that have animated Tunisian politics for over a hundred years and remain relevant areas of political and social research today. However, for historical institutions, events, and individuals to exert a legacy on Tunisia's post-revolution politics, the mechanisms of historical persistence need to be clearly identified and examined. Returning to Hibou's critique of culturalist explanations of autocratic persistence: 'If there is indeed reproduction, what does it mean, and how is it carried out?'[52]

Many of the social and political outcomes discussed have been attributed to historical persistence or path dependence. Paul Pierson summarizes path dependence as the idea that 'particular courses of action, once introduced, can be virtually impossible to reverse; and consequently, political development is often punctuated by critical moments or junctures that shape the basic contours of social life.'[53]

Path dependence, however, should not be understood to mean that places or political dynamics are inevitable or cannot change but rather that there are costs to reversing course, particularly once certain institutional arrangements or patterns of behavior become entrenched. There are several mechanisms of persistence that help explain why certain events or policies continue to exercise an enduring effect on Tunisian political life. In this section, I discuss two broad mechanisms of persistence: institutional path dependence and behavioral path dependence or socialization. I offer examples for how the political outcomes described above are the results of replication through these mechanisms.

Institutional Path Dependence

Historical persistence often results from institutions that, once in place, create incentives for a certain type of behavior and norms to persist. One common example is the historical legacy of legal institutions, such as colonial legal systems, which can continue to influence outcomes like property rights and women's rights, even after the colonial administration has departed.[54] This type of institutional path dependence through legal institutions may be relevant for understanding why Tunisia's state centralization and bureaucratization during the colonial period have such significance today. As Khellaf illustrates, many of the challenges for decentralization efforts in Tunisia are the result of administrative and legal structures that supported centralization and were reinforced during the colonial period.[55] Similarly, institutional path dependence and Pierson's concept of increasing returns may explain Tunisia's steady commitment to women's rights. The personal status laws promulgated by Bourguiba helped to elevate the social status of women and ensured that—at least a subset of—women became an important political constituency. As women gained further social and political bargaining power as a result of the personal status laws, a reversal of these laws became increasingly costly. For instance, while there was some opposition to reforms, the laws also empowered certain women, developing a constituency who would balk at any reversals to those laws and, over time, might make demands for further reforms.

199

Institutional path dependence also operates through investments in infrastructure and public goods, including schooling and education. In their study of inequality in the Americas, Stanley Engerman and Kenneth Sokoloff show the persistence of early colonial investments in education,[56] and in her work Elise Huillery finds that French colonial investments in education in West Africa continue to have an effect on local educational outcomes today, in part because of the significance of the initial physical infrastructure.[57] This type of mechanism is important for understanding the persistence of colonial educational investments, which I will discuss below, as well as for understanding the persistence of regional inequality, whether resulting from uneven colonial investments in infrastructure like roads and railroads or exacerbated by Ben Ali's unequal distribution of economic resources such as foreign investment. Likewise, institutional path dependence can also operate through the lack of investment in a particular institution. For instance, creating a new independent financial base for the Zeitouna Mosque and University system is only more challenging today because the public *habous* system that had supported it was dismantled. Many of the historical legacies identified above result from a form of institutional path dependence, whether through laws or the creation (or dismantling) of particular institutions. Future work should examine precisely how new institutions arise and how those institutions alter the incentives that political actors face over the short and long term.

Behavioral Path Dependence

In addition to institutional path dependence, historical persistence can also operate through the transmission of norms, beliefs, and behaviors.[58] In their study of the legacy of slavery in the American South, Acharya, Blackwell, and Sen find that in the areas where slavery was more prevalent in the nineteenth century, whites today are more conservative, specifically on issues of race. They argue that this legacy of slavery exists because of family and community socialization, or what they call behavioral path dependence.[59] In her study of the protest movement in Morocco, Adria Lawrence suggests that the protest leaders are motivated to lead current protests because they learned political values and activism from their parents (intergenerational transmission) who had previously suffered repression for political activism.[60] Wendy Pearlman finds that protest leaders can attract new protest participants through appeals to moral identity and demonstrations of the joy of agency (community transmission).[61]

Experiences like conscription for war can lead to the development and transmission of new norms and political beliefs. Conscripted soldiers may be affected by their service through learning and training, exposure to a broader national 'imagined community,' and the development of new grievances against mistreatment by the colonial administration. These values can then be shared with family and community members. Similarly, norms associated with secularist or Islamist ideology are likely to be transmitted through behavioral path dependence. Once an individual has adopted a set of political beliefs, there is evidence that they often share them with their family through conversations at home and through modeled behavior by the parents. In their study of the United States, Jennings, Stoker, and Bowers find that political and religious orientations are some of the beliefs most likely to be transmitted from parent to child.[62]

Additionally, research has shown that attitudes related to experiences with repression, in particular, tend to be shared among a broader community and transmitted within families. Lisa Blaydes shows that repression in Iraq reinforced communal identities and the group members' sense of 'linked fate.'[63] In the case of Ben Ali's Tunisia, Nugent finds that shared experiences of repression and imprisonment reduced both affective and preference polarization between opposition groups.[64] These extra-institutional mechanisms for the reproduction of historical legacies, particularly within families, warrant further exploration in the Tunisian context. Future research should examine how and why certain beliefs are transmitted within families and communities.

In the next section, I examine two political trends in Tunisia; regional inequality and the Islamist–secular cleavage. I explore these institutional and extra-institutional mechanisms in the context of those two political issues.

What Can History Teach Us about Tunisia Today?

There are many contemporary political patterns and current events that researchers seek to understand by examining the critical junctures, individuals, or policies that preceded them. But not everything that precedes an important political outcome has some direct effect on ensuring or realizing that specific political or social development. Instead, new policies may in fact be endogenous to a historical trend that is already operative. And many phenomena have multiple historical causes that feed into each other. For instance, some researchers argue that the Sahel region of Tunisia is more developed than the interior regions primarily because Bourguiba and Ben Ali favored their home regions along the coast.[65] As I discuss below, however, there is also evidence that changes in the colonial settlement patterns around World War I led to greater colonial investments in the coastal regions. Thus, regional inequality existed to some degree before independence, but was likely exacerbated by post-independence policies. Work on historical legacies in Tunisia can help to identify how important issues like regional inequality are reproduced over multiple regimes through both self-reinforcing institutions and other forms of path dependence.

I selected the examples of regional inequality and the Islamist–secularist cleavage in this section not only because of their continued importance in Tunisian politics but also because the post-revolutionary period represents an opportunity for a break with past patterns. These political issues, I argue, can be traced back to the colonial period, if not earlier. I examine some of the ways that regional inequality and the Islamist–secularist cleavage were reinforced through policies pursued by both the Bourguiba and Ben Ali regimes through until today.

Regional Inequalities: A Case Study in Historical Legacy

Research on early state development in North Africa and the impact of the centralized colonial administration suggests that state penetration in Tunisia was quite high compared to its neighbors, and, thus, the disparities between the center and periphery were, relatively speaking, smaller.[66] While this is true in contrast to Algeria and Libya, regional inequalities in Tunisia remain an issue of central importance, having gained a renewed focus particularly after the 2010 uprising. As several recent reports show, these regional disparities encompass a wide range of outcomes, from significant differences in unemployment rates and rates of educational attainment to disparate poverty rates and levels of economic investment.[67] By almost all of these measures, the Sahel region on Tunisia's eastern coast performs better than nearly all other regions, particularly the western and southern regions of the country. These regional inequalities have implications beyond current economic and educational outcomes. Work by Berman and Nugent shows that the historical patterns of regional favoritism and marginalization produce heterogeneity in voters' attitudes toward redistribution.[68]

How has Tunisia's history shaped these regional inequalities and what does that history suggest about efforts to address these disparities now? Many researchers have highlighted the regional favoritism displayed under the previous autocratic regimes, particularly under the rule of Ben Ali. In his study of smuggling along the Tunisian border, Hamza Meddeb highlights how many Tunisians recognize that the interior or border regions suffered significantly under Ben Ali.[69] Berman and Nugent attribute the regional differences in voters' preferences to unequal redistributive policies enacted by the previous regime.

And the evidence *does* suggest that Ben Ali exacerbated regional inequalities through policies that favored or punished certain regions. However, these same patterns of regional inequality were evident long before Ben Ali assumed power. As Khellaf demonstrates, the decentralization of reforms introduced in the 1970s—which were largely unsuccessful—were aimed in part at trying to reduce regional disparities, particularly in the ability of municipalities to raise revenue. Khellaf writes:

> In the early 1970s, the Tunisian government started giving particular attention to the issue of regional economic development and institutional development of the local and regional administrations. According to official documents, the

203

factors that have pushed the Tunisian government to give so much attention to these issues were the growing economic disparities between regions, the excessive centralization of public functions and congestion of the central administration, and the lack of citizen participation in the public life at the local level.[70]

While Khellaf is focused on the Bourguiba era, how the urbanization and local development of many of Tunisia's coastal regions had already begun to accelerate under French colonial rule deserves close attention.[71]

At the beginning of the French protectorate in Tunisia, the French colonial administration was not formally involved in the process of land colonization, in contrast to the land settlement policies pursued in Algeria. However, as French control and interest in Tunisia grew, so did the pressure to make land, particularly prime agricultural land, available to more French citizens.[72] To meet growing French demand for access to land in Tunisia, the colonial administration established a Colonization Service in Tunisia in February 1898. Gustave Wolfrom, the inaugural head of the Colonialization Service, was eager to expand the Colonization Service and French access to rural, agricultural land, including *habous* lands. Under Wolfrom's leadership, the French protectorate's Directorate for Agriculture and Commerce greatly expanded its efforts to produce agricultural land surveys and widely publicized lists of properties available for purchase. These catalogs provided details on each property, including its precise location, its agricultural suitability, average rainfall, and price per hectare.[73] These land surveys facilitated the identification and expropriation of the most valuable lands, particularly in terms of greater potential agricultural productivity.

The French appetite for control of land in Tunisia continued to evolve following World War I and the demands for land redistribution to French citizens grew for several reasons, including, notably, because the number of war veterans seeking concessions from the state increased and the new economic opportunities in the periphery of the French Empire.[74] This meant not only that the French population expanded, but that the form of the colonization and the type of settlers also changed. As Julia Clancy-Smith notes, changes in the colonial period reflect the intersection of colonialism, globalization, and 'coastalization' at play in Tunisia at that time.[75]

Until the early 1930s, Italian settlers in Tunisia outnumbered French settlers, but this pattern rapidly changed amid the rising nationalism of the early twentieth century and the growing French settlement that followed World War I. Figure 9.1 shows the Tunisian, French, and Italian populations in the country between 1871 and 1966. Prior to World War I, the French and Italian populations were growing rapidly, although the Italian population exceeded that of the

Figure 9.1: French, Italian, and Tunisian Populations in Tunisia, 1871–1966[76]

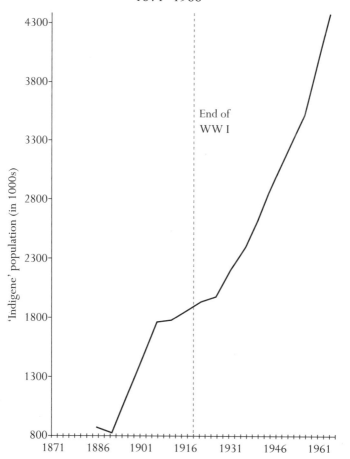

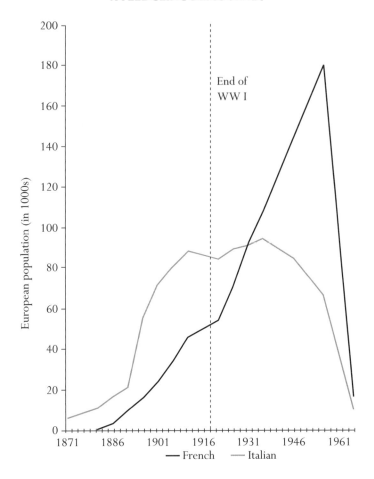

French. After the war, however, the Italian population plateaued and then contracted; at the same time, the French population continued to expand, overtaking the Italian population in absolute terms by the time of the 1931 census.[77]

The rapid settlement of Tunisia by the French after World War I did not affect all regions of Tunisia equally. Notably, prior to World War I, many of the rural interior regions of the northwest were heavily colonized by French agricultural settlers. Although prior to World War I there were more French colonists in Tunisia's coastal region, it was only after World War I that a large gap developed in the French settlement populations of the coastal regions versus the interior regions. This change marks an important shift in terms of Tunisian regional development, with the coastal areas moving further ahead of the interior regions in terms of colonial investments, particularly infrastructure. This differential colonial investment is an example of institutional path dependence; in this case, coastal regions that received a greater share of these investments could continue to build on these investments in the colonial and post-independence periods.

Figure 9.2 contrasts the pre- and post-war French population in the coastal regions with that of Tunisia's interior regions.[78] While the pre-war trends in population growth are comparable in coastal and interior regions, albeit higher along the coast, in the post-World War I period, French settlement in the coastal regions rapidly accelerated, while settlement in the interior regions continued to grow at its slower pre-war pace.

Figure 9.2: Pre- and Post-World War I French Population in Coastal Regions versus in Interior Regions

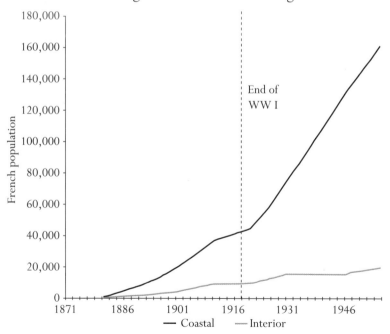

Following World War I, new French settlement was concentrated in the more coastal *contrôles* like Sousse and Bizerte. This agglomeration effect to the already urbanized and suburbanized areas is significant because it suggests that the post-war French population not only expanded, but also changed in form. Instead of individuals involved in farming and agriculture making up the bulk of new arrivals to Tunisia, the post-war immigration included more individuals involved in commerce and industry. Accordingly, these new settlers were less interested in large agricultural plots, instead seeking smaller properties closer to existing urban and industrial centers, particularly close to the port cities. Chomiak describes how colonization exacerbated the country's regional inequalities: 'The re-organization of the economy from a pre-colonial integrated system linking the countryside to major towns and cities into a centralized colonial export-oriented economy based on industrialization of the coastal littoral, increased rural/urban inequalities.'[79]

Over the medium to long term, these changes had a significant impact on the Tunisian population, including rural displacement and urban migration to the larger local economies along the coasts. Figure 9.3 depicts the pre- and post-war Tunisian population in Tunisia's coastal versus interior regions. In the 1930s and 1940s, the Tunisian population in the coastal regions was growing more rapidly and overtook the interior regions.

While growing regional inequalities were already apparent during the colonial period and particularly after World War I, the legacy of colonial investments in local infrastructure and institutions, along with policies adopted by the Bourguiba and Ben Ali regimes, further reinforced these regional disparities. The newly independent regime built its economic plans on top of the pre-existing colonial economies. According to Chomiak, post-independence policies 'perpetuated colonial-era wealth accumulation in major cities and port-towns.'[80] Dirk Vandewalle notes that some of the economic successes of the Bourguiba era masked 'a growing disparity between an affluent urban society and the rest of the country.'[81]

In addition to building upon the economic orientation of the colonial administration, there is evidence that the Sahel region became a favored region of both the Bourguiba and Ben Ali

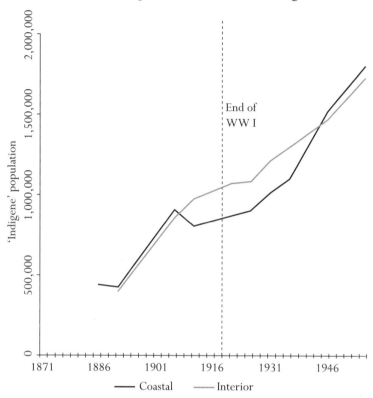

Figure 9.3: Pre- and Post-World War I North African Population in Coastal Regions versus in Interior Regions

administrations because both presidents and many ministers in the government hailed from the coast. This type of favoritism is well-documented, with the Ben Ali era in particular witnessing the rise in wealth of the Ben Ali family and their affiliated companies.[82]

This discussion of the history of regional disparities is important because it continues to reverberate in post-revolutionary Tunisian politics. As Irene Weipert-Fenner points out in Chapter 6 of this volume, regional inequalities remain highly salient today and often serve to mobilize social movements and protests. Frustrations over persistent patterns of regional wealth distribution and infrastructure investments were reflected in campaigns like Winou el Pétrole and Manich Msameh, which drew nationwide support.

The issue raised by these campaigns has a long history based on years of uneven development in Tunisia's regions. The historical approach highlights how these long-run patterns are often reinforced through policymaking across multiple administrations. By identifying that these regional inequalities are caused only in part by the Ben Ali regime's regional favoritism, this discussion highlights that the issue of regional inequalities will not disappear as a result of his removal from power alone. More work needs to be done to understand the complex set of institutions, such as investments in education and local infrastructure, that reinforce these disparities.

The Islamist–Secularist Cleavage: A Case Study in Historical Legacy

In October 2013, Tunisia's National Constituent Assembly opened debate on a draft law introduced by the Islamist movement, Ennahda. The bill proposed restoring the country's *habous* system, which Bourguiba had abolished at independence. The draft law sparked immediate controversy. Houcine Dimassi, a Tunisian politician affiliated with the main secular party at the time, Nidaa Tounes, warned the public that, if passed, the law would create a 'religious state in the state.'[83] While supporters of the draft law believed that the re-establishment of the *habous* system was a symbol of religious liberty and the freedom of religious institutions in the country, the law's critics argued that it represented an existential threat to the Tunisian state's commitment to secular values. Ultimately, the draft law failed, but the controversy regarding the *habous* system illustrates the deep disagreement in Tunisia regarding the appropriate relationship between the state and religious institutions, the main basis of the cleavage between Tunisia's Islamist and secular factions.[84]

This deep ideological rift between those advocating for greater freedom for religious institutions to influence public life and those calling for religious authority to be completely subordinated to political authority is not a new feature of politics in Tunisia. In 1939, Henri de Montety described the Tunisian intellectual elite as divided between those affiliated with Zeitouna Mosque and

University and the 'Gallicized' elite connected to the country's French institutions.[85] How does this Tunisian history shed new light on the country's Islamist–secularist cleavage? Importantly, looking at the early development of this split, it is clear that issues like the *habous* draft law reflect long-run disagreements between Islamists and secularists about the appropriate relationship between the state and religious institutions. These competing visions are grounded in each side's historical experience and in the ambitions each faction had for Tunisia at independence. A historical lens suggests that these political preferences, both for the secularists and the Islamists, are a meaningful dimension of their political ideologies, with similar debates recurring in different periods of Tunisian history. Additionally, a historical view highlights that the secular political parties today are not simply the residual category for non-Islamist parties, but in fact articulate a clear ideology that has its roots in the colonial era.

In the following section, I examine the early development of this Islamist–secular cleavage and its connection to today.[86] I argue that the differential provision of French and Islamic education under colonial rule gave rise to regional variation in the development and spread of secular and Islamist ideas among the Tunisian population. Moreover, the historical patterns of support for Bourguiba's secular faction of the nationalist movement correspond to areas of support for the current secular parties, and the views articulated by Tunisian secularists both historically and today focus on many of the same ideas about the role of the state in controlling religious institutions.

Prior to the arrival of the French in Tunisia, the education system largely consisted of a network of primary schools (*kuttabs*) and mosques that provided education and were funded primarily through the *habous* system, through which individuals could endow the revenue from their land or property to finance a school or mosque in perpetuity. While the Ottoman elite endowed some of these institutions and the Ottoman administration managed the Habous Administration, the state had a fairly limited role in education at that time.

Upon the establishment of the protectorate, the French immediately began to transform the education sector in Tunisia.

When the French created a Directorate of Public Education in 1883, there were only 24 schools with French-language instruction in the country and approximately 500 *kuttabs*.[87] Of the 24 French schools, 20 were religious and only 4 followed a secular (*laïc*) curriculum. However, the number of French secular schools rapidly increased, while the number of French religious schools remained low. By 1890, there were 61 secular French schools and, by 1900, there were approximately 130 French secular schools with more than 5,000 Tunisian students enrolled.

The impact of French colonization on Tunisian access to secular education was uneven across the country. In localities with high numbers of French settlers, the impact of colonization was two-fold. First, the settlers brought with them demands for French education, thus the French administration was more likely to install French secular schools in those locations. Second, high levels of local French colonization often disrupted the local Islamic school system because *habous* properties, which funded Islamic education, were more likely to be expropriated in places with the higher French demand for land. Accordingly, in high French settlement areas, more Tunisians were enrolled in secular schools than in areas with lower levels of French settlement.

The differential access to secular and Islamic education across Tunisia created lasting differences in the social and political attitudes of the individuals trained in each system. This was as a result of the French secular schooling emphasis on values of the French Third Republic, such as *laïcité*, and the subordination of religious institutions to the state. These values were in tension with the relatively decentralized Islamic education system funded through the Habous Administration that favored less centralized state control over education. The role of learning and sharing secular values within a community and family that underpins the long-run impact of colonial schooling on secularist attitudes is an example of behavioral path dependence as a mechanism of historical persistence. These divisions in the Tunisian population are reflected in de Montety's observation about the Zeitouna-affiliated elite and the 'Gallicized' Tunisian elite, as well as in the divisions that developed among the leadership of the nationalist Neo-Destour. They are also evident in the regional patterns of support for the Islamist and secular factions of the Neo-Destour movement.

The divisions within the nationalist movement were embodied in the ideological orientations of two of the movement's leaders, Bourguiba and his contemporary, Salah Ben Youssef. While Bourguiba articulated values consistent with the more secular, Western-oriented faction of the Neo-Destour party, Ben Youssef maintained close ties with the Zeitouna-affiliated elite and adopted a more pan-Islamic and pan-Arab nationalist ideology that wanted to see Tunisia's religious elite given more power. Observers at the time noted the strain between some of the Neo-Destour's more secular members and the Zeitouna-affiliated members: 'the Zaytouna bloc "[finds itself] completely alienated by the Neo-Destourian tendency to adopt western modes of thought. They are essentially arabophones as against the gallophones of the Neo-Destour."'[88]

Following one of Ben Youssef's speeches in which he criticized Bourguiba's negotiations with the French government, Bourguiba removed Ben Youssef from the Neo-Destour's political bureau. However, Ben Youssef maintained a significant base of support, particularly among the religious establishment and a more religious subset of the population. Examining regional levels of political mobilization for the Bourguiba and Ben Youssef factions during Tunisia's first National Constituent Assembly elections in March 1956, I find that mobilization for the secular Bourguibist faction is higher in regions with greater French settlement (Figure 9.4).[89] This pattern of support for Bourguiba's more secular nationalism maps onto the patterns of Tunisian access to secular education indicating an ideological dimension to Bourguiba's support base.

Moreover, this positive correlation between French colonial settlement and local support for secularism carries over to contemporary patterns of electoral support for Tunisia's secular political parties. Specifically, when examining the results of the 2014 election, greater French settlement is positively correlated with support for Nidaa Tounes, the primary secular political party during the 2014 elections.[90] Notably, the regional pattern of support for secularist and Islamist parties in 2014 corresponds to the regional patterns of support for Bourguiba and Ben Youssef in 1956. Figure

9.5 displays the bivariate correlation between Ennahda's share of the 2014 two-party vote and 1914 levels of French settlement.[91] These patterns of support persist even though Bourguiba, with the backing of the French administration, ultimately defeated Ben Youssef's Islamist-oriented faction,[92] and despite the Ben Ali's regime's two decades of harsh repression of Islamists. So how has this Islamist–secular cleavage persisted?

Figure 9.4: Political Mobilization for the Secular and Islamist Factions of the Nationalist Movement, March 1956

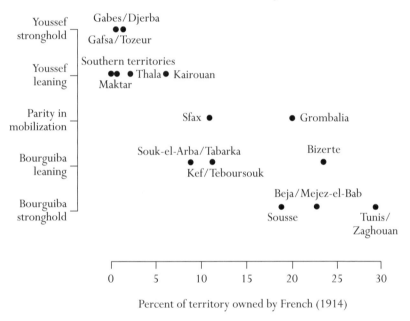

In addition to religious institutions, this historical perspective suggests that other institutions may have played an important role in the transmission of Islamist and secular values. The initial investments in French secular education (or lack thereof in certain regions) may operate as a mechanism of persistence. For example, secular Tunisian schooling may have been more available even after independence in the regions that had historically higher levels of French secular schooling as a result of earlier investments in school infrastructure

Figure 9.5: Ennahda Share of the Two-Party Vote
(versus Nidaa Tounes), 2014

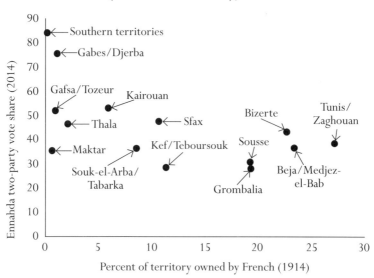

(e.g., buildings and teachers). In fact, there is evidence in Tunisia of persistent regional inequalities in educational attainment, despite the nationalization of the education system at independence.[93]

Additionally, there are non-institutional modes of reproduction that likely played a role in the transmission of secular and Islamist values over the course of the Bourguiba and Ben Ali regimes through until today: intergenerational transmission and community socialization. Community socialization and reproduction of secular and Islamist values may have occurred through the repression of Ben Youssef and his allies. As Elizabeth Nugent and Lisa Blaydes each find, group-level repression and targeting by the state can increase group members' identification with that group identity and group solidarity.[94] Instead of eliminating a more Islamist orientation, experiences with repression may have strengthened that identity for some.

While the broad patterns of Islamist and secularist support signal continuity between the past and the present, there are also important discontinuities in the post-revolutionary period. For instance, the examples of cooperation between Islamist and secularist parties within the government mark a clear break with past patterns of conflict between the two groups and with the secularists' dominance of Tunisian state institutions.

This discussion of the distinct ideological orientations that constitute the Islamist–secular cleavage and the mechanisms through which they are reproduced highlights the persistence of this dimension of Tunisian politics. It also suggests that, even amid compromise, Islamist and secular political parties may struggle over certain issues, such as laws that challenge or change the relationship of the state to religious institutions. Importantly, this is not just because of a certain interpretation pursued by the Islamists—it also results from the secular faction's strong ideological commitments on issues pertaining to religion that have developed over the last century.

Conclusion

There are, as this chapter illustrates, some long-run political patterns or critical junctures that continue to shape Tunisian politics today, even a decade after the country's revolution. These long-run legacies often persist because a political decision or critical policy change a century ago established a set of self-reinforcing behaviors or institutions that raise the cost of reversing course. For instance, the pattern of regional inequalities in infrastructure and levels of education continues to attract organizations looking to invest in Tunisia to coastal regions, only further exacerbating coastal and interior regions' disparate levels of development.

Despite the important continuities between Tunisia's pre-revolution past and today, the revolution marked a significant departure from the way politics was previously exercised in the country, and the post-revolutionary period was characterized by notable discontinuities as well. One of the most important discontinuities is the transformation of Tunisia's political institutions and changes to the processes of both formal and informal politics. With the opening up of the political sphere, Tunisia has now held several democratic elections, including the country's first free and fair municipal elections in 2018, in which local councils and mayors were democratically elected in each of Tunisia's 350 municipalities.

In addition to formal politics, Tunisia has also witnessed important changes in the realm of informal politics; while some of the demands and tactics of the protest movements remain the same, the post-revolutionary period experienced a drastic increase in the number of protest events.[95] With regard to challenges like persistent regional inequalities, these changes to both formal and informal politics have created new pathways for citizens to hold the government accountable and keep attention on addressing these long-run challenges. Over time, these changes could alter the current status quo of regional inequalities through the transformation of the political ruling class, a shift in incentives for investment, or simply holding politicians accountable for inaction.

The changes to the Tunisian political system also highlight another important discontinuity with the pre-revolutionary period: the cooperation between Islamist and secularist political parties and the peaceful transition of power between different governing coalitions over the last decade. As noted above, although Bourguiba and Ben Ali did, at times, accommodate the Islamist opposition, Ennahda and its predecessor, Mouvement de la Tendance Islamique (MTI), had a primarily adversarial relationship with both regimes and were not permitted to participate formally in politics and governing. Thus, while the Islamist–secular cleavage persists, the process through which the different sides interact and resolve disagreements has changed. In the medium to long term, this change in the process of interacting could potentially undermine that particular political cleavage rather than reinforce it. Thus, the full impact of the revolution may not come into view for another several decades.

NOTES

CHAPTER 1. POST-AUTHORITARIAN GOVERNANCE AND
ELUSIVE STABILITY

1. Inmaculada Szmolka, 'Political Change in North Africa and the Arab Middle East: Constitutional Reforms and Electoral Processes,' *Arab Studies Quarterly* 36, no. 2 (2014): 128–148.
2. See, for instance, Alfred Stepan, 'Tunisia's Transition and the Twin Tolerations,' *Journal of Democracy* 23, no. 2 (2012): 89–103; Borzou Daragahi, 'Tunisia is a Shining Example of Democracy in a World Hellbent on Backsliding into Chaos: Why is the West Ignoring it?,' *Independent*, July 28, 2019, www.independent.co.uk/voices/tunisia-beji-essebsi-democracy-middle-east-us-aid-a9024036.html.
3. These range from 'Doustourna,' which played an important role during the drafting of the Constitution, and 'I-Watch,' an anti-corruption watchdog organization, to 'Baswala,' which works to enhance transparency and improve the work of the parliament.
4. Katharina Natter, 'Revolution and Political Transition in Tunisia: A Migration Game Changer,' *Migration Information Source*, May 28, 2015, www.migrationpolicy.org/article/revolution-and-political-transition-tunisia-migration-game-changer.
5. Habiba Boumlik and Joni Schwartz, 'Conscientization and Third Space: A Case Study of Tunisian Activism,' *Adult Education Quarterly* 66, no. 4 (2016): 321.
6. See Safwan M. Masri, *Tunisia: An Arab Anomaly* (New York, NY: Columbia University Press, 2017), 293, 95; Emma C. Murphy, 'The Tunisian Elections of October 2011: A Democratic Consensus,' *Journal of North African Studies* 18, no. 2 (2013): 242–243; and Sharan Grewal, 'Tunisian Democracy at a Crossroads,' Brookings, *Policy Brief*, February 2019,

www.brookings.edu/wp-content/uploads/2019/02/FP_20190226_tunisia_grewal.pdf.

7. Murphy, 'The Tunisian Elections of October 2011,' 234.
8. Ibid., 237.
9. Masri, *Tunisia: An Arab Anomaly*, 69.
10. Amel Boubekeur, 'Islamists, Secularists and Old Regime Elites in Tunisia: Bargained Competition,' *Mediterranean Politics* 21, no. 1 (2016): 107–127.
11. Grewal, 'Tunisian Democracy at a Crossroads.'
12. Boubekeur, 'Islamists, Secularists and Old Regime Elites in Tunisia,' 108; Sharan Grewal and Shadi Hamid, 'The Dark Side of Consensus in Tunisia: Lessons from 2005–2019,' Brookings, January 2020, www.brookings.edu/wp-content/uploads/2020/01/FP_20200131_tunisia_consensus_grewal_hamid.pdf.
13. Lamine Ghanmi, 'Tunisian Islamist Figure Resigns from Party in Widening Split in Ennahda's Leadership,' *Arab Weekly*, March 8, 2020, https://thearabweekly.com/tunisian-islamist-figure-resigns-party-widening-split-ennahdas-leadership.
14. Anne Wolfe, 'Is Rached Ghanouchi Ennahda's President for Life: Leadership Struggles Pose Challenge to Tunisia's Largest Party,' Washington, DC: Project of Middle East Democracy, 2021, https://pomed.org/wp-content/uploads/2021/07/Anne-Wolf_Ghannouchi-Report_proof_FINAL_reduced.pdf?x18047.
15. Hind Ahmed Zaki, 'Resisting and Redefining State Violence: The Gendered Politics of Transitional Justice in Tunisia,' *The Journal of the Middle East and Africa* 9, no. 4 (2018): 376.
16. Farah Samti, 'In Tunisia, a New Reconciliation Law Stokes Protest and Conflict Instead,' *Foreign Policy*, September 15, 2015, https://foreignpolicy.com/2015/09/15/in-tunisia-a-new-reconciliation-law-stokes-protest-and-conflict-instead; Sarah Yerkes and Marwan Muasher, 'Tunisia's Corruption Contagion: A Transition at Risk,' Carnegie Endowment for International Peace, October 25, 2017, https://carnegieendowment.org/2017/10/25/tunisia-s-corruption-contagion-transition-at-risk-pub-73522.
17. Kora Andrieu, 'Confronting the Dictatorial Past in Tunisia: Human Rights and the Politics of Victimhood in Transitional Justice Discourses since 2011,' *Human Rights Quarterly* 38, no. 2 (2016): 261–293.
18. Ibid.
19. Omar Belhaj Salah, 'Tunisia: A Democracy and a Police State?', *Middle East Eye*, February 26, 2015, www.middleeasteye.net/opinion/tunisia-democracy-and-police-state; Alex Walsh, 'Restarting Police Reform in Tunisia: The Importance of Talking about Everyday Security,'

Middle East Institute, March 26, 2019, www.mei.edu/publications/restarting-police-reform-tunisia-importance-talking-about-everyday-security.

20. Amnesty International, 'Tunisia: Members of Parliament Must Reject Legalizing Impunity for Security Forces,' October 5, 2020, www.amnesty.org/en/latest/news/2020/10/tunisia-members-of-parliament-must-reject-legalizing-impunity-for-security-forces.

21. Frederic Wehrey, 'Tunisia's Wake-Up Call: How Security Challenges from Libya are Shaping Defense Reforms,' Carnegie Endowment for International Peace, March 18, 2020, https://carnegieendowment.org/2020/03/18/tunisia-s-wake-up-call-how-security-challenges-from-libya-are-shaping-defense-reforms-pub-81312.

22. International Crisis Group, 'Tunisia: Violence and the Salafi Challenge,' *Middle East and North Africa Report* no. 137, February 13, 2013, https://d2071andvip0wj.cloudfront.net/tunisia-violence-and-the-salafi-challenge.pdf.

23. Moncef Kartas, 'Foreign Aid and Security Sector Reform in Tunisia: Resistance and Autonomy of the Security Forces,' *Mediterranean Politics* 19, no. 3 (2014): 373–391.

24. Ruth Hanau Santini and Giulia Cimini, 'The Politics of Security Reform in Post-2011 Tunisia: Assessing the Role of Exogenous Shocks, Domestic Policy Entrepreneurs and External Actors,' *Middle Eastern Studies* 55, no. 2 (2019): 225–241.

25. Ishac Diwan, 'Tunisia's Upcoming Challenge: Fixing the Economy Before it is Too Late,' *Arab Reform Initiative*, September 23, 2019, www.arab-reform.net/wp-content/uploads/pdf/Arab_Reform_Initiative_en_tunisias-upcoming-challenge-fixing-the-economy-before-its-too-late_6582.pdf?ver=a1af2da58abe0ab2dfcbffaab21f9e99.

26. Ken Roberts, Siyka Kovacheva, and Stanimir Kabaivanov, 'Still Troubled: Tunisia's Youth During and Since the Revolution of 2011,' *Societies* 7, no. 4 (2017): 1–14.

27. Khaled Tababi, 'Al-taqrir al-sanawi lil-hijra 2019' (Migration Annual Report 2019), Forum *Tunisien* pour les Droits Economiques et Sociaux (FTDES), 2019, http://ftdes.net/rapports/migration2019.pdf.

28. Youssef Cherif, 'Tunisia: Activism on the Rise,' *Global Civic Activism in Flux*, ed. Richard Youngs, Carnegie Endowment for International Peace, March 17, 2017, http://carnegieeurope.eu/2017/03/17/global-civic-activism-in-flux-pub-68301.

29. Hatem Chakroun, 'Rights and Politics: Human Rights Action and Socio-Economic Struggles in Tunisia,' *Arab Reform Initiative*, January 26, 2018, www.arab-reform.net/wp-content/uploads/pdf/Arab_Reform_Initiative_en_rights-and-politics-human-

rights-action-and-socio-economic-struggles-in-tunisia_2637.
pdf?ver=acabc1f9f7815722d6b67f8a4e9ffdeb.

30. Anna Antonakis-Nashif, 'Contested Transformation: Mobilized Publics in Tunisia between Compliance and Protest,' *Mediterranean Politics* 21, no. 1 (2016): 128–149.

31. Karim Mezran and Elissa Miller, 'Tunisia's 2017 Budget: The Rocky Way Ahead,' Atlantic Council, December 12, 2016, www.atlanticcouncil. org/blogs/menasource/tunisia-s-2017-budget-the-rocky-way-ahead.

32. Kamel Laroussi, *Parallel Trade and Smuggling at the Tunisian-Libyan Border Space (1988–2012): Status Quo and Prospects within a Concealed Globalization* (Beirut: Arab Center for Research and Policy Studies, 2018); Kamel Laroussi, 'L'Espace frontalier tuniso-libyen dans la tourmente de la mondialisation et prospection conceptuelle des nouvelles formes d'urbanités et de gouvernances dans les nouvelles "régions économiques"' [The Tunisian-Libyan border area in the turmoil of globalization and conceptual exploration of new forms of urbanity and governance in the new 'economic regions'], *Revue des Régions Arides*, no. 31 (2013): 131–148; and Yerkes and Muasher, 'Tunisia's Corruption Contagion: A Transition at Risk.'

33. Mongi Boughzala and Mohamed Tlili Hamdi, 'Promoting Inclusive Growth in Arab Countries: Rural and Regional Development and Inequality in Tunisia,' Brookings Global Economy & Development, working paper no. 71, February 2014, www.brookings.edu/wp-content/uploads/2016/06/Arab-EconPaper5Boughzala-v3.pdf.

34. Ibid.

35. Ragnar Weilandt, 'Socio-Economic Challenges to Tunisia's Democratic Transition,' *European View* 17, no. 2 (2018): 214.

36. Transparency International, 'Corruption Perceptions Index 2019,' 2019, www.transparency.org/en/cpi/2019/results.

37. Youssef Cherif, 'Tunisia's Risky War on Corruption,' Carnegie Endowment for International Peace, July 18, 2017, https://carnegieendowment. org/sada/71569.

38. Yerkes and Muasher, 'Tunisia's Corruption Contagion: A Transition at Risk.'

39. International Monetary Fund (IMF), 'Tunisia: Fiscal Transparency Evaluation,' *IMF Country Report*, no. 16/339, November 2016, www. imf.org/external/pubs/ft/scr/2016/cr16339.pdf; Lamine Ghanmi, 'Tunisia Enters Debt-to-Repay Cycle,' *The Arab Weekly*, November 3, 2019, https://thearabweekly.com/tunisia-enters-debt-repay-cycle.

40. Chakroun, 'Rights and Politics: Human Rights Action and Socio-Economic Struggles in Tunisia,' 4.

CHAPTER 2. THE TUNISIAN TRANSITION AND AUTHORITARIANISM IN THE MIDDLE EAST

1. Guillermo A. O'Donnell, Philippe C. Schmitter, and Laurence Whitehead, *Transitions from Authoritarian Rule: Tentative Conclusions about Uncertain Democracies* (Baltimore, MD: Johns Hopkins University Press, 1986). See also John Higley and Michael G. Burton, 'The Elite Variable in Democratic Transitions and Breakdowns,' *American Sociological Review* 54, no. 1 (1989): 17–32.

2. O'Donnell, Schmitter, and Whitehead, *Transitions from Authoritarian Rule*, 5; see also Jon C. Pevehouse, 'Democracy from the Outside-in? International Organizations and Democratization,' *International Organizations* 56, no. 3 (2002): 515–549.

3. Hassan Hamdan al-Alkim, 'The Prospect of Democracy in the GCC Countries,' *Critique: Critical Middle Eastern Studies* 5, no. 9 (1996): 29–41.

4. For a summary of the arguments on the persistence of authoritarianism, see Raymond Hinnebusch, 'Authoritarian Persistence, Democratization Theory and the Middle East: An Overview and Critique,' *Democratization* 13, no. 3 (2006): 373–395. See also Eva Bellin, 'The Robustness of Authoritarianism in the Middle East: Exceptionalism in Comparative Perspective,' *Comparative Politics* 36, no. 2 (2004): 139–157; Eva Bellin, 'Reconsidering the Robustness of Authoritarianism in the Middle East,' *Comparative Politics* 44, no. 2 (2012): 127–149; and F. Gregory Gause III, 'Why Middle East Studies Missed the Arab Spring: The Myth of Authoritarian Stability,' *Foreign Affairs* 90, no. 4 (2011): 81–90.

5. See, for example, Isobel Coleman and Terra Lawson-Remer, 'A User's Guide to Democratic Transitions,' *Foreign Policy*, June 18, 2013, https://foreignpolicy.com/2013/06/18/a-users-guide-to-democratic-transitions. She argues that mass movements help transitions, but violence does not. O'Donnell, Schmitter, and Whitehead, on the other hand, consider all mass movements detrimental to democratic transitions (see O'Donnell, Schmitter, and Whitehead, *Transitions from Authoritarian Rule*). Evidence from many countries outside the Middle East suggests that mass movements can facilitate transitions. For example, in Poland the trade union federation Solidarity was an instrumental grassroots movement in democratic transition; similarly, in Indonesia, widespread street protests in 1997–98 and high voter turnout in 1999 gave citizens power in the democratization process.

6. On Islam in Tunisia, see Marina Ottaway, 'Religious Conservativism, Religious Extremism, and Secular Civil Society in North Africa,' in *The Lure of Authoritarianism: The Maghreb after the Arab Spring*, eds., Stephen J.

King and Abdeslam M. Maghraoui (Bloomington, IN: Indiana University Press, 2019), 15–41.

7. Following Independence, the Tunisian General Labor Union (UGTT) formed a coalition with the employers' union (UTICA), the women's organization (UNFT) and the Union of Agriculture and Fisheries (UTAP) with the purpose of 'supporting economic and social programmes of the state.' See Sami Adouani and Saïd Ben Sedrine, 'Trade Union Power and Democratic Transition in Tunisia-The UGTT: A Unique Story, an Unprecedented Experience,' *Friedrich Ebert Stiftung*, January 2018, http://library.fes.de/pdf-files/iez/14064.pdf.

8. Zeitouna, or Ez-Zituna, was the second Mosque built in the Maghreb region with most scholars agreeing its origins begin around 703 CE. Starting in the thirteenth century, Tunis became the capital under Almohad and Hafsid rule and the subsequent shift in power allowed Zeitouna to flourish into the major center of Islamic learning in the region.

9. On the weakness of donor-sponsored civil society, see Marina Ottaway and Thomas Carothers, eds., *Funding Virtue: Civil Society Aid and Democracy Promotion* (Washington, DC: Carnegie Endowment for International Peace, 2000); Michael Edwards, *Civil Society* (Cambridge: Polity Press, 2009); Jude Howell, 'In Their Own Image: Donor Assistance to Civil Society,' *Lusotopie*, no. 9 (2002): 117–130.

10. Ansar al-Shari'a is a Salafi militant group that advocates for strict adherence of Shari'a across Libya and is designated as a terrorist organization by the UN and US. This violent group emerged during the 2011 uprisings has been associated with the 2012 Benghazi attack as well as the assassination of Chokri Belaïd and Mohamed Brahmi in Tunisia in 2013.

11. On the role of the UGTT in turning the self-immolation of a vegetable vendor in Sidi Bouzid into a national uprising, see Kasper Ly Netterstrøm, 'The Tunisian General Labor Union and the Advent of Democracy,' *Middle East Journal* 70, no. 3 (2016): 383–398. The crucial role of the organization is confirmed by the fact that, earlier that year, another case of self-immolation took place in the coastal city of Monastir; it was briefly reported in local newspapers, but had no political repercussions.

12. In November 2009, a wave of small-scale demonstrations and strikes swept through North African countries. The Carnegie Endowment for International Peace, where I directed the Middle East program at the time, invited the leaders of protests in several countries to a seminar in Beirut. A heated discussion broke out among participants about the best way to organize. Some, particularly those coming from the labor unions, favored the traditional method of creating formal organizations. Others, particularly in youth movements, argued that formal organizations were

too vulnerable to government repression and that the best approach was to organize informal and loosely structured networks. Subsequent events in many countries showed that networks could mobilize people quickly, but that formal organizations had more staying power, and thus were ultimately more effective.

13. George Packer, 'Exporting Jihad: The Arab Spring has Given Tunisians the Freedom to Act on their Unhappiness,' *New Yorker*, March 21, 2016, www.newyorker.com/magazine/2016/03/28/tunisia-and-the-fall-after-the-arab-spring; Farida Dahmani, 'Tunisie: Hafedh Caïd Essebsi ou la tentation dynastique' [Tunisia: Hafedh Caïd Essebsi or the Dynastic Temptation], *Jeune Afrique*, June 20, 2018, www.jeuneafrique.com/mag/575907/politique/tunisie-hafedh-caid-essebsi-ou-la-tentation-dynastique.

14. Larbi Sadiki, 'Intra-Party Democracy in Tunisia's Ennahda: Ghannouchi and the Pitfalls of "Charismatic" Leadership,' Middle East Institute, November 25, 2020, www.mei.edu/publications/intra-party-democracy-tunisias-ennahda-ghannouchi-and-pitfalls-charismatic-leadership.

15. Constitute Project, 'Morocco's Constitution of 2011,' trans. Jefri J. Ruchti, 2012, 3, www.usc.es/export9/sites/webinstitucional/gl/institutos/ceso/descargas/Const-Morocco_2011.pdf.

16. Samuel P. Huntington, *The Third Wave: Democratization in the Late Twentieth Century* (Norman, OK: University of Oklahoma Press, 1991).

17. See, for example, Wolfgang Merkel, Raj Kollmorgen, and Hans-Jurgen Wagener, eds., *Handbook of Political, Social and Economic Transformation* (Oxford: Oxford University Press, 2019); see also James L. Payne, 'Did the United States Create Democracy in Germany?', *Independent Review* 11, no. 2 (2006): 209–221.

CHAPTER 3. TRANSITIONAL BODIES, PARTY POLITICS, AND ANTI-DEMOCRATIC POTENTIAL IN TUNISIA

1. Larbi Chouikha and Eric Gobe, 'Politique de l'indépendance en conjoncture politique fluide: Le cas de la Tunisie post-Ben Ali' [The politics of independence in a fluid political context: The case of post-Ben Ali Tunisia], January 10, 2020, https://halshs.archives-ouvertes.fr/halshs-02435218. All quotes from non-English sources were translated by the author.

2. Juan J. Linz, *Totalitarian and Authoritarian Regimes* (Boulder, CO: Lynne Rienner Publishers, 2000).

3. Daniel C. Hallin and Paolo Mancini, *Comparing Media Systems: Three Models of Media and Politics* (Cambridge: Cambridge University Press, 2004), 59.

4. Jean-Pierre Gaudin, *Gouverner par contrat* [Governing by contract] (Paris: Presses de Sciences Po, 1999).

5. Philippe Bezes and Christine Musselin, 'Le New Public Management: Entre rationalisation et marchandisation?' [New Public Management: Between rationalization and commodification?], in *Une 'French Touch' dans l'analyse des politiques publiques?* [A 'French Touch' in the analysis of public policies?], eds. Laurie Boussaguet, et al. (Paris: Presses de Sciences Po, 2015), 125.

6. Philippe Bezes, 'Le tournant néomanagérial de l'administration française' [The neo-managerial turn of the French administration], in *Politiques publiques I: La France dans la gouvernance européenne* [Public policies I: France in European governance], eds. Olivier Borraz and Virginie Guiraudon (Paris: Presses de Sciences Po, 2008), 215.

7. Gilles Massardier, 'Les espaces non pluralistes dans les démocraties contemporaines' [Non-pluralistic spaces in contemporary democracies], in *Autoritarismes démocratiques et démocraties autoritaires au XXIe siècle: Convergences Nord-Sud* [Democratic authoritarianisms and authoritarian democracies in the 21st century: North-South convergences], eds. Olivier Dabène, Vincent Geisser, and Gilles Massardier (Paris: La Découverte, 2008), 33.

8. Pierre Rosanvallon, *La légitimité démocratique: Impartialité, réflexivité, proximité* [Democratic legitimacy: Impartiality, reflexivity, proximity] (Paris: Seuil, 2010), 159.

9. Yannis Papadopoulos, 'Démocratie, gouvernance et "management de l'interdépendance": Des rapports complexes' [Democracy, governance, and the 'management of interdependence': Complex relationships], in *À la recherche de la démocratie* [In search for democracy], ed. Javier Santiso (Paris: Karthala, 2002), 135. In the case of the HAICA, this lack of visibility is reflected in the professional secrecy imposed on its members during the exercise of their mandate and within two years following its expiry (Article 12, DL116).

10. Massardier, 'Les espaces non pluralistes,' 43.

11. Ibid., 39.

12. Philippe Bezes, 'Construire des bureaucraties wébériennes à l'ère du New Public Management ?' [Building Weberian bureaucracies in the era of New Public Management?], *Critique internationale* 35, no. 2 (2007): 19.

13. Ibid., 20.

14. Ibid.

15. Articles 43–45 and 53, and chapter IV of DL116.

16. Mohamed Rami Abdelmoula, 'Tunisie: La mort au coin du verre' [Tunisia: Death at the corner of the glass], *Orient XXI*, June 18, 2020, https://orientxxi.info/magazine/tunisie-la-mort-au-coin-du-verre,3966.

17. One can refer to the polemics surrounding the drama series *Awled Moufida* (Moufida's children), which revolves around the turbulent life of three brothers, including one born out of wedlock, or the series *Nouba*, broadcast in 2019 and 2020, whose characters evolve in the shady environment of the Mezoued music scene.

18. I refer here to Dominique Mehl, *La fenêtre et le miroir: La télévision et ses programmes* [The window and the mirror: Television and its programs] (Paris: Payot, 1992).

19. Jean-Matthieu Méon, 'Contrôle concerté ou censure? L'euphémisation du contrôle public des médias et sa légitimation' [Concerted control or censorship? The euphemization of public control of the media and its legitimation], *Raisons politiques* 1, no. 17 (2005): 150.

20. Jean-Matthieu Méon, 'L'euphémisation de la censure: Le contrôle des médias et la protection de la jeunesse, de la proscription au conseil' [The euphemization of censorship: Media control and youth protection, from proscription to counseling] (PhD diss., University of Strasbourg III, 2003).

21. Méon, 'Contrôle concerté ou censure,' 150.

22. Ibid., 152.

23. See Article 5 of the HAICA guidelines and Article 13 of the annex on children's rights.

24. Méon, 'Contrôle concerté ou censure,' 152.

25. Ibid., 157.

26. Ibid., 159.

27. David P. Dolowitz and David Marsh, 'Learning from Abroad: The Role of Policy Transfer in Contemporary Policy-Making,' *Governance* 13, no. 1 (2000): 16.

28. Transitional organizations and international aid agencies can be identified as agents of coercive policy transfer that 'compel governments to adopt programs and policies against their will;' Dolowitz and Marsh, 'Learning from Abroad,' 14.

29. Michel Dobry, *Sociologie des crises politiques: La dynamique des mobilisations multisectorielles* [Sociology of political crises: The dynamics of multisectoral mobilizations] (Paris: Presses de Sciences Po, 2009).

30. Bilel Kchouk, '"Si vous votez la loi d'exclusion aujourd'hui, c'est vous qui serez exclus demain"' ['If you vote for the exclusion law today, you will be the one excluded tomorrow'], *L'Année du Maghreb* 16 (2017): 319–339.

31. DL116 is often associated with DL115 on freedom of the press. The latter provides for the creation of a Press Council, which is yet to be instituted.

32. Quoted by Rachida Ennaïfer, interview with author, Tunis, December 19, 2016.

33. Republic of Tunisia, *Debates of the High Commission for the Protection of the*

Objectives of the Revolution, Political Reform, and Democratic Transition (in Arabic) (Tunis: Republic of Tunisia, 2012), 931–935; 958–962.

34. Jean-Philippe Bras, 'Le peuple est-il soluble dans la constitution? Leçons tunisiennes' [Can the people be dissolved in the constitution? Tunisian lessons], *L'Année du Maghreb* VIII (2012): 103–119.

35. Nicolas Beau, 'Quand Béji Caïd Essebsi gérait la transition post-Ben Ali' [When Béji Caïd Essebsi was managing the post-Ben Ali transition], *Mondafrique.com*, July 25, 2019, https://mondafrique.com/quand-beji-caid-essebsi-gerait-la-transition-post-ben-ali. Mebazaa was the head of security when Essebsi served as minister of interior (1965–69).

36. In an interview with *La Presse* (06/09/2017), quoted in *Leaders*, Essebsi criticized the independent bodies, which abused their prerogatives, in his view, to the point of threatening the state. Hechmi Nouira, 'Le président Béji Caïd Essebsi à Assahafa et à La Presse: "Le système politique actuel ne peut assurer le développement et la stabilité du pays"' [President Béji Caïd Essebsi to Assahafa and *La Presse*: 'The current political system cannot ensure the development and stability of the country'], *Leaders*, November 6, 2017, www.leaders.com.tn/article/22971-le-president-beji-caid-essebsi-a-assahafa-et-a-la-presse-le-systeme-politique-actuel-ne-peut-assurer-le-developpement-et-la-stabilite-du-pays.

37. Emmanuel Taïeb, '*House of Cards*: Qu'est-ce qu'un coup politique fictionnel?' [*House of Cards*: How far can fiction depict political moves?], *Quaderni* 88 (2015): 67.

38. At the end of April 2012, the Jebali government convened a national consultation on media reform that sparked controversy because it was held before the INRIC report was released and in the presence of caciques in the sector under the former regime. Lilia Weslaty, 'Tunisie: Démarrage très controversé de la consultation nationale sur les medias' [Tunisia: A very controversial start of the national media consultation], *Nawaat*, April 27, 2012, https://nawaat.org/2012/04/27/tunisie-demarrage-tres-controverse-de-la-consultation-nationale-sur-les-medias.

39. The president of the republic appoints the chair of the HAICA, while the head of parliament appoints two members. The Association of Tunisian Magistrates (AMT) appoints two others, the Journalists' Union (SNJT), two more, the UGTT culture subcommittee one, and the media owners' union (STDM) appoints another one (Article 7 DL 116).

40. At the call of many civil society organizations to implement DL115 and DL116, the first was organized on October 17, 2012, and the second on December 13, 2012.

41. The HAICA chair: Nouri Lajmi; deputy-chair: Raja Chaouachi. Members: Mouna Ghariani, Riadh Ferjani, Rachida Ennaïfer, Mohsen Riahi, Habib Belaïd, Hichem Senoussi, and Radhia Saïdi.

42. It was also during that year that various partisan formations or coalitions came into being: the Republican Party (April 9), Nidaa Tounes (June 16), the Popular Front (October 7), and the Democratic Alliance (November 8).

43. Michaël Ayari and Thierry Brésillon, 'Le "retour" du parti Ennahda sur la scène politique: De la normalisation démocratique au compromis autoritaire?' [The 'return' of Ennahda party to the political arena: From democratic normalization to authoritarian compromise?], in *Tunisie: Une démocratisation au-dessus de tout soupçon?* [Tunisia: Democratization above all suspicion?], eds. Amin Allal and Vincent Geisser (Paris: CNRS Éditions, 2018), 91. The two 'general strikes' by journalists are to be seen as episodes of this 'relentless pressure.'

44. Interview with Riadh Ferjani, La Goulette, June 24, 2015.

45. Richard Martinez, 'Préparer le statut de l'Instance de bonne gouvernance et de lutte contre la corruption' [Preparing the founding articles of the Good Governance and Anti-Corruption Instance], technical document, Council of Europe, Strasbourg, October 6, 2014: 7, https://rm.coe.int/16806d8b4e.

46. See, for instance, Riadh Ferjani, 'Internationalisations du champ télévisuel en Tunisie' [Internationalizations of the television field in Tunisia], in *La mondialisation des médias contre la censure: Tiers Monde et audiovisuel sans frontières* [Media globalization against censorship: The Third World and audiovisual without borders], ed. Tristan Mattelart (Brussels: De Boeck Supérieur, 2002), 155–175.

47. *Hakaek*, 'Mohsen al-Riahi yastaqil min al-HAICA' [Mohsen al-Riahi resigns from the HAICA], July 8, 2014, https://bit.ly/39qV56B.

48. *Business News*, 'Tunisie: Raja Chaouachi quitte la HAICA' [Tunisia: Raja Chaouachi quits HAICA], August 21, 2014, www.businessnews.com.tn/tunisie-raja-chaouachi-quitte-la-haica,520,48828,3.

49. With the exception of the STDM appointee, three new recruits were appointed on June 23, 2015: Assia Laabidi (AMT), Amel Chahed (SNJT), and Adel B'sili (ARP).

50. Interview with Riadh Ferjani, La Goulette, June 24, 2015 and interview with Rachida Ennaïfer, Tunis, December 19, 2016.

51. Rachida Ennaifer and Riadh Ferjani, 'Démission de la HAICA, deux ans après' [Resignation from HAICA, two years after], Facebook, May 3, 2017, www.facebook.com/notes/rachida-ennaifer/d%C3%A9mission-de-la-haica-deux-ans-apr%C3%A8s/1321518681250074.

52. Rachida Ennaïfer, 'Ma mission à la HAICA prend fin aujourd'hui,' [My mission with the HAICA comes to an end today] Facebook, April 27, 2014, https://m.facebook.com/story.php?story_fbid=102056906335 38912&id=1647145563&tra=1&__tn__=%2As%2As-R.

53. Samira Dami, 'Combler la vacance pour éviter l'anarchie' [Fill the vacancy to avoid anarchy], *Turess*, May 5, 2015, www.turess.com/fr/lapresse/99320.

54. At the end of April 2014, its representatives met with NCA chair, Mustapha Ben Jafaar, the head of the provisional government, Mehdi Jomaa and President Marzouki.

55. *Kapitalis*, 'Tunisie-Médias: Nabil Karoui menace de priver les Tunisiens de "Harim Soltan"' [Tunisia-Media: Nabil Karoui threatens to deprive Tunisians of 'Harim Soltan'], April 19, 2014, www.kapitalis.com/medias/21852-tunisie-medias-nabil-karoui-menace-de-priver-les-tunisiens-de-harim-soltan.html.

56. Reporters Without Borders and El Khatt Association, 'Media Ownership Monitor: Tunisia,' 2016, www.mom-rsf.org/en/countries/tunisia.

57. Hallin and Mancini, *Comparing Media Systems*, 140.

58. Ibid.

59. Haute Autorité de la Communication Audiovisuelle (HAICA), *La couverture des élections de 2014 dans les médias audiovisuels tunisiens: Rapport analytique* [The coverage of the 2014 elections in the Tunisian audiovisual media: An Analytical report] (Tunis: HAICA, 2015), http://haica.tn/media/Livre-Monitoring-en-Fran%C3%A7ais.pdf, 122.

60. Rosanvallon, *La légitimité démocratique*, 150.

61. It amounted to TND 50,000 for five TV channels (Nessma, Hannibal, Al Janoubiya, Tunisna, and Zitouna) and to TND 20,000 for four radio stations.

62. Paolo Mancini, 'Instrumentalization of the Media vs. Political Parallelism,' *Chinese Journal of Communication* 5, no. 3 (2012): 262–280.

63. Anja Wollenberg and Carola Richter, 'Political Parallelism in Transitional Media Systems: The Case of Libya,' *International Journal of Communication* 14 (2020): 1174.

64. Ibid.

65. *Liqâ' Khass* [Special Encounter], Nessma, April 19, 2015.

66. I Watch, 'Nessma Network: What Lies Behind the Karoui Brothers' TV,' July 11, 2016, www.iwatch.tn/ar/article/60.

67. The recording was released to the public on April 23, 2017. See also Maher Zid, 'Nabil al-Karoui muhadidan "adadan min al-qudat w al-nushata": lamma nahram 'alayhim al-khuruj min diarihim' [Nabil Karoui threatening a number of judges and activists: When we forbid them to leave their homes], YouTube, August 2, 2019, www.youtube.com/watch?v=b_5--W1sYsg&fbclid=IwAR2nAwxBp089Smn5_xgcc6n_w2C6pN3zr3ZAmupevDoGqoDx_SD3epFhh3E.

68. Frida Dahmani, 'Tunisie: fermeture de Nessma pour diffusion illégale' [Tunisia: closure of Nessma for illegal broadcasting], *Jeune Afrique*,

April 25, 2019, www.jeuneafrique.com/767323/politique/tunisie-les-autorites-ordonnent-larret-de-nessma-tv-pour-diffusion-illegale.

69. Réalités, 'HAICA: On a tellement fermé les yeux sur Nessma TV' [HAICA: We turned a blind eye to Nessma TV], April 25, 2019, www.realites.com.tn/2019/04/haica-on-a-beau-ferme-les-yeux-sur-nessma-tv.

70. Hajer Ajroudi, 'BCE reçoit Nebil Karoui dans le cadre de l'affaire Nessma' [BCE receives Nabil Karoui in connection with the Nessma affair], *Espace Manager*, April 29, 2019, www.espacemanager.com/bce-recoit-nebil-karoui-dans-le-cadre-de-laffaire-nessma.html.

71. David Rose, 'Tunisian President Kais Saied removes State TV Chief,' *Times*, July 29, 2021, www.thetimes.co.uk/article/tunisian-president-kais-saied-removes-state-tv-chief-amid-accusations-of-coup-snwl6mhv6.

72. Samir Dridi, 'Fermeture de Zitouna TV : d'autres chaînes dans le collimateur' [Closure of Zitouna TV: Other channels in the sights], *La Presse*, October 10, 2021, https://lapresse.tn/111156/fermeture-de-zitouna-tv-dautres-chaines-dans-le-collimateur/.

73. Nabil Karoui was imprisoned during an investigation of money laundering and tax evasion accusations from August 29 to October 26, 2021, and then from December 24, 2020 to June 15, 2021. After the July 25 events, he was imprisoned again (from August 29 to October 26, 2021) for illegally crossing the Algerian border.

74. Sihem Ben Sedrine, 'Tunisie: Les autorités publiques indépendantes, ces îlots "d'état dans l'état" qui dérangent tant' [Tunisia: Independent public authorities, these islands of 'state within the state' that are so disturbing], *Le Club de Médiapart*, September 10, 2020, https://blogs.mediapart.fr/sihem-bensedrine/blog/100920/tunisie-les-api-ces-ilots-d-etat-dans-l-etat-qui-derangent-tant. Sihem Ben Sedrine uses the term 'independent public authorities,' while I use 'independant administrative authorities' to refer to the same institutions.

75. Ibid.

76. Ghassan Salamé, *Democracy Without Democrats? The Renewal of Politics in the Muslim World* (London: I.B. Tauris, 1994).

77. Alfred Stepan, 'Tunisia's transition and the twin tolerations,' *Journal of Democracy* 23, no. 2 (2012): 89–103.

78. Pierre Rosanvallon, *La légitimité démocratique*, 159.

79. Auksė Balčytienė, 'Market-Led Reforms as Incentives for Media Change, Development and Diversification in the Baltic States: A Small Country Approach,' *International Communication Gazette* 71, nos. 1–2 (2009): 39–49; Helena Sousa and Elsa Costa e Silva, 'Keeping Up Appearances: Regulating Media Diversity in Portugal,' *International Communication Gazette* 71, nos. 1–2 (2009): 89–100.

80. In addition to this list are the Supreme Council of the Judiciary and the Constitutional Council.
81. Larry J. Diamond, 'Elections Without Democracy: Thinking About Hybrid Regimes,' *Journal of Democracy* 13, no. 2 (2002): 23–24.
82. Philippe Droz-Vincent, 'Quel avenir pour l'autoritarisme dans le monde arabe?' [What future for authoritarianism in the Arab world?], *Revue française de science politique* 54, no. 6 (2004): 963.

CHAPTER 4. POST-ISLAMISM POLITICS IN TUNISIA

1. This chapter is the outcome of a shared and intense exchange of ideas that I had with Ester Sigillò, who shared with me the conclusions of her fieldwork on Ennahda's *da'wa* activism. The Justice and Development Party in Morocco, in power since 2011, might be another example of democratic, formerly Islamist, parties. See Sami Zemni, 'Moroccan Post-Islamism: Emerging Trend or Chimera?,' in *Post-Islamism: The Changing Faces of Political Islam*, ed. Asef Bayat (Oxford: Oxford University Press, 2013), 134–156.
2. Rached Ghannouchi, 'From Political Islam to Muslim Democracy: The Ennahda Party and the Future of Tunisia,' *Foreign Affairs* 95, no. 5 (2016): 58–67.
3. Ali Larayedh, 'Al-Baiyyan al-Khitami lil-mo'tamar al-'Am al-'Ashir lil-Harakat al-Nahdha' [The conclusive statement of the tenth congress of the Ennahda Movement], Ennahda Movement, May 25, 2016, https://bit.ly/3gGam4Y. Author's translation from Arabic.
4. See David Hearst and Peter Oborne, 'Rached Ghannouchi Q&A: Thoughts on Democratic Islam,' *Middle East Eye*, June 13, 2016, www.middleeasteye.net/news/rached-ghannouchi-qa-thoughts-democratic-islam-0. See also Ghannouchi, 'From Political Islam to Muslim Democracy,' 63.
5. Roel Meijer, 'Commanding Right and Forbidding Wrong as a Principle of Social Action: The Case of the Egyptian al-Jama'a al-Islamiyya,' in *Global Salafism: Islam's New Religious Movement*, ed. Roel Meijer (London: Hurst, 2009), 189–220.
6. Michael Cook, *Commanding Right and Forbidding Wrong in Islamic Thought* (Cambridge: Cambridge University Press, 2001), 9.
7. Ghannouchi, 'From Political Islam to Muslim Democracy,' 58.
8. Francesco Cavatorta and Fabio Merone, 'Moderation Through Exclusion? The Journey of the Tunisian *Ennahda* from Fundamentalist to Conservative Party,' *Democratization* 20, no. 5 (2013): 857–875.
9. Antonio Gramsci, *Selections from the Prison Notebooks* (London: Lawrence and Wishart, 1971); Ali Shariati, *On the Sociology of Islam: Lectures*, trans. Hamid Algar (Berkeley, CA: Mizan Press, 1979).

10. Asef Bayat, 'The Coming of a Post-Islamist Society,' *Critique: Journal for Critical Studies of the Middle East* 5, no. 9 (1996): 43–52.

11. Jillian Schwedler, 'A Paradox of Democracy? Islamist Participation in Elections,' *Middle East Report* no. 209 (1998): 25–29.

12. Khalil Al-Anani, 'Islamist Parties Post-Arab Spring,' *Mediterranean Politics* 17, no. 3 (2012): 466–472.

13. Olivier Roy, *L'échec de l'islam politique* [The failure of political Islam] (Paris: Editions du Seuil, 1992).

14. Ibid., 40.

15. Bayat, *Post-Islamism*, 8.

16. Roy, *L'échec de l'islam politique*, 36.

17. Bayat, *Post-Islamism*, 8.

18. Karl Mannheim, *Ideology and Utopia: An Introduction to the Sociology of Knowledge* (London: Routledge, 2013), 61.

19. Gramsci, *Selections from the Prison Notebooks*, 155.

20. Ibid., 377.

21. Thomas J. Butko, 'Revelation or Revolution: A Gramscian Approach to the Rise of Political Islam,' *British Journal of Middle Eastern Studies* 31, no. 1 (2004): 145.

22. Mustapha Kamal Pasha, 'Political Theology and Sovereignty: Sayyid Qutb in Our Times,' *Journal of International Relations and Development* 22, no. 2 (2019): 346–363.

23. Massimo Campanini, '"Ali Shari'ati e la filosofia della prassi' ['Ali Shari'ati and the philosophy of praxis], *Storia del pensiero politico* 8, no. 2 (2019): 323–336.

24. Accepting liberal-democracy can be considered an ideological change as well. It can be argued that Islamism is a conservative democratic ideology (see, for example, Luca Ozzano, 'The Many Faces of the Political God: A Typology of Religiously Oriented Parties,' in *Religiously Oriented Parties and Democratization*, eds. Luca Ozzano and Francesco Cavatorta (Abingdon: Routledge, 2014), 9–32). It is post-ideological only in the sense that it is not a transformative ideology.

25. For a study on Salafism and how it filled the void of the moderation of MB-linked traditional Islamist parties, see Francesco Cavatorta and Fabio Merone, *Salafism after the Arab Awakening: Contending with People's Power* (London: Hurst, 2016).

26. Larayedh, 'Al-Baiyyan al-Khitami lil-mo'tamar al-'Am al-'Ashir lil-Harakat al-Nahdha.'

27. Hearst and Oborne, 'Rached Ghannouchi Q&A.'

28. Bayat, *Post-Islamism*, 8.

29. Hearst and Oborne, 'Rached Ghannouchi Q&A.' See also Ghannouchi, 'From Political Islam to Muslim Democracy,' 63.

30. G.N. Sfeir, 'The Tunisian Constitution,' *Middle East Journal* 13, no. 4 (1959): 443–448. For an overview of the constitutional debate, see Hédi Abdelkefi, 'The Tunisian Constitution: The Evolution of a Text,' in *The Constitution of Tunisia: Process, Principles and Perspectives* (New York, NY: United Nations Development Programme, 2016), www.undp.org/content/dam/rbas/doc/Compendium%20English/Part%202/13%20H%c3%a9di%20Abdelkefi%20EN.pdf.

31. Mohamed-Chérif Ferjani, 'Tunisia: Between Freedom of Conscience and Protection of the Sacred,' *OASIS*, April 18, 2018, www.oasiscenter.eu/en/tunisia-freedom-of-conscience-protection-of-sacred.

32. Ibid.

33. Reuters, 'Tunisia's Ennahda to Oppose Sharia in Constitution,' March 26, 2012, www.reuters.com/article/us-tunisia-constitution/tunisias-ennahda-to-oppose-sharia-in-constitution-idUSBRE82P0E820120326.

34. Monica L. Marks, 'Convince, Coerce, or Compromise? Ennahda's Approach to Tunisian Constitution,' Brookings Doha Center, analysis paper no. 10, February 2014, 20, www.brookings.edu/wp-content/uploads/2016/06/Ennahda-Approach-Tunisia-Constitution-English.pdf.

35. Raja Bahlul, 'Religion, Democracy and the "*Dawla Madaniyya*" of the Arab Spring,' *Islam and Christian Muslim Relations* 29, no. 3 (2018): 331–347.

36. Rory McCarthy, 'Protecting the Sacred: Tunisia's Islamist Movement Ennahda and the Challenge of Free Speech,' *British Journal of Middle Eastern Studies* 42, no. 4 (2015): 447–448.

37. ConstitutionNet, 'Draft Tunisian Constitution,' August 14, 2012, unofficial translation prepared on behalf of the International Institute for Democracy and Electoral Assistance, https://constitutionnet.org/sites/default/files/2012.08.14_-_draft_constitution_english.pdf

38. Quoted in Abdelkefi, 'The Tunisian Constitution.'

39. McCarthy, 'Protecting the Sacred,' 471.

40. The last part of Article 6 of the Tunisian Constitution states: '*Takfir* and the incitement of violence are prohibited' (*Takfir* means in Qur'anic language, declaring someone unbeliever). Article 2 states instead: 'Tunisia is a civil state based on citizenship, the will of the people, and the supremacy of law.'

41. Mohammad Hashim Kamali, 'Citizenship: An Islamic Perspective,' *Journal of Islamic Law and Culture* 11, no. 2 (2009): 121–153.

42. Sami Zemni, 'From Revolution to Tunisianité: Who is the Tunisian People? Creating Hegemony through Compromise,' *Middle East Law and Governance* 8, nos. 2–3 (2016): 131–150.

43. Ennahda International Page, 'Concluding Statement of the 9th Ennahda Party Conference, 12th,' July 18, 2012, www.facebook.com/Nahdha.International/posts/245449198891679.

44. Constituteproject.org, 'Tunisia's Constitution of 2014,' 2014, 3, www. constituteproject.org/constitution/Tunisia_2014.pdf.

45. Its most important codifier was the Andalus scholar Abu Ishaq al-Shatibi (1320–88 CE) and its contemporary refounder, the Tunisian and Zeitunian scholar Tahar Ben Achour (1879–1973). The latter initiated the Tunisian reformist tradition to which now Ennahda intellectuals want to reconnect their own history.

46. Interview with Abdelmajid al-Najjar, April 16, 2014, Bardo.

47. Interview with Salma Sarsut, April 4, 2014, Hammam-Lif, Tunisia.

48. Ibid.

49. Sayyed Qutb, *Ma'alam fiy-l-tariq* [Milestones on the way] (Doha: Al-markaz al-arabi lil-dirasat wal abahath, 2009), 9.

50. Ibid., 7–9.

51. Campanini calls it a 'counter-utopia.' See Massimo Campanini, 'The Utopian Dimension of a (Possible) Islamic Philosophy of History,' in *Utopia in the Present: Cultural Politics and Change*, ed. Claudia Gualtieri (Peter Lang: Bern, 2018), 43–56.

52. Ali Abdel Razek, *Islam and the Foundations of Political Power*, trans. Maryam Loutfi, ed. Abdou Filali-Ansary (Edinburgh: Edinburgh University Press, 2012).

53. Ghannouchi, 'From Political Islam to Muslim Democracy,' 58.

54. Rory McCarthy, 'When Islamists Lose: The Politicization of Tunisia's Ennahda Movement,' *The Middle East Journal* 72, no. 3 (2018): 383.

55. Cavatorta and Merone, 'Moderation Through Exclusion?,' 866.

56. Michel Camau and Vincent Geisser, *Le syndrome autoritaire: Politique en Tunisie de Bourguiba à Ben Ali* [The authoritarian syndrome: Politics in Tunisia from Bourguiba to Ben Ali] (Paris: Presses de Sciences Politiques, 2003), 277.

57. It is a missionary nonpolitical Indian movement. It was established in India in 1926 and spread thereafter all over the world. See, for example, Farish A. Noor, *Islam on the Move: The Tablighi Jama'at in Southeast Asia* (Amsterdam: Amsterdam University Press, 2012).

58. Interview with Abdel Fettah Mourou, cofounder of Ennahda movement, November 7, 2012, La Marsa, Tunisia.

59. McCarthy, 'When Islamists Lose,' 371.

60. Ibid., 373.

61. Ghannouchi, 'From Political Islam to Muslim Democracy,' 59.

62. McCarthy, 'When Islamists Lose,' 382.

63. Ester Sigillò, 'Going Professional: The Evolution of Islamic Charities in Post-Authoritarian Tunisia,' *Manshurat*, December 2019, https:// manshurat.org/node/64484.

235

64. Fabio Merone, 'Politicians or Preachers? What Ennahda's Transformation Means for Tunisia,' Carnegie Middle East Center, January 31, 2019, https://carnegieendowment.org/files/1-31_Merone_Ennahda.pdf.

65. Sigillò, 'Going Professional,' 11.

66. Fabio Merone, Ester Sigillò, and Damiano De Facci, 'Nahda and Tunisian Islamic Activism,' in *New Opposition in the Middle East*, eds. Dara Conduit and Shahram Akbarzadeh (Singapore: Palgrave Macmillan, 2018), 186–190.

67. Ester Sigillò, 'Shifting from Party Politics to Civil Society, Political Islam and Hybrid Trajectories of Tunisian Islamic Activism in Tunisia,' MWP working paper, European University Institute, May 2020 (I would like to thank the author for sharing the manuscript).

68. Fabio Merone, 'Enduring Class Struggle in Tunisia: The Fight for Identity Beyond Political Islam,' *British Journal of Middle Eastern Studies* 42, no. 1 (2015): 74–87.

69. BBC, 'Tunisia Declares Ansar al-Sharia a Terrorist Group,' August 27, 2013, www.bbc.com/news/world-africa-23853241.

70. Merone, Sigillò, and De Facci, 'Nahda and Tunisian Islamic Activism,' 191.

71. Ghannouchi, 'From Political Islam to Muslim Democracy,' 60.

72. From 2011 to 2014, Ennahda led a three-party coalition government that included two secular parties, the Congress for the Republic and Ettakatol. From 2015 to 2018, it was part of the national unity coalition with Nidaa Tounes. After the 2019 election, it supported in the parliament a technocrat government.

73. Carnegie Endowment for Peace, 'Result's from Tunisia's 2018 Municipal Elections,' August 15, 2018, https://carnegieendowment. org/2018/08/15/results-from-tunisia-s-2018-municipal-elections-pub-77044.

74. It chose to give up the battle against secular forces in 2013 ceded power in favor of a technocratic government in 2014. See Anne Wolf, *Political Islam in Tunisia: The History of Ennahda* (London: Hurst, 2017), 152–156.

75. Larayedh, 'Al-Baiyyan al-Khitami lil-mo'tamar al-'Am al-'Ashir lil-Harakat al-Nahdha.'

76. Laura Guazzone, 'Ennahda Islamists and the Test of Government in Tunisia,' *International Spectator* 48, no. 4 (2013): 30–50.

77. Alia Gana and Ester Sigillò, 'Les mobilisations contre le rapport sur les libertés individuelles et l'égalité (COLIBE): Vers une spécialisation du parti Ennahda dans l'action partisane?' [The mobilizations against the report on individual freedoms and equality (COLIBE): Toward a specialization of the Ennahda party in partisan action?], *L'Année du Maghreb* 21 (2019): 377–383.

78. Ester Sigillò, 'Going Professional,' 13.
79. Fabio Merone and Damiano De Facci, 'The New Islamic Middle Class and the Struggle for Hegemony in Tunisia,' *Afriche o Orienti* XVIII, nos. 1–2 (2015): 56–69.
80. Hamza Meddeb, 'Ennahda's Uneasy Exit from Political Islam,' Carnegie Middle East Center, September 5, 2019, 16, https://carnegieendowment.org/files/WP_Meddeb_Ennahda1.pdf.
81. Ibid., 18.
82. Ibid., 17.
83. Ibid.
84. Ennahda won 52 seats (out of 217) compared to 62 in the previous election in 2014.
85. Resorting to emergency powers under Article 80 of the 2014 Constitution, the president assumed all three constitutional powers (executive, legislative, and judicial). Since then, he has been ruling by decrees and holding the office of general attorney. While the president seems willing to modify part of the Constitution, the September 22 decree provisionally reorganized the public powers and sealed the de facto presidential grip on the executive and legislative branches. On October 11, a 'nonpolitical' government was appointed, which reported to the president.
86. El Watan.com, 'Crise politique en Tunisie: Un Parlement émietté et source de tous les maux.'
87. Tunisie Numérique, 'Le 25 Juillet propulse la popularité de Kaïs Saïed et Rached Ghannouchi creuse toujours.'
88. In a statement on September 25, 113 senior officials announced their resignation over the failure to confront President Saied's coup.
89. Guliz Dinc Belcher, 'Journey from Islamism to Conservative Democracy: The Politics of Religious Party Moderation in Turkey' (PhD diss., University of Massachusetts, 2014).
90. Mohammad Affan, 'The Ennahda Movement... A Secular Party?,' Al Sharq Expert Brief, June 14, 2016, https://research.sharqforum.org/2016/06/14/the-ennahda-movement-a-secular-party.

CHAPTER 5. TUNISIA'S RE-INVIGORATED CIVIL SOCIETY

1. The quartet includes the Tunisian General Labor Union (UGTT), the employers' Tunisian Union of Industry, Trade, and Handicrafts (UTICA), the Tunisian Bar Association (ONAT), and the Tunisian Human Rights Association (LTDH).
2. Norwegian Nobel Committee, 'The Nobel Peace Prize for 2015,' press release, October 10, 2015, www.nobelprize.org/nobel_prizes/peace/laureates/2015/press.html.

3. Michael W. Foley and Bob Edwards, 'The Paradox of Civil Society,' *Journal of Democracy* 7, no. 3 (1996): 38–52.
4. Larry Diamond, 'Rethinking Civil Society: Toward Democratic Consolidation,' *Journal of Democracy* 5, no. 3 (1994): 4–17; Axel Hadenius and Frederik Uggla, 'Making Civil Society Work, Promoting Democratic Development: What Can States and Donors Do?,' *World Development* 24, no. 10 (1996): 1621–1639; Juan Linz and Alfred Stepan, 'Toward Consolidated Democracies,' *Journal of Democracy* 7, no. 2 (1996): 14–33; Alexis de Tocqueville, *Democracy in America*, vol. 2, trans. Henry Reeve (London: Saunders and Otley, 1840); Robert Putnam, *Making Democracy Work: Civic Traditions in Modern Italy* (Princeton, NJ: Princeton University Press, 1993); and Robert Putnam, *Bowling Alone: The Collapse and Revival of American Community* (New York, NY: Simon & Schuster, 2000).
5. Guillermo O'Donnell and Philippe Schmitter, *Transitions from Authoritarian Rule: Tentative Conclusions about Uncertain Democracies* (Baltimore, MD: Johns Hopkins University Press, 1986); Adam Michnik, *Letters from Prison and Other Essays*, trans. Maya Latynski (Berkeley, CA: University of California Press, 1985); Michael Bernhard, 'Civil Society and Democratic Transition in East Central Europe,' *Political Science Quarterly* 108, no. 2 (1993): 307–326; and Diamond, 'Rethinking Civil Society.' These accounts have since been re-evaluated as exaggerated. See, for example, Clive Tempest, 'Myths from Eastern Europe and the Legends of the West,' *Democratization* 4, no. 1 (1997): 132–144; Jean Grugel, 'Romancing Civil Society: European NGOs in Latin America,' *Journal of Inter-American Studies and World Affairs* 42, no. 2 (2000): 87–107; and Stephen Kotkin, *Uncivil Society: 1989 and the Implosion of the Communist Establishment* (New York, NY: Random House, 2010).
6. For a more critical view of civil society's potential for democratization, see, for example, Ariel Armony, *The Dubious Link: Civic Engagement and Democratization* (Stanford, CA: Stanford University Press, 2004); and David Lewis, 'Civil Society and the Authoritarian State: Cooperation, Contestation and Discourse,' *Journal of Civil Society* 9, no. 3 (2013): 325–340. For civil society's role in the Arab world prior to the 2011 uprisings, see Sean L. Yom, 'Civil Society and Democratization in the Arab World,' *Middle East Review of International Affairs* 9, no. 4 (2005): 15–33; Steven Heydemann, 'Upgrading Authoritarianism in the Arab World,' Brookings, analysis paper no. 13, October 2007, www.brookings.edu/~/media/research/files/papers/2007/10/arabworld/10arabworld.pdf.
7. Anthony Spires, 'Contingent Symbiosis and Civil Society in an Authoritarian State: Understanding the Survival of China's Grassroots NGOs,' *American Journal of Sociology* 117, no. 1 (2011): 1–45; Janine Clark,

'Relations between Professional Associations and the State in Jordan,' in *Civil Society Activism Under Authoritarian Rule: A Comparative Perspective*, ed. Francesco Cavatorta (London: Routledge, 2013), 158–180.

8. Quintan Wiktorowicz, 'Civil Society as Social Control: State Power in Jordan,' *Comparative Politics* 33, no. 1 (2000): 43–61.
9. Heydemann, 'Upgrading Authoritarianism.'
10. Carlos Forment, *Democracy in Latin America: Civic Selfhood and Public Life in Mexico and Peru, 1760–1900* (Chicago, IL: University of Chicago Press, 2003).
11. Omar Encarnación, *The Myth of Civil Society: Social Capital and Democratic Consolidation in Spain and Brazil* (New York, NY: Palgrave Macmillan, 2003).
12. Sheri Berman, 'Civil Society and the Collapse of the Weimar Republic,' *World Politics* 49, no. 3 (1997): 401–429; Dylan Riley, *The Civic Foundations of Fascism in Europe: Italy, Spain, and Romania, 1870–1945* (Baltimore, MD: Johns Hopkins University Press, 2010).
13. This is in line, for example, with the approach taken by Francesco Cavatorta and Vincent Durac, eds., *Civil Society and Democratization in the Arab World* (London: Routledge, 2010).
14. For an overview of how the concept of 'civil society' has been used historically, see, for example, John Keane, *Democracy and Civil Society* (London: Verso, 1988).
15. One or more of these forms of action are sometimes included in the conception of civil society, but are excluded here to avoid creating a catch-all category that includes virtually any type of collective action.
16. On this point, see, for example, Petr Kopecký and Cas Mudde, *Uncivil Society? Contentious Politics in Post-Communist Europe* (London: Routledge, 2003); Yom, 'Civil Society and Democratization'; and Amaney Jamal, *Barriers to Democracy: The Other Side of Social Capital in Palestine and the Arab World* (Princeton, NJ: Princeton University Press, 2007).
17. Zuzana Hudáková, 'Civil Society in Tunisia: From Islands of Resistance to Tides of Political Change,' *Journal of North African Studies* 26, no. 3 (2021): 498–526.
18. This was in line with the developments in other MENA countries. See Vickie Langohr, 'Too Much Civil Society, Too Little Politics: Egypt and Liberalizing Arab Regimes,' *Comparative Politics* 36, no. 2 (2004): 181–204.
19. Hèla Yousfi, *L'UGTT, une passion tunisienne: Enquête sur les syndicalistes en révolution 2011–2014* [The UGTT, a Tunisian passion: Survey on trade unionists in revolution 2011–2014] (Tunis: Institut de Recherche sur le Maghreb Contemporain and Med Ali éditions, 2015), 241.
20. Ibid.

21. I am here referring to the 'Black Thursday' of February 26, 1978, the January 1984 bread riots, and the 2008 Gafsa popular uprising.

22. Larbi Chouikha and Vincent Geisser, 'Retour sur la révolte du bassin minier: Les cinq leçons politiques d'un conflit social inédit' [A reading of the revolt in the Gafsa mining basin: The five policy lessons of a unique social conflict], *L'Année du Maghreb* VI (2010): 415–426.

23. Bourguiba's own epitaph, inscribed on his mausoleum in Monastir, proclaimed him 'The supreme combatant, builder of modern Tunisia, liberator of women.'

24. Clement H. Moore, 'Tunisia and Bourguibisme: Twenty Years of Crisis,' *Third World Quarterly* 10, no. 1 (1988): 176–190.

25. Larbi Sadiki, 'The Search for Citizenship in Bin Ali's Tunisia: Democracy versus Unity,' *Political Studies* 50, no. 3 (2002): 497–513.

26. Bourguiba was declared 'President for life' in 1974 and political parties other than the ruling Neo-Destour, later renamed Socialist Destourian Party (Parti socialiste destourien, PSD), were banned between 1963 and 1981.

27. Eva Bellin, 'Civil Society in Formation: Tunisia,' in *Civil Society in the Middle East*, ed. Augustus R. Norton (Leiden: Brill, 1995), 127–128.

28. Ibid., 141.

29. Kevin Dwyer, *Arab Voices: The Human Rights Debate in the Middle East* (Berkeley, CA: University of California Press, 1991).

30. Bellin, 'Civil Society in Formation,' 128.

31. Law no. 59–154 of November 7, 1959.

32. Bellin, 'Civil Society in Formation,' 128.

33. Moore, 'Tunisia and Bourguibisme,' 180.

34. Organic Law no. 88–90 of August 2, 1988.

35. Foundation for the Future, 'Study on Civil Society Organizations in Tunisia,' January 2013, 7, https://africanphilanthropy.issuelab.org/resource/study-on-civil-society-organizations-in-tunisia.html.

36. Ibid., 8.

37. The former was allowed to run in the 1989 elections as an independent, while the latter was legalized in 1988.

38. Organic Law no. 92–25 of April 2, 1992.

39. Ibid.

40. Bellin, 'Civil Society in Formation,' 138.

41. Hudáková, 'Civil Society in Tunisia.'

42. Oliver Schlumberger, 'The Arab Middle East and the Question of Democratization: Some Critical Remarks,' *Democratization* 7, no. 4 (2000): 104–132; Wiktorowicz, 'Civil Society as Social Control;' Yom, 'Civil Society and Democratization;' and Heydemann, 'Upgrading Authoritarianism.'

43. Christopher Alexander, 'Back from the Democratic Brink: Authoritarianism and Civil Society in Tunisia,' *Middle East Report* no. 205 (1997): 35. Tellingly, 1988 and 1989 witnessed the creation of almost the same number of associations as the following twenty years of Ben Ali's rule.

44. Ibid. Indeed, Tunisia under Ben Ali was widely considered a prime example of a police state. See, for example, Derek Lutterbeck, 'Tool of Rule: The Tunisian Police under Ben Ali,' *Journal of North African Studies* 20, no. 5 (2015): 813–831.

45. Hudáková, 'Civil Society in Tunisia,' 504.

46. Ragnar Weilandt, 'Divisions within Post-2011 Tunisia's Secular Civil Society,' *Democratization* 26, no. 6 (2019): 962–963.

47. Éric Gobe and Michaël B. Ayari, 'Les avocats dans la Tunisie de Ben Ali: Une profession politisée?' [Lawyers in Ben Ali's Tunisia: A politicized profession], *L'Année du Maghreb* III (2007): 105–132; Éric Gobe, *Les avocats en Tunisie de la colonisation à la révolution (1883–2011): Sociohistoire d'une profession politique* [Lawyers in Tunisia from colonization to revolution (1883–2011): Sociohistory of a political profession] (Paris: Karthala, 2013).

48. Hudáková, 'Civil Society in Tunisia.'

49. Mehdi Mabrouk, 'A Revolution for Dignity and Freedom: Preliminary Observations on the Social and Cultural Background to the Tunisian Revolution,' *The Journal of North African Studies* 16, no. 4 (2011): 625–635; Hudáková, 'Civil Society in Tunisia.'

50. Foundation for the Future, 'Study on Civil Society Organizations,' 7.

51. Ibid., 12. Each of the three categories was responsible for around one fifth of the newly created CSOs.

52. For a detailed breakdown of the change in civil society composition in the first two years following the revolution, see Foundation for the Future, 'Study on Civil Society Organizations.'

53. Source: Centre d'Information, de Formation, d'Études et de Documentation sur les Associations, IFEDA [Centre for Information, Training, Research and Documentation on Associations]. Pre-2013 data is cited in Foundation for the Future 'Study on Civil Society Organizations,' 7, post-2013 data was collected by the author.

54. International Center for Non-Profit Law (ICNL), Beyond Reform & Development (BRD), and Menapolis, 'The State of Civic Freedoms in the Middle East and North Africa: Access to Associational Rights in Morocco, Tunisia, Lebanon, Jordan and Kuwait,' June 2018, 16, https://mk0rofifiqa2w3u89nud.kinstacdn.com/wp-content/uploads/The-State-of-Civic-Freedoms-in-MENA-FINAL.pdf.

55. Decree-Law no. 2011–88 of September 24, 2011.

56. ICNL, BRD, and Menapolis, 'The State of Civic Freedoms,' 34–35.

57. Silvia Colombo and Hamza Meddeb, 'Fostering Inclusiveness: A New Roadmap for EU–Tunisia Relations and the Engagement with Civil Society,' in *The EU-Tunisia Privileged Partnership:What Next?*, ed. Emmanuel Cohen-Hadria, EUROMESCO *Joint Policy Study* 10 (Barcelona: European Institute of the Mediterranean, 2018), 47.

58. Ibid.

59. Personal interviews with a range of civil society actors, Tunis, April 2016.

60. Colombo and Meddeb, 'Fostering Inclusiveness,' 47.

61. IFEDA, June 26, 2020, www.ifeda.org.tn/stats/francais.pdf.

62. Source: IFEDA. Data from 2010 and 2012 (which contains four unaccounted for CSOs, hence the discrepancy in totals for those years) is cited in Foundation for the Future 'Study on Civil Society Organizations,' 12. Subsequent data was collected by the author.

63. Pietro Marzo, 'Supporting Political Debate While Building Patterns of Trust: The Role of the German Political Foundations in Tunisia (1989–2017),' *Middle Eastern Studies* 55, no. 4 (2019): 621–637.

64. Colombo and Meddeb, 'Fostering Inclusiveness,' 39.

65. Marzo, 'Supporting Political Debate.'

66. This tendency was observed already during the authoritarian period. See Richard Gillespie and Laurence Whitehead, 'European Democracy Promotion in North Africa: Limits and Prospects,' *Democratization* 9, no. 1 (2002): 192–206; personal interviews with civil society activists, Tunis, April 2016.

67. Ester Sigillò, 'Tunisia's Evolving Islamic Charitable Sector and Its Model of Social Mobilization,' *Middle East Institute*, September 15, 2016, www.mei.edu/publications/tunisias-evolving-islamic-charitable-sector-and-its-model-social-mobilization.

68. Weiland, 'Divisions,' 965.

69. Colombo and Meddeb, 'Fostering Inclusiveness,' 39–40.

70. Personal interviews with civil society activists, Tunis, April 2016.

71. ICNL, BRD, and Menapolis, 'The State of Civic Freedoms,' 58. For comparison, this is less than in Lebanon or Jordan, where a significantly higher percentage of CSOs receive foreign funding (Ibid., 37).

72. This was particularly visible during the authoritarian period, when democracy promotion tended to strengthen regime control over civil society rather than contribute to its autonomous development. See for example Vincent Durac and Francesco Cavatorta, 'Strengthening Authoritarian Rule through Democracy Promotion? Examining the Paradox of the US and EU Security Strategies: The Case of Bin Ali's Tunisia,' *British Journal of Middle Eastern Studies* 36, no. 1 (2009): 3–19.

73. Personal interview with UNFT President Radhia Jerbi, Tunis, April 2016.

74. Other oppositional CSOs, like CNTL, ATFD, SJNT, and the LTDH, participated in its creation, but subsequently withdrew. For more information, see International Crisis Group, 'Popular Protest in North Africa and the Middle East (IV): Tunisia's Way,' Middle East/North Africa *Report* no. 106, April 28, 2011, www.crisisgroup.org/middle-east-north-africa/north-africa/tunisia/popular-protests-north-africa-and-middle-east-iv-tunisia-s-way.

75. Decree-Law no. 2011–6 of February 18, 2011.

76. The represented CSOs included, among others, the UGTT, ONAT, AMT, LTDH, ATFD, AFTURD, CNLT, AISPP, and SNJT.

77. ICG, 'Popular Protest,' 19–20.

78. For more information about the first phase of the Tunisian political transition, see Emma C. Murphy, 'The Tunisian Elections of October 2011: A Democratic Consensus,' *The Journal of North African Studies* 18, no. 2 (2013): 231–247.

79. Mounira Charrad and Amina Zarrugh, 'Equal or Complementary? Women in the New Tunisian Constitution after the Arab Spring,' *Journal of North African Studies* 19, no. 2 (2014): 230–243.

80. Ibid., 239–240.

81. Sami Zemni, 'The Extraordinary Politics of the Tunisian Revolution: The Process of Constitution Making,' *Mediterranean Politics* 20, no. 1 (2015): 1–17.

82. International Crisis Group, 'Tunisia: Violence and the Salafi Challenge,' Middle East/North Africa Report no. 137, February 13, 2013, https://d2071andvip0wj.cloudfront.net/tunisia-violence-and-the-salafi-challenge.pdf.

83. Anna Antonakis-Nashif, 'Contested Transformation: Mobilized Publics in Tunisia between Compliance and Protest,' *Mediterranean Politics* 21, no. 1 (2016): 131.

84. Earlier unilateral attempts by the UGTT to launch a 'National Dialogue' process were unsuccessful.

85. Created in 2012 by former interim Prime Minister Essebsi, Nidaa Tounis presented a popular, secular anti-pole to Ennahda until its progressive decline following the 2014 legislative elections.

86. The most notable exception was President Moncef Marzouki's CPR party—a member of the ruling Troika coalition government.

87. Freedom House, 'Freedom in the World 2015. Discarding Democracy: A Return to the Iron Fist,' 2015, www.freedomhouse.org/report/freedom-world/freedom-world-2015.

88. Personal interviews with civil society activists, Tunis, 2015–2016.

89. Irene Weipert-Fenner, 'Unemployed Mobilisation in Times of Democratisation: The Union of Unemployed Graduates in Post-Ben Ali Tunisia,' *The Journal of North African Studies* 25, no. 1 (2018): 53–75.
90. Weilandt, 'Divisions.'
91. Ibid.
92. Personal interview, Tunis, April 2016.
93. For more information, see the Al-Bawsala website, 2020, www.albawsala.com.
94. The I-Watch I Assist project platform is available at I-Watch I Assist, 2018, https://iassist.tn.
95. Available, in Arabic, at I-Watch Meter, n.d., https://meter.iwatch.tn.
96. Personal interviews with members of ATFD and UNFT executive boards, Tunis, 2015–2016.
97. The UNFT membership fell from around 180,000 members at the end of 2010 to less than 40,000 in 2016.
98. Amel al-Hilali, 'LGBTQ Association Achieves Major Legal Milestone in Tunisia,' *Al-Monitor*, March 10, 2020, www.al-monitor.com/pulse/originals/2020/03/tunisia-shams-association-gay-rights-legal-presence.html.
99. For more information, see Mash'hed, 2020, www.mashhed.org.
100. Hudáková, 'Civil Society in Tunisia.'
101. This is true for all three waves of Arab Barometer survey in which the question was asked, with the mistrust in CSOs increasing from 40 percent in 2011 to 56 percent in 2018. See Arab Barometer, 'Survey Data,' 2020, www.arabbarometer.org/survey-data. The lack of trust in CSOs' ability to protect their rights and freedoms was also confirmed by another recent survey, which found that Tunisians were twice as likely to distrust CSOs as they were to trust them, with the highest levels of trust reserved for NGOs and unions and the lowest for social enterprises. See ICNL, BRD, and Menapolis, 'The State of Civic Freedoms,' 41–42.

CHAPTER 6. MOBILIZATION IN TUNISIA POST-2011

1. Amin Allal, 'Becoming Revolutionary in Tunisia, 2007–2011,' in *Social Movements, Mobilization, and Contestation in the Middle East and North Africa*, eds. Joel Beinin and Frédéric Vairel (Stanford, CA: Stanford University Press, 2019), 185–204; Laryssa Chomiak, 'Architecture of Resistance in Tunisia,' in *Taking to the Streets: The Transformation of Arab Activism*, eds. Lina Khatib and Ellen Lust (Baltimore, MD: The John Hopkins University Press, 2014), 22–51; and Eric Gobe, 'The Gafsa Mining Basin between Riots and a Social Movement: Meaning and Significance of a Protest

Movement in Ben Ali's Tunisia,' HAL working paper, 2010, https://halshs.archives-ouvertes.fr/halshs-00557826/document.

2. Julius Dihstelhoff and Katrin Sold, 'The Carthage Agreement Under Scrutiny,' *Carnegie Endowment for International Peace*, November 29, 2016, https://carnegieendowment.org/sada/66283.

3. Guillermo O'Donnell and Philippe C. Schmitter, *Transitions from Authoritarian Rule: Tentative Conclusions about Uncertain Democracies* (Baltimore, MD: John Hopkins University Press, 2013).

4. Jack A. Goldstone, 'Rethinking Revolutions: Integrating Origins, Processes, and Outcomes,' Comparative Studies of South Asia, Africa and the Middle East 29, no. 1 (2009): 18–32. https://doi.org/10.1215/1089201X-2008-040.

5. Chantal Berman, 'When Revolutionary Coalitions Break Down: Polarization, Protest, and the Tunisian Political Crisis of August 2013,' *Middle East Law and Governance* 11, no. 2 (2019): 146.

6. Clionadh Raleigh et al., 'Introducing ACLED: An Armed Conflict Location and Event Dataset,' *Journal of Peace Research* 47, no. 5 (2010): 651–660.

7. Armed Conflict Location & Event Data Project (ACLED), 'Guide to Dataset Use for Humanitarian and Development Practitioners,' April 2019, https://acleddata.com/acleddatanew/wp-content/uploads/dlm_uploads/2019/04/ACLED_User-Guide-for-Humanitarians_2019FINAL.pdf. I only follow ACLED's terminology in this section. In the rest of the chapter, I use protests for both non-violent as well as disruptive and violent, yet unarmed, forms of contentious collective actions. See Charles Tilly, *The Politics of Collective Violence* (Cambridge: Cambridge University Press, 2003).

8. Latest research has pointed to several coverage biases in off-the-shelf protest event datasets including ACLED (see Killian Clarke, 'Which Protests Count? Coverage Bias in Middle East Event Datasets,' *Mediterranean Politics* 47, no. 3 (2021): 1–27.). As locally-coded protest event data for Tunisia is not yet available for the period under study, I use ACLED data here with great caution and for illustrative purposes of my qualitative findings only. I also reflect on potential biases below.

9. Source: Armed Conflict Location & Event Data Project (2020), acleddata.com

10. Prisca Joest and Jan-Philipp Vatthauer, 'Socioeconomic Contention in Post-2011 Egypt and Tunisia: A Comparison,' in *Socioeconomic Protests in MENA and Latin America: Egypt and Tunisia in Interregional Comparison*, eds. Irene Weipert-Fenner and Jonas Wolff (Basingstoke: Palgrave Macmillan, 2020), 71–104.

11. Dana R. Fisher et al., 'The Science of Contemporary Street Protest: New Efforts in the United States,' *Science Advances* 5, no. 10 (2019): 2.

12. Carola Richter, 'Media Policy in Times of Transition: Tunisia's Bumpy Road to Democracy,' *Publizistik* 62, no. 3 (2017): 325–333. See also Enrique Klaus in this volume.

13. See Nils B. Weidmann and Espen Geelmuyden Rød, *The Internet and Political Protest in Autocracies* (New York, NY: Oxford University Press, 2019).

14. Francesca Governa and Matteo Puttilli, 'After a Revolution: Public Spaces and Urban Practices in the Core of Tunis,' in *Rethinking Life at the Margins: The Assemblage of Contexts, Subjects, and Politics*, ed. Michele Lancione (London: Routledge, 2016), 44; Choukri Hmed, '"Le peuple veut la chute du régime": Situations et issues révolutionnaires lors des occupations de la place de la Kasbah à Tunis, 2011' ['The people want the fall of the regime': Revolutionary situations and issues during the occupations of the Kasbah square in Tunis, 2011], *Actes de la recherche en sciences sociales* 211, nos. 1–2 (2016): 72.

15. Hmed, '"Le peuple veut la chute du régime."'

16. Berman, 'When Revolutionary Coalitions Break Down,' 146.

17. Hmed, '"Le peuple veut la chute du régime"' 78–88.

18. Ibid., 84. English translations from French by the author.

19. For detailed analyses, see Amel Boubekeur, 'Islamists, Secularists and Old Regime Elites in Tunisia: Bargained Competition,' *Mediterranean Politics* 21, no. 1 (2016): 107–127; Sami Zemni, 'The Extraordinary Politics of the Tunisian Revolution: The Process of Constitution Making,' *Mediterranean Politics* 20, no. 1 (2015): 1–17.

20. Berman, 'When Revolutionary Coalitions Break Down,' 149.

21. Boubekeur, 'Islamists, Secularists and Old Regime Elites,' 113.

22. Ibid., 117.

23. Anna Antonakis-Nashif, 'Contested Transformation: Mobilized Publics in Tunisia Between Compliance and Protest,' *Mediterranean Politics* 21, no. 1 (2016): 128–149.

24. Ibid.

25. Joel Beinin, *Workers and Thieves: Labor Movements and Popular Uprisings in Tunisia and Egypt* (Stanford, CA: Stanford University Press, 2016).

26. Berman, 'When Revolutionary Coalitions Break Down,' 156–161.

27. For a detailed analysis of the UGTT's different roles in the transition process, see Bassem Karray, 'The Tunisian Labor Union and the Constitutional Transformation,' in *Socioeconomic Protests in MENA and Latin America*, eds. Weipert-Fenner and Wolff, 123–144.

28. Boubekeur, 'Islamists.'

29. Ibid., 118 and 122–124.

30. Dihstelhoff and Sold, 'The Carthage Agreement Under Scrutiny.'

31. Farah Samti, 'Tunisia's Ruling Party is Falling Apart,' *Foreign Policy*,

December 3, 2015, https://foreignpolicy.com/2015/12/03/tunisias-ruling-party-is-falling-apart.

32. Fabio Merone, 'Between Social Contention and Takfirism: The Evolution of Salafi-Jihadi Movement in Tunisia,' *Mediterranean Politics* 22, no. 1 (2016): 71–90.

33. Beinin, *Workers and Thieves*.

34. Irene Weipert-Fenner, 'Unemployed Mobilisation in Times of Democratisation: The Union of Unemployed Graduates in Post-Ben Ali Tunisia,' *Journal of North African Studies* 25, no. 1 (2020): 53–75.

35. Nadia Marzouki, 'Tunisia's Rotten Compromise,' *Middle East Research and Information Project*, July 10, 2015, www.merip.org/mero/mero071015.

36. Nadia Marzouki and Hamza Meddeb, 'The Struggle for Meanings and Power in Tunisia after the Revolution,' *Middle East Law and Governance* 8, nos. 2–3 (2016): 124.

37. Also, activists themselves saw the year 2014 as a turning point that brought routine politics back and replaced non-routine mobilization between 2011 and 2013. See, for instance, Arab Reform Initiative, 'Tunisian Engaged Youth New Approaches to Political Action,' October 1, 2018, www.arab-reform.net/event/tunisian-engaged-youth-new-approaches-to-political-action.

38. Prisca Jöst, 'Mobilization without Organization: Grievances and Group Solidarity of the Unemployed in Tunisia,' *Mobilization: An International Quarterly* 25, no. 2 (2020): 265–283.

39. Kristina Dietz and Bettina Engels, 'Contested Extractivism: Actors and Strategies in Conflicts over Mining,' *DIE ERDE* 148, nos. 2–3 (2017): 111–120.

40. Samiha Hamdi and Irene Weipert-Fenner, 'Unemployed Protests in Tunisia: Between Grassroots Activism and Formal Organization,' in *Socioeconomic Protests in MENA and Latin America*, eds. Weipert-Fenner and Wolff, 195–219.

41. Lorenzo Feltrin, 'The Struggles of Precarious Youth in Tunisia: The Case of the Kerkennah Movement,' *Review of African Political Economy* 45, no. 155 (2017): 44–63.

42. Youssef Cherif, 'The Kamour Movement and Civic Protests in Tunisia,' *Carnegie Endowment*, August 8, 2017, https://carnegieendowment.org/2017/08/08/kamour-movement-and-civic-protests-in-tunisia-pub-72774.

43. Weipert-Fenner, 'Unemployed Mobilisation in Times of Democratisation,' 53–75.

44. Hamdi and Weipert-Fenner, 'Unemployed Protests in Tunisia,' 195–219.

45. Jöst, 'Mobilization without Organization,' 265–283.

46. Jan-Philipp Vatthauer and Irene Weipert-Fenner, 'The Quest for Social Justice in Tunisia: Socioeconomic Protest and Political Democratization Post 2011,' *Peace Research Institute Frankfurt (PRIF) Report* 143 (2017): 1–39.

47. Fedia Gasmi, 'Winou El Petrol?!: A Debate on Transparency of Natural Resource Extraction in Tunisia,' Heinrich Böll Foundation, December 12, 2016, https://lb.boell.org/en/2016/12/12/perspectives-9-winou-el-petrol-debate-transparency-natural-resource-extraction-tunisia#_ftnref2.

48. Vanessa Szakal, '"Where's our Oil?": The (Continued) Confusion of Politics and Resource Management in Tunisia,' *Nawaat*, June 16, 2015, http://nawaat.org/portail/2015/06/16/wheres-our-oil-the-continued-confusion-of-politics-and-resource-management-in-tunisia.

49. Gasmi, 'Winou El Petrol?!'

50. See, for example, Leaders, 'Winou el petrol: La vérité' [Where is the oil: The truth], July 6, 2015, www.leaders.com.tn/article/17432-winou-el-petrol-la-verite.

51. Sarah Yerkes and Marwan Muasher, 'Tunisia's Corruption Contagion: A Transition at Risk,' *Carnegie Endowment*, October 25, 2017, https://carnegieendowment.org/2017/10/25/tunisia-s-corruption-contagion-transition-at-risk-pub-73522.

52. Monica Marks, '"Letting Go of Every Principle": Tunisia's Democratic Gains Under Threat,' *Middle East Eye*, July 24, 2017, www.middleeasteye.net/opinion/letting-go-every-principle-tunisias-democratic-gains-under-threat.

53. Mariam Salehi, 'Designing Transitional Justice: Problems of Planning Political & Institutional Change in Volatile Political Contexts,' in *POMEPS Studies 37 Challenges to the Middle East North Africa Inclusionary State* (Washington, DC: POMEPS, 2020), 41–45, https://pomeps.org/wp-content/uploads/2020/02/POMEPS_Studies_37_Web.pdf.

54. Yerkes and Muasher, 'Tunisia's Corruption Contagion,' 20.

55. Laryssa Chomiak, 'The Revolution in Tunisia Continues,' *Middle East Institute*, September 22, 2016, www.mei.edu/publications/revolution-tunisia-continues.

56. Marks, 'Letting Go of Every Principle.'

57. For a detailed account, see Amal Amraoui, '#Manich_Msamah: Les mouvements de protestation entre le 8 et le 21 septembre' [#Manich_Msamah: Protest movements between September 8 and 21], *Nawaat*, September 23, 2015, http://nawaat.org/portail/2015/09/23/manich_msamah-les-mouvements-de-protestation-entre-le-8-et-le-21-septembre.

58. Vanessa Szakal, 'Manich Msamah Declares a "Grassroots State of

Emergency,'" *Nawaat*, July 27, 2016, https://nawaat.org/portail/2016/07/27/manich-msamah-declares-a-grassroots-state-of-emergency.

59. Oussama Kardi, 'Tunisia's Parliament Delays Vote on Amnesty Law as Protests Erupt,' *Middle East Eye*, July 29, 2017, www.middleeasteye.net/news/tunisias-parliament-delays-vote-amnesty-law-protests-erupt.

60. Hamadi Lassoued, 'Manich Msamah: Raghm khasarat rundat, tatawasal al-ta'bi'at w al-nidhal' [Manich Msamah: Mobilization continues despite losing the battle], *Nawaat*, September 14, 2017, https://bit.ly/3oOlqju.

61. Yerkes and Muasher, 'Tunisia's Corruption Contagion,' 20.

62. Soufiane Jaballah, '"Manish Msamih, Fish Nistanaw, Basta": Muqaraba susiyulujiyya li-l-hamalat al-shababiyya fi Tunis ['Manish Msamih, Fish Nistanaw, Basta': A sociological approach to youth campaigns in Tunisia], *Forum Tunisien pour les Droits Economiques et Sociaux (FTDES)*, August 6, 2019, https://ftdes.net/ar/the-new-forms-of-protests-and-bothold-and-new-actors.

63. Layla Riahi, 'Manich Msamah: Retour critique sur un moment politique' [Manich Msamah: Critical review of a political moment], *Nawaat*, February 9, 2018, http://nawaat.org/portail/2018/02/09/manich-msamah-retour-critique-sur-un-moment-politique.

64. Sharan Grewal and Shadi Hamid, 'The Dark Side of Consensus in Tunisia: Lessons from 2015–2019,' Foreign Policy at Brookings, January 2020, 1–32, www.brookings.edu/research/the-dark-side-of-consensus-in-tunisia-lessons-from-2015-2019.

65. Youssef Cherif, 'Why are Tunisians Protesting?,' *Al Jazeera*, January 14, 2018, www.aljazeera.com/indepth/opinion/tunisians-protesting-180114082908910.html.

66. Mounir Saidani and Fouad Gharbali, 'Al-harakat al-ijtima'iyya fi Tunis al-siyaqat, al-fa'ilun, al-af'al, wa-sinariyuhat at-tatawwur al-muhtamila' [Social movements in Tunisia: Contexts, actors, actions, and potential development scenarios], *Forum Tunisien pour les Droits Economiques et Sociaux (FTDES)*, September 12, 2018, https://ftdes.net/ar/mvtssociauxtunisie; Jaballah, '"Manish Msamih, Fish Nistanaw, Basta."'

67. Mohammed Samih Beji Okkez, 'Map of Protests: Increased Prices Galvanize Streets Across Tunisia,' *Nawaat*, January 12, 2018, https://nawaat.org/portail/2018/01/12/map-of-protests-increased-prices-galvanize-streets-across-tunisia.

68. Cherif, 'Why are Tunisians Protesting?'

69. Weipert-Fenner, 'Unemployed Mobilisation in Times of Democratisation,' 53–75.

70. Yasmine Berriane and Marie Duboc, 'Allying Beyond Social Divides: An

Introduction to Contentious Politics and Coalitions in the Middle East and North Africa,' *Mediterranean Politics* 24, no. 4 (2019): 399–419, 403.

71. See, for instance, the official Facebook post: UGTT, 'Abassi: Le FMI n'a pas imposé le report des augmentations salariales' [Abassi: The IMF did not impose the postponement of wage increases], Facebook, November 13, 2016, www.facebook.com/ugtt.page.officielle/posts/1325368510870904.

72. Frida Dahmani, 'Tunisie – Noureddine Taboubi (UGTT): "Le gouvernement navigue à vue"' [Tunisia – Noureddine Taboubi (UGTT): 'The government is sailing on sight'], *Jeune Afrique*, January 18, 2019, www.jeuneafrique.com/707750/societe/tunisie-noureddine-taboubi-ugtt-le-gouvernement-navigue-a-vue.

73. Tula Connell, 'Tunisia Public Workers Win Wage Increases,' *Solidarity Center*, February 7, 2019, www.solidaritycenter.org/tunisia-public-workers-win-wage-increases.

74. Mohammed Samih Beji Okkez, 'Professors Raise Red Flag Against Marginalization of Tunisia's Public Universities,' trans. Vanessa Szakal, *Nawaat*, April 19, 2019, https://nawaat.org/portail/2019/04/19/professors-raise-red-flag-against-marginalization-of-tunisias-public-universities.

75. *France 24*, 'Tunisia Teachers Protest After Months on Strike,' February 6, 2019, www.france24.com/en/20190206-tunisia-teachers-protest-after-months-strike.

76. *African Manager*, 'Tunisia-IMF: They Talk, Without Breaking Off, While Waiting for the Next Government,' February 17, 2020, https://en.africanmanager.com/tunisia-imf-they-talk-without-breaking-off-while-waiting-for-the-next-government.

77. International Crisis Group, 'Tunisie: éviter les surenchères populistes' [Tunisia: Avoiding populist escalation], Briefing No. 73, March 4, 2020, www.crisisgroup.org/fr/middle-east-north-africa/north-africa/tunisia/b73-tunisie-eviter-les-surencheres-populistes.

78. Robert P. Parks and Tarek Kahlaoui, 'Populist Passions or Democratic Aspirations? Tunisia's Liberal Democracy in Crisis,' *Middle East Report Online*, October 26, 2021, https://merip.org/2021/10/populist-passions-or-democratic-aspirations-tunisias-liberal-democracy-in-crisis/.

79. International Monetary Fund (IMF), 'IMF Executive Board Approves a US$745 Million Disbursement to Tunisia to Address the COVID-19 Pandemic,' *IMF Press Release* no. 20/144, April 10, 2020, www.imf.org/en/News/Articles/2020/04/10/pr20144-tunisia-imf-executive-board-approves-a-us-745m-disbursement-address-covid19-pandemic.

80. Irene Weipert-Fenner and Jonas Wolff, 'Introduction: Socioeconomic

Protests in Times of Political Change:Studying Egypt and Tunisia from a Comparative Perspective,' in *Socioeconomic Protests in MENA and Latin America*, eds. Weipert-Fenner and Wolff, 28–29.

CHAPTER 7. THE VIOLENCE OF ENDURANCE

1. Benoît Challand, 'Current Legacies of Colonial Violence and Racialization in Tunisia,' *Comparative Studies of South Asia, Africa, and the Middle East* 40, no. 2 (2020): 248–255. See also Lisa Anderson, *The State and Social Transformation in Tunisia and Libya, 1830–1980* (Princeton, NJ: Princeton University Press, 1986).

2. Najem Dhaher, 'L'aménagement du territoire tunisien: 50 ans de politiques à l'épreuve de la mondialisation' [Spatial planning in Tunisia: 50 years of policies put to the test of globalization], *EchoGéo* 13 (2010).

3. Bilel Kchouk, 'Les "anciennes" élites économiques et le changement de régime en Tunisie: De l'incertitude vers la consolidation politico-économique des positions' [The 'former' economic elites and the change of regime in Tunisia: On the uncertainty surrounding the political and economic consolidation of positions], *Politix* 4, no. 120 (2017): 157–178.

4. Nate Grubman and Aytuğ Şaşmaz, 'The Collapse of Tunisia's Party System and the Rise of Kais Saied,' *Middle East Report Online*, August 17, 2021, https://merip.org/2021/08/the-collapse-of-tunisias-party-system-and-the-rise-of-kais-saied/.

5. Project on Middle East Democracy, *Tunisia Update*, newsletter, November 23, 2021.

6. Sami Zemni, 'Tunisia's Marginalized Redefine the Political,' *Middle East Report* 293 (Spring 2021),

7. Bandy X. Lee, 'Structural Violence,' in *Violence: An Interdisciplinary Approach to Causes, Consequences, and Cures* (Hoboken, NJ: John Wiley and Sons, 2019), 123.

8. Ibid.

9. Donatella Della Porta, *Social Movements in Times of Austerity: Bringing Capitalism Back into Protest Analysis* (Cambridge: Polity Press, 2015).

10. While this may be true of much academic theorizing of precarity, Maribel Casas-Cortés has shown how the precarity concept evolved in movement spaces to include gendered and racialized forms of labor that were never protected under Keynesianism. See Maribel Casas-Cortés, 'A Genealogy of Precarity: A Toolbox for Rearticulating Fragmented Social Realities in and out of the Workplace,' *Rethinking Marxism* 26, no. 2 (2014): 206–226.

11. Brett Neilson and Ned Rossiter, 'Precarity as a Political Concept, or,

Fordism as Exception,' *Theory, Culture & Society* 25, nos. 7–8 (2008): 51–72.

12. Joel Beinin, *Workers and Thieves: Labor Movements and Popular Uprisings in Tunisia and Egypt* (Stanford, CA: Stanford University Press, 2016); Sadri Khiari, *Tunisie, le délitement de la cité: Coercition, consentement, résistance* [Tunisia, the disintegration of the city: Coercion, consent, resistance] (Paris: Karthala, 2003).

13. Khiari, *Tunisie, le délitement de la cité*, 76.

14. Lorenzo Feltrin, 'The Struggles of Precarious Youth in Tunisia: The Case of the Kerkennah Movement,' *Review of African Political Economy* 45, no. 155 (2018): 44–63.

15. Khiari, *Tunisie, le délitement de la cité*; Irene Weipert-Fenner, 'Unemployed Mobilisation in Times of Democratisation: The Union of Unemployed Graduates in Post-Ben Ali Tunisia,' *Journal of North African Studies* 25, no. 1 (2020): 53–75.

16. Feltrin, 'The Struggles of Precarious Youth,' 47.

17. Jan Breman, *Footloose Labour: Working in India's Informal Economy* (Cambridge: Cambridge University Press, 1996).

18. Hamza Meddeb, 'L'ambivalence de la "course à el *khobza*": Obéir et se révolter in Tunisie' [The ambivalence of the 'race to el *khobza*': Obedience and revolt in Tunisia], *Politique Africaine* 1, no. 121 (2011): 35–51.

19. Béatrice Hibou, 'Tunisie: Économie politique et moral d'un movement' [Tunisia: The political and moral economy of a social movement], *Politique Africaine* 1, no. 121 (2011): 5–22; Béatrice Hibou et al., 'Introduction: S'affranchir d'un événement qui fait date' [Introduction: Breaking free from a landmark event], in *L'état d'injustice au Maghreb: Maroc et Tunisie* [The state of injustice in the Maghreb: Morocco and Tunisia] (Paris: Karthala, 2015), 5–22.

20. Béatrice Hibou, *The Force of Obedience: The Political Economy of Repression in Tunisia* (Cambridge: Polity Press, 2011).

21. Deborah Cowen and Amy Siciliano, 'Surplus Masculinities and Security,' *Antipode* 43, no. 5 (2011): 1516–1541. It is worth noting that the oft-used descriptor for socioeconomic precarity in Tunisian Arabic, *hash* (as in *al-'amal al-hash*), has also been used to designate 'at-risk' youth in post-2011 Countering Violent Extremism (CVE) programming.

22. Hibou, 'Tunisie: Économie politique.'

23. Hamza Meddeb, 'L'attente comme mode de gouvernement en Tunisie' [Waiting as a mode of government in Tunisia], in *L'état d'injustice au Maghreb*, 345–377; see also Amin Allal, 'Le "prix" de la révolution en Tunisie' [The 'price' of revolution in Tunisia], *Savoir/Agir* 4, no. 34 (2015): 117–122.

24. Meddeb, 'L'attente comme mode de gouvernement en Tunisie.'

25. Weipert-Fenner, 'Unemployed Mobilisation,' 53–75.
26. Alcinda Honwana, *The Time of Youth: Work, Social Change, and Politics in Africa* (Boulder, CO: Kumarian Press, 2012).
27. Weipert-Fenner, 'Unemployed Mobilisation,' 53–75.
28. Zemni, 'Tunisia's Marginalized Redefine the Political.'
29. Allal, 'Le "prix" de la révolution en Tunisie,' 117–122.
30. Corinna Mullin and Brahim Rouabah, 'Discourse of Power and State Formation: The State of Emergency from Protectorate to Post-Uprising Tunisia,' *Middle East Law and Governance* 8, nos. 1–2 (2016): 151–178; Saerom Han, 'Securitization of the Unemployed and Counter-Conductive Resistance in Tunisia,' *Security Dialogue* (2020): 1–18.
31. The recruitment list had been drawn up to resolve an earlier sit-in, underscoring the cyclical nature of such protest actions.
32. Vanessa Szakal and Mohammed Samih Beji Okkez, 'After Kasserine, Protests Break Out in 16 Governorates,' Nawaat, January 22, 2016, https://nawaat.org/2016/01/22/after-kasserine-protests-break-out-in-16-governorates.
33. Han, 'Precarity, Precariousness, and Vulnerability,' 331–343.
34. Ibid., 339.
35. Elizabeth Povinelli, *Economies of Abandonment: Social Belonging and Endurance in Late Liberalism* (Durham, NC: Duke University Press, 2011), 32.
36. Zemni, 'Tunisia's Marginalized Redefine the Political.'
37. Povinelli, *Economies of Abandonment*, 132.
38. For similar sentiments in Zarzis, see Valentina Zagaria, 'The Morally Fraught *Harga*: Migration Blame Games in a Tunisian Border Town,' *Cambridge Journal of Anthropology* 37, no. 2 (2019): 57–73.
39. Ghassan Hage, 'Bearable Life,' *Suomen Antropologi* 44, no. 2 (2019): 81–83. My turn to Hage here is indebted to Zargaria 2019.
40. The Care Collective, *The Care Manifesto; The Politics of Interdependence* (London: Verso, 2020).
41. For a vivid description of the revolution in Kasserine, see Mustafa Aloui, 'Kasserine and January,' *Boundary 2* 39, no. 1 (2012): 55–67.
42. Michael Denning, 'Wageless Life,' *New Left Review* 66 (2010): 79–97.
43. Messaoud Romdhani, 'The Region as Victim: Transitional Justice as Class Action in Tunisia,' Brookings, November 24, 2020, www.brookings.edu/opinions/the-region-as-victim-transitional-justice-as-class-action-in-tunisia.
44. Rebecca Galemba, '"Corn is Food, not Contraband": The Right to "Free Trade" at the Mexico-Guatemala Border,' *American Ethnologist* 39, no. 4 (2012): 716–734; Hamza Meddeb, *Young People and Smuggling in the Kasserine Region of Tunisia* (London: International Alert, 2016),

www.international-alert.org/wp-content/uploads/2021/08/Tunisia-Young-People-Smuggling-EN-2016.pdf.

45. International Crisis Group, 'Tunisia's Borders: Jihadism and Contraband,' *Middle East/North Africa Report* No. 148, 2013, https://d2071andvip0wj. cloudfront.net/tunisia-s-borders-jihadism-and-contraband.pdf; Meddeb, *Young People and Smuggling*.

46. Pseudonyms have been used throughout to protect interlocutors' anonymity. All direct quotes have been translated into English by the author.

47. Meddeb, *Young People and Smuggling*.

48. Ibid.

49. Hassen Boubakri, 'Les migrations en Tunisie après la revolution' [Migration in Tunisia after the revolution], *Confluences Méditerranée* 4, no. 87 (2013): 31–46.

50. Sarah Barrières and Abir Kréfa, 'Des rapports du genre inchangés? Enquête sur le mouvement pour le droit au travail dans la région de Kasserine' [Unchanged gender relations? Survey on the movement for the right to work in the Kasserine region], in *Tunisie: Une démocratisation au-dessus de tout soupçon?* [Tunisia: A democratization above all suspicion?], eds. Amin Allal and Vincent Geisser (Paris: CNRS Éditions, 2018), 313–330.

51. Barrières and Kréfa, 'Des rapports du genre inchangés?

52. Farha Ghannam, *Live and Die Like a Man: Gender Dynamics in Urban Egypt* (Stanford, CA: Stanford University Press, 2013).

53. Statements made to Radhia Nasraoui during her July 27 visit to the sit-in.

54. Weipert-Fenner puts such feelings of entitlement into perspective, describing an earlier era in which a university degree practically guaranteed employment. See 'Unemployed Mobilisation,' 53–75.

55. Kamel Chachoua, 'Brahim: Autopsie d'un suicide en Kabylie (Algérie)' [Brahim: Autopsy of a suicide in Kabylia (Algeria)], in *Jeunesses Arabes: Du Maroc au Yémen: Loisirs, cultures et politiques* [Arab Youth: From Morocco to Yemen: Leisure, Cultures and Politics], eds. Laurent Bonnefoy and Myriam Catusse (Paris: La Découverte, 2013), 256–263.

56. Radhia Nasraoui is a widely respected lawyer and human rights activist who was targeted by the Ben Ali regime for her activism. No stranger to endurance tactics, she went on hunger strike in 2002 to protest the imprisonment of her husband Hamma Hammami, head of the Communist Worker's Party. She did so again in 2003, citing surveillance and harassment of her family life and work, sustaining the strike for fifty-seven days.

57. Michael Denning, 'Wageless Life,' *New Left Review* 66 (2010): 79–97.

58. Ilana Feldman, 'Looking for Humanitarian Purpose: Endurance and the

Value of Lives in a Palestinian Refugee Camp,' *Public Culture* 27, no. 3 (2015): 429.

CHAPTER 8. CHANGING SECURITY DYNAMICS IN TUNISIA

1. Siad Darwish, 'Balad el-Ziblé (Country of Rubbish): Moral Geographies of Waste in Post-Revolutionary Tunisia,' *Anthropological Forum* 28, no. 1 (2018): 64.
2. Ibid., 65.
3. Pierre Robert Baduel, 'Le temps insurrectionnel comme "moment politique": Tunisie 2011' [Insurrectionary time as a 'political moment': Tunisia 2011], *Revue internationale de politique comparée* 20, no. 2 (2013): 49.
4. Layna Mosley, *Interview Research in Political Science* (Ithaca, NY: Cornell University Press, 2015).
5. Janine Clark and Francesco Cavatorta, eds., *Political Science and Research in the Middle East and North Africa: Methodological and Ethical Challenges* (New York, NY: Oxford University Press, 2018), 5.
6. Paul Kingston, 'Playing with Positionality? Reflections on "Outsider/Insider" Status in the Context of Fieldwork in Lebanon's Deeply Divided Polity,' in *Political Science and Research in the Middle East and North Africa: Methodological and Ethical Challenges*, eds., Janine Clark and Francesco Cavatorta (New York, NY: Oxford University Press, 2018), 242–253.
7. Stefano Maria Torelli, 'The Ben Guerdane Attack and Tunisia's Tackling of Terrorism,' *Terrorism Monitor* 14, no. 6 (2016), https://jamestown. org/program/the-ben-guerdane-attack-and-tunisias-tackling-of-terrorism/#.VvFisOIrKUk.
8. Corinna Mullin and Brahim Rouabah, 'Decolonizing Tunisia's Border Violence: Moving Beyond Imperial Structures and Imaginaries,' *Viewpoint Magazine*, February 1, 2018, https://viewpointmag.com/2018/02/01/decolonizing-tunisias-border-violence-moving-beyond-imperial-structures-imaginaries.
9. Presidency of Tunisia, 'Mutābi'a Ra'īs al-Jumhūriyya li-saīr al-'amaliyyāt al-'amaniyya wa al-'askariyya al-Jāriyya bi-Bin Qardān Mubāshira Min Qā'a al-'Amaliyyāt al-Markaziyya bi-Thakna al-'Awina' [The President of the Republic Monitors the Evolution of Security and Military Operations in Ben Gardane from the Operation Centre in Al-Awina], March 7, 2016, https://bit.ly/3o9qQoG.
10. Elhiwar Ettounsi, 'Interview du président de la République tunisienne' [Statement of the President of the Republic Béji Caïd Essebsi on the Events of Ben Gardane], YouTube, March 7, 2016, www.youtube.com/watch?v=a-ipZ_jTSnw.

11. Hamza Meddeb, 'Young People and Smuggling in the Kasserine Region of Tunisia: Stories of Dispossession and the Dynamics of Exclusion,' International Alert, May 2016, www.international-alert.org/sites/default/files/Tunisia_YoungPeopleSmuggling_EN_2016.pdf.

12. Ruth Hanau Santini and Giulia Cimini, 'Intended and Unintended Consequences of Security Assistance in Post-2011 Tunisia,' *Contemporary Arab Affairs* 12, no. 1 (2019): 91–106.

13. Lydia Letsch, 'Countering Violent Extremism in Tunisia: Between Dependency and Self-Reliance,' *Journal for Deradicalization*, no. 17 (2018): 163–195.

14. United Nations Development Program, 'Vers la généralisation du modèle de police de proximité sur tout le territoire Tunisien' [Toward the generalization of the community policing model across the entire Tunisian territory], UNDP Tunisia, December 4, 2018, www.tn.undp.org/content/tunisia/fr/home/presscenter/articles/2018/vers-la-generalisation-du-modele-de-police-de-proximite-sur-tout.html.

15. Kyle Peyton, Michael Sierra-Arévalo, and David G. Rand, 'A Field Experiment on Community Policing and Police Legitimacy,' *Proceedings of the National Academy of Sciences* 116, no. 40 (2019): 19894–19898.

16. Zoltan Barany, 'Comparing the Arab Revolts: The Role of the Military,' *Journal of Democracy* 22, no. 4 (2011): 24–35.

17. Marsad, '98% des Tunisiens font confiance à l'armée selon Sigma Conseil' [98% of Tunisians trust the army according to Sigma Conseil], April 26, 2018, www.observatoire-securite.tn/fr/2018/04/26/98-des-tunisiens-font-confiance-larmee-selon-sigma-conseil.

18. Interview, UNDP, Tunis, May 2020.

19. Pinar Bilgin, 'Individual and Societal Dimensions of Security,' *International Studies Review* 5, no. 2 (2003): 203–222.

20. Barry Buzan, Ole Wæver, and Jaap de Wilde, *Security: A New Framework for Analysis* (Boulder, CO: Lynne Rienner, 1997).

21. Ole Wæver, 'World Conflict over Religion: Secularism as a Flawed Solution,' in *Constituting Communities: Political Solutions to Cultural Conflicts*, eds., Per Mouritsen and Knud E. Jørgensen (London: Palgrave Macmillan, 2008), 208–235.

22. Béatrice Hibou, *The Force of Obedience: The Political Economy of Repression in Tunisia* (Cambridge: Polity Press, 2011).

23. Ruth Hanau Santini, *Limited Statehood in Post-Revolutionary Tunisia: Citizenship, Economy, and Security* (London: Palgrave, 2018).

24. Ibid.

CHAPTER 9. WHAT CAN TUNISIA'S PAST TELL US ABOUT
ITS FUTURE?

1. Béatrice Hibou, *The Force of Obedience: The Political Economy of Repression in Tunisia*, trans. Andrew Brown (Cambridge: Polity Press, 2011), 271.

2. Despite President Kais Saied's suspension of the parliament and seizure of power in July 2021, Tunisia has experienced several free and fair elections, as well as the peaceful transfer of power between administrations.

3. For reviews of recent work on historical legacies in the social sciences, see Nathan Nunn, 'Historical Development,' in *Handbook of Economic Growth*, vol. 2, eds. Philippe Aghion and Steven N. Durlauf (Oxford: North Holland, 2014), 347–402; Alberto Simpser, Dan Slater, and Jason Wittenberg, 'Dead but Not Gone: Contemporary Legacies of Communism, Imperialism, and Authoritarianism,' *Annual Review of Political Science* 21 (2018): 419–439. For a small sample of historical legacies work focused on the Middle East, see Lisa Anderson, *The State and Social Transformation in Tunisia and Libya, 1830–1980* (Princeton, NJ: Princeton University Press, 1987); Steven Brooke and Neil Ketchley, 'Social and Institutional Origins of Political Islam,' *American Political Science Review* 112, no. 2 (2018): 376–394; Anthony Gill and Arang Keshavarzian, 'State Building and Religious Resources: An Institutional Theory of Church-State Relations in Iran and Mexico,' *Politics & Society* 27, no. 3 (1999): 431–465; Timur Kuran, *The Long Divergence: How Islamic Law Held Back the Middle East* (Princeton, NJ: Princeton University Press, 2011); Timur Kuran, 'Legal Roots of Authoritarian Rule in the Middle East: Civic Legacies of the Islamic Waqf,' *American Journal of Comparative Law* 64, no. 2 (2016): 419–445; and Adria K. Lawrence, 'Repression and Activism among the Arab Spring's First Movers: Evidence from Morocco's February 20th Movement,' *British Journal of Political Science* 47, no. 3 (2017): 699–718.

4. For an example that examines the rise of cosmopolitanism in Tunis during the Ottoman period, see Abdelhamid Larguèche, 'The City and the Sea: Evolving Forms of Mediterranean Cosmopolitanism in Tunis, 1700–1881,' trans. Julia Clancy-Smith and Caroline Audet, *Journal of North African Studies* 6, no. 1 (2001): 117–128.

5. Lisa Blaydes, 'State Building in the Middle East,' *Annual Review of Political Science* 20 (2017): 487–504.

6. Anderson, *The State and Social Transformation*, 32; Julia Clancy-Smith, *Tunisian Revolutions: Reflections on Seas, Coasts, and Interiors* (Washington, DC: Georgetown University Press and Center for Contemporary Arab Studies, 2014).

7. Alfred Stepan, 'Tunisia's Transition and the Twin Tolerations,' *Journal of Democracy* 23, no. 2 (2012): 94–97.

8. The 1861 Constitution established courts for litigation between Muslims and non-Muslims, established a Grand Council, and established foreigners' right to land ownership in Tunisia. However, not all research views this as a purely inclusive document. Anderson argues the *bey* (the Ottoman leader in Tunisia) and his close allies were the main beneficiaries of the 1861 Constitution (Anderson, *The State and Social Transformation*).

9. Stepan, 'Tunisia's Transition and the Twin Tolerations,' 97; Larguèche, 'The City and the Sea.' This type of inclusionary political legacy is also referred to as a legacy of political pluralism, as Marina Ottaway discusses in her chapter in this volume, albeit in reference to the twentieth century and not the Ottoman era.

10. Henri de Montety, 'Old Families and New Elites in Tunisia,' in *Man, State, and Society in the Contemporary Maghrib*, 1st ed., I. William Zartman (New York, NY: Praeger Publishers, 1973), 171–180. Mamluks were captured slaves who worked for the ruling Ottoman families and were trained to be 'loyal servants' of the Ottoman rulers, often holding important positions in the state administration (Anderson, *The State and Social Transformation*, 40). See also: Blaydes, 'State Building in the Middle East' for further discussion of the use of Mamluks and their legacy in the region.

11. Lily Fletcher, 'Beji Caid Essebsi: Tunisian President Who Oversaw Country's Transition to Democracy,' *Independent*, August 8, 2019, www.independent.co.uk/news/obituaries/beji-caid-essebsi-death-tunisia-president-arab-spring-north-africa-dead-a9040051.html.

12. Clement Henry Moore, *Tunisia since Independence: The dynamics of One-Party Government* (Berkeley, CA: University of California Press, 1965); Leon Carl Brown, 'The Many Faces of Colonial Rule in French North Africa,' *Revue de l'Occident musulman et de la Méditerranée* nos. 13–14 (1973): 171–191.

13. Anderson, *The State and Social Transformation*, 4 and 8.

14. Mounira M. Charrad, *States and Women's Rights: The Making of Postcolonial Tunisia, Algeria, and Morocco* (Berkeley, CA: University of California Press, 2001).

15. Robert P. Parks, 'Local-National Relations and the Politics of Property Rights in Algeria and Tunisia' (PhD dissertation, University of Texas at Austin, 2011).

16. Importantly, colonization in this context is the direct intervention of the French government in efforts to redistribute land to colons, who in the Tunisian context were typically French citizens from the French métropole who wanted to resettle permanently in North Africa and work in the agricultural sector.

17. Broadly, there were four categories of landholding at the time the French Protectorate was established: 1) *melk* or private property; 2) *habous* or religious endowment property, also referred to as waqf; 3) *'arsh* or collectively-held tribal land; and 4) *ardh al-bey* or property of the Ottoman ruler.

18. Décret du 31 janvier 1898 [Decree of 31 January 1898], *Journal official* [Official Journal], 1898.

19. Moore, *Tunisia since Independence*, 27.

20. Assia Khellaf, 'Decentralization and centralization of local public services in Tunisia' (PhD dissertation, Massachusetts Institute of Technology, 1992), 29.

21. Éric Deroo and Antoine Champeaux, 'Panorama des troupes coloniales françaises dans les deux guerres mondiales' [An overview of French colonial troops in the two world wars], *Revue historique des armées* 271 (2013): 72–88; Paul Azan, *L'Armée indigène nord-africaine* [The North African indigenous army] (Paris: Charles-Lavauzelle, 1925); and François Arnoulet, 'Les Tunisiens et la première guerre mondiale (1914–1918)' [Tunisians and the World War I (1914–1918)], *Revue de l'Occident musulman et de la Méditerranée* 38 (1984): 47–61.

22. James Cooke, 'Paul Azan and l'Armée indigène Nord-Africaine' [Paul Azan and the North African indigenous army], *Military Affairs* 45, no. 3 (1981): 133–137; Leon Carl Brown, 'The Islamic Reformist Movement in North Africa,' *Journal of Modern African Studies* 2, no. 1 (1964): 55–63.

23. Adria K. Lawrence, *Imperial Rule and the Politics of Nationalism: Anti-Colonial Protest in the French Empire* (Cambridge: Cambridge University Press, 2013).

24. Intissar Kherigi, 'Municipal Boundaries and the Politics of Space,' The Program on Governance and Local Development at Gothenburg, working paper no. 38, 2021, https://gld.gu.se/media/2032/gld-working-paper-38.pdf.

25. Alexandra Domike Blackman and Marlette Jackson, 'Gender Stereotypes, Political Leadership, and Voting Behavior in Tunisia,' *Political Behavior* 43 (2021): 1037–1066. Charrad, *States and Women's Rights*; and Emma C. Murphy, 'Women in Tunisia: Between State Feminism and Economic Reform,' in *Women and Globalization in the Arab Middle East*, eds. Eleanor Abdella Doumato and Marsha Pripstein Posusney (Boulder, CO: Lynne Rienner, 2003), 169–194.

26. See Mounira M. Charrad, 'Policy Shifts: State, Islam, and Gender in Tunisia, 1930s–1990s,' *Social Politics: International Studies in Gender, State & Society* 4, no. 2 (1997): 284–319; Mounira M. Charrad and Amina Zarrugh, 'Equal or Complementary? Women in the New Tunisian Constitution after the Arab Spring,' *Journal of North African Studies* 19,

no. 2 (2014): 230–243; and Aili Mari Tripp, *Seeking Legitimacy: Why Arab Autocracies Adopt Women's Rights* (Cambridge: Cambridge University Press, 2019).

27. Mark A. Tessler, Janet Rogers, and Daniel Schneider, 'Women's Emancipation in Tunisia: Changing Policies and Popular Responses,' in *Women in the Muslim World*, eds. Lois Beck and Nikki Keddie (Cambridge, MA: Harvard University Press, 1978), 141–158; Adrian M. Morse, Jr., and Leila P. Sayeh, 'Tunisia: Marriage, Divorce, and Foreign Recognition,' *Family Law Quarterly* 29, no. 3 (1995): 701–720; and Thomas F. Brady, 'Bourguiba Toasts Modernism with Fruit Juice at Time of Fast; Deplores Traditional Rite of Ramadan—Says Tunisians Tolerate Non-Observance,' *New York Times*, March 6, 1962, www.nytimes.com/1962/03/06/archives/bourguiba-toasts-modernism-with-fruit-juice-at-time-of-fast.html.

28. Victoria Chambers and Clare Cummings, 'Building Momentum: Women's Empowerment in Tunisia,' *Overseas Development Institute Report*, November 2014, www.odi.org/sites/odi.org.uk/files/odi-assets/publications-opinion-files/10319.pdf.

29. Blackman and Jackson, 'Gender Stereotypes, Political Leadership, and Voting Behavior'; Chambers and Cummings, 'Building Momentum.' This includes the elections for the National Constituent Assembly (NCA) in 2011, as well as the elections for the national parliament in 2014 and 2019.

30. *Al Jazeera*, 'Tunisia Lifts Ban on Muslim Women Marrying Non-Muslims,' September 14, 2017, www.aljazeera.com/news/2017/09/tunisia-lifts-ban-muslim-women-marrying-muslims-170914154657961.html; *BBC News*, 'Tunisian Women Free to Marry Non-Muslims,' September 15, 2017, www.bbc.com/news/world-africa-41278610.

31. *UN Women*, 'Tunisia Passes Historic Law to End Violence Against Women and Girls,' August 10, 2017, www.unwomen.org/en/news/stories/2017/8/news-tunisia-law-on-ending-violence-against-women.

32. Brady, 'Bourguiba Toasts Modernism,' 8; Lisa Anderson, 'Political Pacts, Liberalism, and Democracy: The Tunisian National Pact of 1988,' *Government and Opposition* 26, no. 2 (1991): 251.

33. Elizabeth R. Nugent, *After Repression: How Polarization Derails Democratic Transition* (Princeton, NJ: Princeton University Press, 2020); Sharan Grewal, 'From Islamists to Muslim Democrats: The Case of Tunisia's Ennahda,' *American Political Science Review* 114, no. 2 (2020): 519–535.

34. Some researchers do not classify Bourguiba as a secularist because he did not call for the complete separation between religion and politics (see for example: Rory McCarthy, 'Re-Thinking Secularism in Post-Independence Tunisia,' *Journal of North African Studies* 19, no. 5 (2014):

733–750). While I agree with McCarthy that Bourguiba's goal was to subordinate of religious institutions and symbols to political authority, I argue that the subordination of religion to political authority is a form of secularist ideology akin to that practiced by the French Third Republic (for a full discussion, see Alexandra Domike Blackman, 'The Politicization of Faith: Settler Colonialism, Education, and Political Identity in Tunisia' (PhD dissertation, Stanford University, 2019)). As Casanova argues: 'the moment the state holds a particular view of "religion" one enters the realm of ideology' (José Casanova, 'The Secular and Secularisms,' *Social Research* 76, no. 4 (2009): 1051). Moreover, there are different forms of secularist ideology that a state can adopt (Ahmet T. Kuru, 'Passive and Assertive Secularism: Historical Conditions, Ideological Struggles, and State Policies toward Religion,' *World Politics* 59, no. 4 (2007): 568–594).

35. Author interview with Mounir Tlili, December 4, 2014; McCarthy, 'Re-Thinking Secularism in Post-Independence Tunisia.'

36. Rachid Ghannouchi, 'Secularism in the Arab Maghreb,' in *Islam and Secularism in the Middle East*, eds. John Esposito and Azzam Tamimi (New York, NY: New York University Press, 2000), 97–123.

37. Brady, 'Bourguiba Toasts Modernism,' 8.

38. Charrad, 'Policy Shifts'; McCarthy, 'Re-Thinking Secularism in Post-Independence Tunisia.'

39. This latter aim is a point of some contention, with researchers like Béatrice Hibou arguing that, even after these reforms, the state remained in control of the economy but the tools of control had changed.

40. Emma C. Murphy, 'Ten Years On: Ben Ali's Tunisia,' *Mediterranean Politics* 2, no. 3 (1997): 114–122.

41. Francesco Cavatorta and Rikke Hostrup Haugbølle, 'The End of Authoritarian Rule and the Mythology of Tunisia under Ben Ali,' *Mediterranean Politics* 17, no 2 (2012): 179–195.

42. Bob Rijkers, Caroline Freund, and Antonio Nucifora, 'All in the Family: State Capture in Tunisia,' *World Bank Policy Research Working Paper*, no. 6810, 2014, https://openknowledge.worldbank.org/bitstream/handle/10986/17726/WPS6810.pdf?sequence=1&isAllowed=y.

43. Chantal E. Berman and Elizabeth R. Nugent, 'Regionalism in New Democracies: The Authoritarian Origins of Voter–Party Linkages,' *Political Research Quarterly* 73, no. 4 (2019): 908–922.

44. Hibou, *The Force of Obedience*.

45. Anderson, 'Political Pacts, Liberalism, and Democracy,' 244–260.

46. Elizabeth R. Nugent, 'The Psychology of Repression and Polarization,' *World Politics* 72, no. 2 (2020): 291–334; Grewal, 'From Islamists to Muslim Democrats.'

47. Hibou, *The Force of Obedience*.

48. Grewal, 'From Islamists to Muslim Democrats.'
49. Nugent, 'The Psychology of Repression and Polarization.'
50. Laryssa Chomiak, 'The Making of a Revolution in Tunisia,' *Middle East Law and Governance* 3, nos. 1–2 (2011): 68–83.
51. Chantal E. Berman, 'Protest, Social Policy, and Political Regimes in the Middle East' (PhD dissertation, Princeton University, 2019).
52. Hibou, *The Force of Obedience*, 271.
53. Paul Pierson, 'Increasing Returns, Path Dependence, and the Study of Politics,' *American Political Science Review* 94, no. 2 (2000): 251.
54. For an example related to women's rights see Siwan Anderson, 'Legal Origins and Female HIV,' *American Economic Review* 108, no. 6 (2018): 1407–1439.
55. Khellaf, 'Decentralization and Centralization of Local Public Services.'
56. Stanley L. Engerman and Kenneth L. Sokoloff, 'Factor Endowments, Inequality, and Paths of Development among New World Economies,' *Economía* 3, no. 1 (2002): 41–88.
57. Elise Huillery, 'History Matters: The Long-Term Impact of Colonial Public Investments in French West Africa,' *American Economic Journal: Applied Economics* 1, no. 2 (2009): 176–215.
58. Alberto Bisin and Thierry Verdier, 'The Economics of Cultural Transmission and the Dynamics of Preferences,' *Journal of Economic Theory* 97, no. 2 (2001): 298–319.
59. Avidit Acharya, Matthew Blackwell, and Maya Sen, *Deep Roots: How Slavery Still Shapes Southern Politics* (Princeton, NJ: Princeton University Press, 2018).
60. Lawrence, 'Repression and Activism among the Arab Spring's First Movers,' 699–718.
61. Wendy Pearlman, 'Moral Identity and Protest Cascades in Syria,' *British Journal of Political Science* 48, no. 4 (2018): 877–901.
62. M. Kent Jennings, Laura Stoker, and Jake Bowers, 'Politics across Generations: Family Transmission Reexamined,' *Journal of Politics* 71, no. 3 (2009): 782–799.
63. Lisa Blaydes, *State of Repression: Iraq under Saddam Hussein* (Princeton, NJ: Princeton University Press, 2018).
64. Nugent, 'The Psychology of Repression and Polarization.'
65. Bourguiba was born in the coastal city of Monastir, and Ben Ali was born in the coastal city of Sousse.
66. Anderson, *The State and Social Transformation*, 17; Parks, 'Local-National Relations and the Politics of Property Rights.'
67. Natsuko Obayashi and Emanuele Santi, 'Tunisia: Economic and Social Challenges Beyond the Revolution,' African Development Bank, 2012, www.afdb.org/sites/default/files/documents/projects-and-

operations/tunisia_economic_and_social_challenges.pdf; Mongi Boughzala and Mohamed Tlili Hamdi, 'Promoting Inclusive Growth in Arab Countries: Rural and Regional Development in Tunisia,' *Brookings Institution Global Economy and Development*, working paper no. 71, 2014, www.brookings.edu/wp-content/uploads/2016/06/Arab-EconPaper5Boughzala-v3.pdf.

68. Berman and Nugent, 'Regionalism in New Democracies.'
69. Hamza Meddeb, 'Young People and Smuggling in the Kasserine Region: Stories of Dispossession and the Dynamics of Exclusion,' *International Alert*, May 2016, www.international-alert.org/sites/default/files/Tunisia_YoungPeopleSmuggling_EN_2016.pdf.
70. Khellaf, 'Decentralization and Centralization of Local Public Services,' 26.
71. Some of the gap between coastal and interior regions also existed under Ottoman rule, but discussion of differential development under Ottoman rule is beyond the scope of this chapter.
72. Brown, 'The Many Faces of Colonial Rule.'
73. See Gustav Wolfrom, 'Comment on peut acquérir une propriété en Tunisie' [How to acquire a property in Tunisia], Service de la Colonisation [Colonization Services], Direction de l'Agriculture et du Commerce [Agriculture and commerce unit], n.d.
74. The Colonization Service actively courted military veterans in its publicity for land sales. The Committee for French Settlement published advertisements for land, some specifically calling for soldiers to settle in Tunisia as a bulwark against social and political upheaval ('Aux Soldats de la Classe,' Le Comité du Peuplement Français).
75. Clancy-Smith, *Tunisian Revolutions*.
76. The axes for the Tunisian and European populations differ. I display them together to show the overall patterns of change for each of the three main populations. Until the 1926 census, the French Administration used the category 'Indigene' for all North Africans in Tunisia. I continue to aggregate the total North African population in Tunisia to make the population measure consistent across multiple time periods. The largest non-Tunisian population included in the 'Indigene' category is Algerian, which typically made up 10,000 to 25,000 of the population in that time period.
77. The increase in the French population was primarily due to new French settlement and not to the naturalization of Italians to French citizenship. While many Italians adopted French citizenship, naturalizations only made up a small portion of new French citizens in Tunisia at this time. The population data comes from French censuses conducted in Tunisia. Between 1891 and 1936, the French conducted and published a national

census every five years, with the exception of 1916 because of World War I. After 1936, the French conducted a census every ten years. In addition to the national census data, the numbers for the Italian population pre-French protectorate are taken from Statistica Generale del Regno D'Italia, *Censimento degli italiani all'estero (31 dicembre 1871)* [Census of Italians abroad (December 31, 1871)] (Rome: Stamperia Reale, 1874) and Statistica Generale del Regno D'Italia, *Censimento degli italiani all'estero (Dicembre 1881)* [Census of Italians abroad (December 1881)] (Rome: Tipografia Nell'ospizio di San Michele, 1884). The decolonization process is manifest in the steep drop between 1956 and 1966.

78. Coastal regions include the northeast and center-east (the historical *contrôle* of Bizerte, Grombalia [Nabeul], Sousse, and Sfax), while the interior regions include the northwest and center-west regions (the historical *contrôle* of Kef, Souk-el-Arba [Jendouba], Beja, Thala [Kasserine], Kairouan, and the combined southern region [Djerba, Gabes, Gafsa, Tozeur, and the southern territories]). Some *contrôles* and *annexes* were merged in order to keep the geographical unit stable and consistent over time. The entire southern region was merged because of changes in how the French reported the population in the south. Zaghouan was merged with Tunis. Beja, Medjez-el-Bab, and Teboursouk were merged. Kef and Maktar were merged, and Souk-el-Arba and Tabarka were merged. The figures include, the Grand Tunis region, but the patterns in the figures are similar if Tunis is excluded.

79. Laryssa Chomiak, 'Tunisia Transitional Justice Case Study,' Centre for the Study of Violence and Reconciliation (CSVR), October 2018, 7, www.csvr.org.za/project-reports/Tunisian-Case-Laryssa-Chomiak.pdf.

80. Ibid., 12.

81. Dirk Vandewalle, 'From the New State to the New Era: Toward a Second Republic in Tunisia,' *Middle East Journal* 42, no. 4 (1988): 606.

82. Rijkers, Freund, and Nucifora, 'All in the Family: State Capture in Tunisia.'

83. Monia Ben Hamadi, 'Tunisie: Au milieu de la cacophonie politique un projet de loi pour restaurer les Habous fait polémique' [Tunisia: In the Midst of the Political Cacophony a Project of Law to Restore the Habous Councils Stirs up Debate], *HuffPost Maghreb*, November 13, 2013. English translation conducted by the author.

84. McCarthy, 'Re-Thinking Secularism in Post-Independence Tunisia'; Cavatorta and Haugbølle, 'The End of Authoritarian Rule and the Mythology of Tunisia under Ben Ali.'

85. De Montety, 'Old Families and New Elites,' 177.

86. This argument is part of my dissertation work. For more details, see: Alexandra Domike Blackman, 'The Politicization of Faith: Settler

Colonialism, Education, and Political Identity in Tunisia' (PhD dissertation, Stanford University, 2019).

87. Ministère des Affaires Étrangères, *Rapport au Président de la République sur la situation de la Tunisie (1881–1890)* [Report to the President of the Republic on the situation in Tunisia (1881–1890)] (Paris: Imprimerie Nationale, 1890); Ministère de l'Instruction Publique et des Beaux-Arts, *Commission de statistique de l'enseignement primaire:Tome sixième (1896–1897)* [Primary education statistics commission: Sixth volume (1896–1897)] (Paris: Imprimerie Nationale, 1900).

88. The quote is from a foreign diplomatic cable quoted in: Anne Wolf, *Political Islam in Tunisia:The History of Ennahda* (Oxford: Oxford University Press, 2017).

89. This is a qualitative measure of support for Bourguiba and Ben Youssef based on confidential French administrative reports that describe local political activities by different political groups during the two-week period around the election. When the local administrator reports elite and/or mass support for Bourguiba but not for Ben Youssef, that region is coded as favoring Bourguiba and vice versa.

90. Nidaa Tounes was founded following the revolution under the leadership of Essebsi, a longtime ally of Bourguiba, as a secular political party.

91. The vote shares are measured at the delegation level and then aggregated to match the historical *contrôle* boundaries.

92. Bourguiba defeated Ben Youssef and his Islamist supporters through a combination of French support, elimination of the independent financial support for Islamic institutions (primarily by nationalizing the *habous* land as discussed above), and harsh repression of Ben Youssef and his supporters.

93. Boughzala and Hamdi, 'Promoting Inclusive Growth in Arab Countries.'

94. Blaydes, *State of Repression*; Nugent, 'The Psychology of Repression and Polarization.'

95. Berman, 'Protest, Social Policy, and Political Regimes.'

INDEX

Note: Page numbers followed by "*n*" refer to notes, "*f*" refer to figures and "*t*" refer to tables

abolition of slavery (1846), 189
ACLED. *See* Armed Conflict Location and Event Data Project (ACLED)
ADAM. *See* Association for Equality and Development (ADAM)
Afek Tounes (political party), 137
Afghanistan, 57
AFTURD, 117
agency and leadership, 41–4
AISPP. *See* International Association for the Support of Political Prisoners (AISPP)
Ajroubi, Mohammed Ayachi, 72
AJT. *See* Association of Tunisian Journalists (AJT)
Al Janoubiya, 73
Al Jomhouri (political party), 10
Al Karama Coalition, 12, 79
Al Moustaqilla TV, 74
al-Najjar, Abdelmajid, 94
Al Quran Al Karim radio station, 79

Al Rahma (political party), 79
Al Wataniya (TV channel), 80
Al-Bawsala (Compass), 120
Al-Fath Mosque, 97
Algeria, 32, 159, 191, 203, 204
ALTT. *See* Association for the Fight against Torture in Tunisia (ALTT)
AMEN program, 147
amnesty law (2015), 14
AMT. *See* Association of Tunisian Judges (AMT)
Anderson, Lisa, 191, 194
annual protests (1998–2019), 131*f*
Ansar al-Shari'a, 45, 98, 224*n*10
anti-austerity protests, 130, 147
anti-corruption campaigns, 21
'anti-Islamist' clan, 75–6
anti-regime movement, 110
anti-revolution, 12
Arab Spring, 118, 152. *See also* Arab uprisings
Arab Barometer surveys, 125, 244*n*101

Arab uprisings (2011), 16, 31, 33, 36, 50. *See also* uprisings
  protester disappointments, 51–2
Armed Conflict Location and Event Data Project (ACLED), 130–1, 132
arms trafficking, 16
Article (1), 91
Article (2), 92, 234*n*40
Article (230), 123
Article (28), 117
Article (6), 92, 234*n*40
Article (80), 12–13, 237*n*85
assassination, 6, 16, 45, 98, 224*n*10
Assembly of the Representatives of the People, 8. *See also* parliament
Association des journalistes tunisiens. *See* Association of Tunisian Journalists (AJT)
Association des magistrats tunisiens. *See* Association of Tunisian Judges (AMT)
Association for Equality and Development (ADAM), 122
Association for the Fight against Torture in Tunisia (ALTT), 109, 119
Association for the Preservation of the Qur'an, 96
Association of Tunisian Journalists (AJT), 110
Association of Tunisian Judges (AMT), 110, 228*n*39
Associations Law, 107–8
attack, 6, 16, 122, 174, 180–1
  Gafsa attack (1980), 177–8
  IS attack on Ben Gardane, 27–8, 177, 186

IS-led attacks (2015), 184–5
  attack on the US Embassy, 70
ATFD. *See* Tunisian Association of Democratic Women (ATFD)
Audiovisual Authority (ICA), 79
audiovisual regulation, 70–1, 80–1
austerity, 18, 26, 128, 144, 196
  anti-austerity protests, 118–19, 130, 146
'authoritarian isolates', 63
authoritarianism, 22–3, 32, 51
autocratic, 53, 104, 187, 193, 198, 203
Avenue Bourguiba, 49, 135
Avenue Habib Bourguiba. *See* Avenue Bourguiba

Baatour, Mounir, 123
Bab al-Assal, 167
Bab al-Khadhra, 164
al-Banna, Hassan, 96
Bardo Museum, 16, 135, 138
Bardo protests, 135
Bardo public square, 7, 117
Bardo Square. *See* Bardo public square
Bardo, 12
Basta (2019 campaign), 146
Bayat, Asef, 91, 233*n*10
behavioral path dependence, 200–1
Belaïd, Chokri, 6, 45, 117, 136
Belvedere Park, 165
Ben Achour, Yadh, 43, 67
Ben Ali, Zine El Abidine, 4, 42, 105, 154–5
  Ben Ali Era, 195–8
  National Pact (1988), 194, 197
  went to Saudi Arabia, 39
Ben Arous, 144–5
Ben Gardane, 16, 27–8, 185
  IS attack on, 173–4, 177–8

Ben Jaafar, Mustafa, 5, 69, 136, 230n54
Ben Sedrine, Sihem, 81
Ben Youssef, Salah, 213–14, 215, 265n89, 265n92
Berber population, 39, 41
Berman, Chantel, 130, 136, 203
Bizerte, 208
black Tunisians, 122–3
Blaydes, Lisa, 188–9, 201, 215
border, 16, 27, 154, 158, 174, 177, 203
  border areas, 183
  border community, 179, 180
  cross-border smuggling, 179, 185
Bouazizi, Mohamed, 110, 156
Bourdieu, Pierre, 80–1
Bourguiba regime, 42
Bourguiba, Habib, 33, 96, 106–7, 154, 175, 240n22, 240n26
Bourguiba era, 193–5
Brady, Thomas, 194
Brahmi, Mohamed, 6, 45, 117, 136
bread riots (1983–84), 127
Brigade anti-terrorisme de la police (BAT), 178
Budget Law (2019), 144, 146
bureaucracy, 20, 37, 141, 189, 192

cahier des charges, 64
Cairo, 37
Cap Bon, 162
Carthage agreement (2016), 128, 137, 146
Carthage II agreement, 144
Carthage, 12, 80
Cavatorta, Francesco, 196
Chahed government, 146, 150

Chahed, Youssef, 77–8, 121, 137, 144
Charrad, Mounira, 191
Chergui gas field, 138–9
chômeur-diplômé (unemployed graduate), 154
Chomiak, Laryssa, 141, 198, 208
CICM. See National Commission of Investigation on Corruption and Malpractice (CICM)
'civic state' (dawla madaniyya), 94
civil society organizations (CSOs), 103–4, 112f, 114t, 120–1, 244n101
  changes in, 113–16
  growth rate, 110–13
civil war, 1, 32, 118
civilian, 33, 38–9, 173, 177, 179–80, 181
clan
  'anti-Islamist' clan, 75–6
  Ben Ali clan, 74
clandestine, 39, 178
Clancy-Smith, Julia, 204–5
Club Africain (2012–17), 74
CNLT. See Council for Liberties in Tunisia (CNLT)
CNPR. See National Council for the Protection of the Revolution (CNPR)
coalition, 24, 40–1, 87, 98, 145
  Al Karama Coalition, 12, 79
  anti-Islamist coalition, 136
  dissolution of, 8
  Ennahda to form, 68–9
  Nidaa Tounes and Ennahda, 128
  Nidaa Tounes, 47–8
  ruling coalition, 5–6, 53–4
  tenuous coalitions, 10, 13
coastal areas, 122, 207
coastal cities, 110, 111, 189

coastal region, 19, 27, 140, 151, 186, 202, 264n78
  conflict between marginalized interior and, 134
  French colonial rule, 204
  French settlement, 206–7, 207*f*
  Tunisian population in, 208
'coastalization', 205
Code of Personal Status, 107
'coercive policy transfer', 66
Cold War, 184
Coleman, Isobel, 35
colonial period, 107, 199, 205
Colonization Service (1898), 191, 204, 263n74
colonialism, 205
commerce, 204, 208
Commission for Political Reform, 116
Commission of Inquiry into Misappropriation and Corruption, 20
Communism, 89
community policing, 182–3
Compagnie phosphate de Gafsa (CPG), 139, 198
consensus, 4, 7, 9, 13–14, 83, 128
  consensus politics, end of, 144
  elite consensus, 137, 141
  Ennahda's attempt to gain, 99–100
conflict, 1, 33, 136, 144, 182, 216
  conflict lines, 134
  identity conflict, 135
  ideological conflicts, 149
  Islamist and secular forces, 128
Congress for the Republic (CPR) (political party), 5
Conseil national pour la protection de la revolution. *See* National

Council for the Protection of the Revolution (CNPR)
Conseil supérieur de l'audiovisuel (CSA), 65
Constitution (1861), 189, 258n8
Constitution (1956), 47
Constitution (1959), 91
Constitution (2014), 60, 82, 84, 152–3
constitutional court, 9, 13, 82
constitutional draft (Article 2.3), 92
'constitutional political pathway', 4
contention, 18, 26, 79, 127, 142
  Islamist contention, 96
  Islamists and secularists, 133
  protests during waves of, 139–40
  public contention, 138, 148
  social contention, 150
'coordinated transition', 66
Copenhagen school, 184
Copernican revolution, 184
corruption, 20–1
Council for Liberties in Tunisia (CNLT), 109
COVID-19 pandemic, 21–2, 100
CPG. *See* Compagnie phosphate de Gafsa (CPG)
CPR. *See* Congress for the Republic (CPR)
crisis, 11–13, 45–6, 77, 118
  COVID-19, 79, 150
  economic crisis, 31
  financial crisis (2008), 153
  political crisis, 7, 12, 16, 104
'critical junctures', 28
CSA. *See* Conseil supérieur de l'audiovisuel (CSA)
CSOs. *See* civil society organizations (CSOs)

culture, 2, 64, 156, 182, 184
  Ottoman political culture, 189
  political culture, 9–10, 81–2
cultural influences, 55
'culture of impunity', 14

Da'wa, 88
da'wa activism, 96–7
da'wa activists, 99
Da'wa wa Islah (DWI), 97–8
dawla, 181
debt, 17, 152
Decree-Law 116 (DL116), 61,
  66–7, 68–9, 79, 227n31,
  228n40
  parliament's handling of, 81
de-ideologization, 88
'democracy without democrats',
  82
democratic backsliding, 15
democratic consolidation, 13, 15,
  29, 104
Democratic Constitutional Rally
  (RCD), 42, 155, 193
Democratic Current, 12
Democratic Front for Labor and
  Liberty (FDTL), 5, 69
democratic process, 32–3
democratic transition, 2–3, 7, 35,
  51, 54–7, 104, 189
  civil society organizations, role
    on, 25, 41, 46
  socioeconomic difficulties
    impacts on, 22
  success of, 15
'democratic' institution card, 68
democratization, 23, 56, 84, 89,
  96
  civil society's role in, 103–4,
    108–9
  impact of protests on, 149

democratizing, 25, 63, 89, 104,
  109, 160
Dilou, Samir, 100
Dimassi, Houcine, 210
Directorate of Public Education
  (1883), 212
diversity, 25, 103, 105, 121, 124,
  143
'division of labor', 109
DL115, 67, 227n31, 228n40
DL116. See Decree-Law 116
  (DL116)
DWI. See Da'wa wa Islah (DWI)

Eastern Europe, 56, 104
Economic and Financial
  Reconciliation Law (2015), 141
economic growth rates, 17
economic hardship, 17–19
economy, 20–1, 22, 106, 171, 179,
  208
  colonial economy, 151
  global economy, 196
  informal economy, 18, 27, 155
  moral economy, 154, 157, 161,
    180
  political economy, 149
  smuggling economy, 159
Egypt, 1, 33, 137
  Cairo, 37
  Mubarak resignation, 38–9
  Tamarod protest movement, 7
  US policy toward democracy
    in, 52
Eid al-Fitr, 167
Eiffel Tower, 170
El Hiwar Ettounsi, 71–2, 74
El Janoubiya TV, 72
Electoral Law, 67, 78, 193–4
election, 9, 48, 117, 152, 194, 213
Ellouz, Habib, 97

employment, 17, 125, 138–9, 147, 150, 165
  formal employment, 155, 159
  See also Ministry of Employment
Engerman, Stanley, 200
Ennahda (political party), 5, 24, 44, 46–7, 69–70, 236n72
  criticism on, 6–7
  draft law introduced by, 210
  Ghannouchi, Rachid, 40, 46, 54
  ideological transformation, 93–4
  Laraydeh's views on, 87–8
  legislative elections (2019), 100
  Montplaisir, 69
  municipal elections (2018), 99
  professionalization of, 98–9
  rapprochement between Nidaa Tounes and, 8–9
  role in parliamentary system, 83–4
  shura council, 11, 92, 99, 141
    See also majlis al-shura
  struggles faced by, 10–11
  2014 two-party vote, 215f
  2016 conference, 95, 99
Ennaïfer, Rachida, 71, 72
Essebsi, Béji Caïd, 4, 40, 67–8, 122, 228n36
  appointed as Prime Minister, 42–3
  views on citizens of Ben Gardane, 179–80
Essid, Habib, 137
Essid, Sami, 73, 74
Ettakatol (political party), 44
EU. *See* European Union (EU)
Europe, 50
European Union (EU), 115
Europeans, 56

Extractive Industries Transparency Initiative (EITI), 140
Extractivisim, 138–9
extremism, 118, 181

Fakhfakh, Elyes, 12, 79–80
'family-dynasty', 54
FDTL. *See* Democratic Front for Labor and Liberty (FDTL)
Fech Nestanaou (FN) (campaign), 143, 144–5
Feltrin, Lorenzo, 154
Ferjani, Riadh, 71, 72
Finance Law (2018), 128, 144
financial crisis (2008), 153
fiscal deficits, 17
fiscal instability, 17
FN. *See* Fech Nestanaou (FN)
'footloose labour', 154
Foreign Affairs (magazine), 95
Foreign aid, 25, 115
foreign investment (FDI), 22
France, 33, 50, 56, 65, 124, 192
Free Destourian Party (political party), 12
Free Patriotic Union (UPL) (political party), 74, 137
French citizens, 190, 191, 204
French colonial administration, 189, 191, 204
French colonial investments, 200
French colonial period, 106
French colonial rule, 204
French colonial subjects, 192
French Empire, 204–5
French invasion, 190–1
French labor unions, 39–40
French Third Republic, 212
French unions, 39–40
Freund, Caroline, 196

G7+. *See* Group of Seven (G7+)
Gaddafi, Muammar, 33–4
Gafsa (city), 123, 138–9
Gafsa attack (1980), 177–8
Gafsa protests (2008), 149,
    240n21
'Gallicized' elite, 211
gender-based violence, 194
general strike (1978), 127
General Tunisian Union of Students
    (UGTE), 108
'generational divide', 120
Germany, 57
Ghannouchi, Mohamed, 4, 42, 133
Ghannouchi, Rachid, 40, 46, 54,
    90–1
globalization, 205
Goldstone, Jack, 130
GONGOs. *See* government-
    organized NGOs (GONGOs)
government-organized NGOs
    (GONGOs), 108
graffiti, 170
Gramsci, Antonio, 88–9
Grewal, Sharan, 197
Group of Destourian Women, 107
Group of Seven (G7+), 181
Groupe d'intervention militaire
    (GIM), 178
Gulf states, 115

Habous Administration, 211, 212
habous system, 191–2, 195, 210
Hage, Ghassan, 157
HAICA. *See* High Independent
    Authority for Audiovisual
    Communication (HAICA)
Hallin, Daniel C., 74
Hamas, 52
El Hamdi, Hachemi, 74
Han, Clara, 157

Hannibal TV, 74
haraka (movement), 97, 99
Harim al-Sultan (Turkish drama
    series), 73, 77
Hassine, Tahar Ben, 71–2, 74
Haugbølle, Rikke Hostrup, 196
Hay Zuhour, 159, 161
Hibou, Béatrice, 154, 187, 196–7
High Commission for Political
    Reform, 4
High Commission for the
    Achievement of the Objectives
    of Revolution, Political Reform
    and Democratic Transition
    (ISROR), 66–7
High Council for the Realization of
    the Goals of the Revolution, 51
High Electoral Commission (ISIE),
    59–60, 78
High Independent Authority for
    Audiovisual Communication
    (HAICA), 23–4, 65, 80, 83,
    228n39
    criticism from STDM, 72–3
    'failed test of public validity', 76
    missions led by, 59–60
High Judicial Council, 142
Higher Authority for the
    Realization of the Objectives
    of the Revolution, Political
    Reform, and Democratic
    Transition (HIROR), 116–17,
    134
Higher Committee on Human
    Rights and Fundamental
    Freedoms, 108
Higher Political Reform Council,
    43
HIROR. *See* Higher Authority for
    the Realization of the Objectives
    of the Revolution, Political

Reform, and Democratic Transition (HIROR)
historical persistence, 198–9
hizb (party), 97, 99
homosexuality, 123
House of Deputies (1997–2011), 67
Huillery, Elise, 200
Human rights, 13–14, 43, 45, 83, 111, 120
Tunisian Human Rights League (LTDH), 7, 107, 136
violations, 137
Huntington, Samuel, 56
'hybrid regimes', 85

IAA. *See* 'independent administrative authorities' (IAA)
Ibn Khaldun, 189
ICA. *See* Audiovisual Authority (ICA)
ideology, 36
illegal immigrants, 16
'imagined community', 201
IMF. *See* International Monetary Fund (IMF)
immigration, 208
independence, 3, 31, 41, 68–70, 106–7, 175
Bourguiba era after, 193–5
education system at, 214–15
habous system abolished at, 210
HAICA, 72–3
post-independence era, 179, 189, 207
post-independence policies, 202, 208
protests for, 127
women's rights after, 191
'independent administrative authorities' (IAA), 60–1, 63, 81

'independent constitutional bodies', 84
India, 35
industry, 7, 53, 118, 208
informal economy, 18–19
inner regions, 3, 16, 17, 19, 26, 28
INRIC. *See* National Information and Communication Reform Commission (INRIC)
institutional path dependence, 199–200
International Association for the Support of Political Prisoners (AISPP), 109
International Monetary Fund (IMF), 128, 144
International Republican Institute (IRI), 50
institution, 70, 116, 157, 181, 200
'democratic' institution card, 68
Tunisian military as most respected, 182
Iran, 57
Iraq, 1, 47
US invasion, 52
Irhal movement, 6
irregular migration (*harga*), 160
IS. *See* Islamic State (IS)
ISIE. *See* High Electoral Commission (ISIE), 59–60
Islam, 88
Islamic education system, 212
Islamic State (IS), 91, 92–3, 173, 181
Islamism, 88, 89–90, 94, 100, 233n24
Islamist ideology, 91
Islamist universalism, 101
Islamists, 96, 133, 216

ISROR. *See* High Commission for the Achievement of the Objectives of Revolution, Political Reform and Democratic Transition (ISROR) Italian, 161, 191, 205, 263–4n77
population, 205–6, 205f
IVD. *See* Truth and Dignity Commission (IVD), 59–60
I-Watch, 20, 121, 219n3

Japan, 57
Jaziri, Said, 79
Jebali, Hamadi, 5
jihadi Salafis, 6
jihadis, 177
Jomaa, Mehdi, 8, 46, 230n54
Jordan, 1
Jöst, Prisca, 131
journalism, 71
journalist, 69, 151, 110, 229n43
Judicial Financial Pole, 20
justice
  restorative justice, 159
  social justice, 3, 21, 27, 130, 152
  socioeconomic justice, 18
  transitional justice, 13–15, 53, 60, 121, 141

Kairouan, 159
Kamour protests, 18
Kamour, 139
Karoui & Karoui, 76
Karoui group, 77
Karoui, Nabil, 68, 73, 74, 76–7, 231n73
Kasbah, 134
Kasbah I (protests), 133–4
Kasbah II (protests), 133–4, 138, 150
Kasbah Square, 133

Kasserine, 27, 140, 151, 166
  'Arts of Revolution', 170
  terrorism in, 158–9
  2016 uprising in, 156–7
Kébili, 140
Kerkennah, 138–9
Khalil Tounes, 77
Khellaf, Assia, 192, 199, 203–4
Kherigi, Intissar, 193
King, Martin Luther, Jr., 35
Ksiksi, Jamila, 123

labor militancy, 154
labor union mobilization (2019), 147
labor unions, 45, 105, 224–5n12. *See also* UGTT
Lampedusa, 161
Larayedh, Ali, 6, 87–8
Latin America, 33, 56, 104, 148
law, 14, 15, 32, 47, 81, 93–4, 121, 152, 260n31
  against racial discrimination, 122–3
  Associations Law, 107–8
  Budget Law (2019), 146
  draft law, 210–11
  Ennahda, 92
  Finance Law (2018), 144
  Financial Reconciliation Law, 141–2
  International Center for Non-Profit Law (ICNL), 241n54
  Islamic law, 117, 197
  Ottoman Land Law (1858), 188–9
  personal status laws, 191, 199–200
  Transitional Justice Law (2013–53), 142–3
  women's rights, 193

Law of Associations (2011), 113
Law on Administrative
  Reconciliation, 141
Lawrence, Adria, 192, 200–1
Lebanon, 1
Levant, 34
LGBTQ rights, 122, 123
Liberal, 8, 37–8, 82, 88, 96, 101,
  233n24
  Ben Achour, 43
  EU, 115
  neoliberal, 18, 129, 144, 150,
    151–2, 196
liberalization, 96, 106, 107,
  108–9
  economic liberalization, 196–7
Libya, 1, 159, 183, 203
Ligue tunisienne des droits de
  l'homme (LTDH), 45
liminal state, 3, 13
local security committees, 182
LTDH. See Tunisian Human Rights
  League (LTDH)

Mabrouk, Mehdi, 159–61
Maghreb, 50
majlis al-shura, 99. See also shura
  council
Makhzen, 38
Maliki law school, 94
Mamluk families, 190, 258n10
Mancini, Paolo, 74
Manich Msameh (MM), 141–3,
  209–10
maqasid al-shari'a, 91, 93–4, 101
marginalization, 17, 27, 28, 125,
  196, 203
Marxism-Leninism, 50
Marzouki, Moncef, 5, 48, 69,
  230n54
Mash'hed, 123–4

Marsad
  Baladia project, 121
  Budget project, 121
  Majles project, 120
Massardier, Gilles, 63
Mebazaa, Fouad, 4, 42, 67
Mechichi, Hichem, 12, 31, 79–80
Meddeb, Hamza, 155, 203
'Media Ownership Monitor'
  report, 73
medina, 94
Mekki, Abdellatif, 100
MENA. See Middle East and North
  Africa (MENA) region
Méon, J.M., 65
Merzouki, Moncef, 5, 10, 26, 48,
  69
MFM (radio station), 73
Middle East, 1, 23, 52
Middle East and North Africa
  (MENA) region, 33, 34, 104,
  108–9, 193
Middle East Eye (online news
  outlet), 90
Military, the, 33, 37–39, 46, 137
  Military and civilian figures, 33,
    39, 41
  Military and civilian victory, 181
  Military and security officials,
    38, 109
  Military barracks, 178
  Military dictatorships, 56
  Military dominated regime,
    32–3
  Military establishment, 38, 45
  Military officers, 34
  Military services, 109
  Military zone, 158–9
  Tunisian military, 41, 182
  Weak military, 39
militant incursions, 16

mining basin, 198, 240n22
Ministry of Education, 195
Ministry of Employment, 164,
    166–7
Ministry of Interior, 107–8, 113
MM. *See* Manich Msameh (MM)
mobilization, 129–30
modern, 8, 14, 36, 95, 106
modernist, 74, 93, 95, 106, 175
modernity, 89, 154
Mohammed VI (Moroccan King),
    37–8
Montety, Henri de, 189–90,
    210–11, 258n10
Moore, Clement Henry, 192
Moroccan constitution (2011), 55
Moroccan monarchy, 34
Morocco, 1, 37, 38, 53, 191
Morsi, Mohamed, 7, 46, 118
mosque, 40, 97, 191–2, 195, 200,
    211
Mount Chaanbi, 6, 16
Mourakiboun (Observers), 120
movement, 134, 156, 195, 211
    anti-colonial movements, 192
    anti-regime movement, 110
    campaign movements, 129
    civil rights movement, 35
    Irhal movement, 6
    Islamist movement, 75, 108,
        210
    Neo-Destour movement, 213
    resistance movement, 181
    social movement, 95, 98–9,
        126, 145–6
    Tamarod protest movement, 7
    women's movements, 193
Movement of Islamic Tendency
    (MTI), 96
MTI. *See* Movement of Islamic
    Tendency (MTI)

Mubarak, Hosni, 37–39
municipal elections (2018), 11
music, 142, 166, 170
Muslim Brotherhood (MB), 37, 45,
    93, 100
'Muslim democratic', 87, 88–9,
    95
'Muslim democrats', 95
Muslim Women's Union of Tunisia,
    107
Muslims, 88

Nasra, Larbi, 74
Nasroui, Radhia, 168, 254n56
National Anti-Corruption
    Commission, 20
National Commission of
    Investigation on Corruption and
    Malpractice (CICM), 59–60
National Constituent Assembly
    (2013), 5, 41, 43–4, 210
National Constitutional Assembly
    (NCA), 87, 117, 134–5
National Council for the
    Protection of the Revolution
    (CNPR), 116
National Democratic Institute
    (NDI), 50
National Dialogue Quartet, 7, 44,
    70, 104, 118
National Guard, 177
National Information and
    Communication Reform
    Commission (INRIC), 66–7,
    69, 228n38
National Union of Tunisian
    Journalists (SNJT), 110, 228n39
National Union of Tunisian Women
    (UNFT), 107, 121–2, 193,
    224n7
nationalism, 192, 205, 213

Natural Resource Governance
  Institute, 140
NCA. *See* National Constitutional
  Assembly (NCA)
Neo-Destour movement, 213
Neo-Destour party, 154, 193, 213
'neo-fundamentalism', 89
neoliberal policies, 150
Nessma (TV channel), 64, 68,
  75–6, 78
New Public Management (NPM),
  63–4
New York Times (newspaper), 194
NGOs. *See* nongovernmental
  organizations (NGOs)
Nidaa Tounes, 8, 47–8, 137, 128,
  210, 243n85
Nobel Peace Prize (2015), 104,
  118, 136–7
nongovernmental organizations
  (NGOs), 43, 50, 105, 140
North Africa, 27, 33, 123, 202
  anti-colonial movements in, 192
  base for IS caliphate, 178
  Gulf countries meddling in, 56
Nour radio stations, 73
NPM. *See* New Public Management
  (NPM)
Nucifora, Antonio, 196
Nugent, Elizabeth, 197–8, 201,
  215

Obama, Barack, 48
ONAT. *See* Tunisian Bar Association
  (ONAT)
ontological security, 185–6
Order of Lawyers, 51
Ordre national des avocats de
  Tunisie. *See* Tunisian Bar
  Association (ONAT)
Ottoman administration, 211

Ottoman elite, 211
Ottoman Empire, 189
Ottoman Land Law (1858), 188–9
Ottoman period, 188–9

P/CVE. *See* preventing and
  countering violent extremism
  (P/CVE)
Palestinian cause, 134
pandemic
  COVID-19, 21, 100, 147–8
Paris school, 184
parliament, 12–13, 48, 79–80,
  128, 137, 142, 194
  Ennahda's loss of seats in, 100
  handling of DL116, 81
  Nidaa Tounes took control of, 8
  suspended by Saied, 31, 54
Parliamentary elections (2014),
  47
Party for Justice and Development,
  38
PASC. *See* Programme to Support
  Civil Society (PASC)
Pearlman, Wendy, 201
People's Movement, 12
periphery, 27, 202–3, 204
  'peripheral Keynesianism', 154
Persian Gulf region, 34
Personal Status Code (1956), 193
Petrofac, 139
'philosophy of praxis', 90
pluralism, 41, 61, 74
polarization, 129–30, 132
'political coup', 68
Political economy, 149
political identities, 41
'political Islam', 88
'political parallelism', 74, 76
Political party, 10, 88, 95, 108,
  196, 213

political pluralism, 41
'political theology', 90
Politics, 44–8, 83, 94, 173–4, 189, 210
  consensus politics, 144
  as da'wa, 95–8
  diaspora politics, 192
  elite politics, 132
  gender politics, 193
  institutional politics, 88
  Islamic politics, 89
  post-ideological politics, 89–90
  relationship between media and, 64
  street politics, 135, 137
  as technocratic professionalization, 98–100
  traditional politics, 125
policies, 27, 32, 62, 107, 196, 197, 202
  colonial policies, 191, 192
  economic policies, 149
  land settlement policies, 204
  neoliberal policies, 129, 150, 151
  protests and campaigns against, 18
Popular Front, 10, 54, 142, 145
population, 32, 88, 125, 154, 179
  Berber population, 39, 41
  French population, 190, 204, 206, 208
  Italian populations, 205–6
  local population, 182, 185
  marginal populations, 180
  marginalized populations, 148
  rural populations, 175
  youth population, 170
post-Islamism, 24, 90, 100
Povinelli, Elizabeth, 157
pragmatism, 7, 8, 10, 22–3, 33

precarity, 26, 153, 157, 171, 251n10
presidential elections (2014), 48
presidential elections (2019), 11
preventing and countering violent extremism (P/CVE), 181
private TV channels, 74, 75t
professional associations, 43
'professionalization', 24
Programme d'appui à la société civile. See PASC
Programme to Support Civil Society (PASC), 115
protests, 14, 26, 110–11, 117, 127, 140–1
  increase in, 129–32
  nationalist protests, 192
  political protests, 128, 133–7
  satellite protests, 162
  socioeconomic protests, 137–9, 143, 145
  UGTT efforts to end, 147
protest actors, 129
protesters, 35–7, 49, 51, 129, 133
  clashes between security forces and, 140
  faced police repression, 145
  Kasserine protest, 156
  struggles faced by, 162–4, 167–71
PVE, 182. See also preventing and countering violent extremism (P/CVE)

Qalb Tounes (political party), 11, 74, 76–7
quartet, 40–1, 45–6, 104, 118, 237n1
Qur'an, 95
Qutb, Sayyed, 94–5

Rally for an International
Development Alternative
(RAID), 109
Ramadan, 195
rap music, 170
Raqabah, 20
Ras Jedir, 174
RCD. *See* Democratic
Constitutional Rally (RCD)
Redeyef, 151
reform, 1, 3, 4, 9, 13, 15–17,
228n38, 261n39
Ben Ali, 196
Bourguiba's territorial reforms,
193–5
economic reforms, 20–2, 25,
124
emergency funding, 148
Ennahda, 68–9
French colonial administration,
189
Moroccan monarchy, 34
neoliberal reforms, 144, 149,
154
political parties, 37
UGTT and, 40
'reform fatigue', 22
regime, 14, 25, 32, 33–5, 36–7, 53,
69, 121, 158, 228n38, 242n72
authoritarian regime, 15
Ben Ali regime, 12, 96, 135,
188, 196–7, 208, 210, 215,
254n56
Bourguiba, 194
change, 42
civil society, 104
constitution, 84
CSOs, 106–10
Germany and Japan, 57
old regime, 61, 65, 129, 133,
141

Ottoman regime, 189–90
'regime security', 27
religion, 14–15, 39, 46–7, 137–8,
189, 195, 216, 260–1n34
Ennahda's post-Islamist
ideology, 90–5
Reporters Without Borders, 73
revolution, 1, 3, 14, 15–16, 17,
19–20, 23, 25–8, 124–6,
265n90
Arab uprisings, 35–8
CSOs, 104, 105
Gafsa mining region, 130–1
precarity and, 153–6, 158
protest outbreaks, 176
revolution (2011), 153
to political protests, 133–7
women's associations, 121–2
'Revolutionary' Islamist politics,
96
Riahi, Laila, 142–3, 145
Riahi, Mohsen, 72
Riahi, Slim, 74
Richter, Carola, 76
Rijkers, Bob, 196
Rosanvallon, 84
rural, 19, 26, 154, 175, 204, 206,
208

Sahel region, 202, 203, 208–9
Saied, Kais, 11–13, 31, 54, 80,
100, 147–8, 152–3
Salafi-Jihadism, 6, 90
Salafi, 98, 117–18, 138
Salafis, 6, 98
Salafism, 6, 90, 233n25
Salem, Mohammed, 100
Salem, Osama Ben, 73
Salsut, Salma, 94
SCAF. *See* Supreme Council of the
Armed Forces (SCAF)

school, 47, 96, 114, 153, 181, 191, 212, 214–15
secularists, 133
'security pact', 154–5
Senoussi, Hichem, 72
Sfax, 97, 144–5
Shams (Shams: Pour la dépénalisation de l'homosexualité en Tunisie), 123
shari'a (Islamic law), 90, 91
Shariati, Ali, 88–9
Shouru, Sadok, 97
Sidi Bouzid, 49, 110
SJT. See Union of Tunisian Journalists (SJT)
SNJT. See National Union of Tunisian Journalists (SNJT)
Social media, 36
'social movement' 95
social pluralism, 41
Sokoloff, Kenneth, 200
Sousse, 16, 138, 144–5, 208
South Africa, 35, 53
STDM. See Tunisian Union of Media Executives' (STDM)
Stepan, Alfred, 189, 258n9
Streets Festival (2013), 170
Sudan, 1
Sunni Islam, 39
Supreme Council of the Armed Forces (SCAF), 37
Syndicat des journalistes tunisiens. See Union of Tunisian Journalists (SJT)
Syndicat national des journalistes tunisiens. See National Union of Tunisian Journalists (SNJT)
Syria, 1, 33

Tamarod protest movement, 7
Tataouine, 139

Tourism, 21
trade, 146, 160, 196
networks of informal trade, 18–19
trade unionists, 133, 135, 139, 182–3
trade unions, 43, 129, 146, 149, 150
transition, 20, 22, 54, 96, 129, 135–6
'coordinated transition', 66
democratic transition, 2–3, 4, 8–9
first phase of, 116
outcome of, 41
political transition, 28
second phase of, 117
transition period, 3–4, 83
Tunisian transition, 49–51, 54–7, 150
transitional, 81, 134, 153
transitional period, 17
transitional process, 3–4, 7, 82
transitional body/bodies, 23, 51, 59, 60–1, 67, 83–4, 135
transitional justice, 13–15, 53, 121
Transitional Institutions, 24, 59–60, 61, 62t, 84
Transparency International, 121
Troika, 6, 44, 48, 73, 87, 97, 134–5
Trump, Donald, 48
Truth and Dignity Commission (IVD), 13–14, 59–60, 141, 142–3, 159
Truth and Reconciliation Commission, 53
Tunis, 7, 144–5, 156–7
Tunisian Association of Democratic Women (ATFD), 108, 117, 119, 121–2, 135

Tunisian Bar Association (ONAT),
45, 109–10, 116, 237*n*1
Tunisian civil society, 106, 107,
115–16
Tunisian Communist Workers'
Party (PCOT), 10, 197–8
Tunisian Constitution, 53, 234*n*40
Tunisian El Khatt Association, 73
Tunisian Front of Islamic
Associations, 97
Tunisian General Labor Union
(UGTT), 7, 18, 35, 117, 224*n*7,
243*n*84
formed National Dialogue
Quartet, 45–6
held general strike (2019),
146–7
relationship with government,
39–40
Tunisian Human Rights League
(LTDH), 7, 107, 108–9, 119,
136, 237*n*1
Tunisian Islamic forces, 97
Tunisian Movement for Freedom
and Dignity, 72
Tunisian Organization Against
Torture, 168
Tunisian Trade Union Federation,
128
Tunisian transition, 54–5
'Tunisian Union of Media
Executives' (STDM), 69–70,
72–3, 228*n*39
Tunisian Women Association, 121
tunisianité, 25, 91, 93, 101
Tunisians, 39, 50–1, 65, 125, 155,
175
colonial education program, 195
economic hardships for, 152
Economic stagnation effects on,
53

racism faced by black Tunisians,
122
World War I participation, 192

UDC. *See* Union of Unemployed
Graduates (UDC)
UGTE. *See* General Tunisian Union
of Students (UGTE)
UGTT. *See* Tunisian General Labor
Union (UGTT)
umma, 90, 91, 93
UN. *See* United Nations (UN)
UNDP. *See* United Nations
Development Program (UNDP)
Unemployed Graduates' Union
(UCD), 161
unemployment, 17, 19
UNFT. *See* National Union of
Tunisian Women (UNFT)
Union des diplômés chômeurs.
See Union of Unemployed
Graduates (UDC)
Union of Tunisian Journalists (SJT),
110
Union of Unemployed Graduates
(UDC), 119, 135, 139
Unité spéciale de la garde nationale
(USGN), 178
United Nations (UN), 181
United Nations Development
Program (UNDP), 182
United States (US), 35, 50, 56–7,
137
invasion of Iraq, 52
unrest, 3, 42, 100, 186
UPL. *See* Free Patriotic Union
(UPL)
uprisings, 179
US Embassy, 70
Urban, 122, 132, 208
urbanized, 19, 208

UTICA (Union Tunisienne de l'industrie, du commerce et de l'artisanat), 45, 118, 136, 224n7

Vandewalle, Dirk, 208
Vatthauer, Jan-Philipp, 131
violence, 16, 117, 157, 166, 180–1
    gender-based violence, 194
    political violence, 6, 173, 179, 186
    structural violence, 153
Voice of the People of Tunisia (political party), 74

war
    civil war (Libya), 32
    civil war (Syria), 1
    proxy war (Yemen), 1
    World War I, 192, 202, 204–5, 206–7, 207f
    World War II, 57, 192
Wæver, Ole, 184
Washington, 50, 52
watan (homeland), 181
women, 121–2, 162, 191, 194, 199
    Bourguiba's control over issues of, 107
    Kasserine protest participation, 165–6

life during transition, 117
Personal Status Code (1956), 193
West Africa, 200
wilaya (governorate), 156
Winou el Pétrole, 209–10
Wolff, Jonas, 148
Wolfrom, Gustave, 204
Wollonberg, Anja, 76
'work, freedom, and national dignity', 152
World War I, 192, 202, 204–5, 206–7, 207f
World War II, 57, 192

Yahyaoui, Ridha, 156
Yemen, 1, 33
youth, 26–7, 65, 153, 196, 224–5n12
    'Arts of Revolution', 170–1
    employment issues, 155–6
    Mash'hed association formation, 123–4
    Rahma's views on, 169
    unmet demands, 17

Zeitouna Mosque and University, 191–2, 195, 200, 210–11
Zeitouna Mosque, 40, 224n8
Zitouna TV, 73, 79, 80, 81